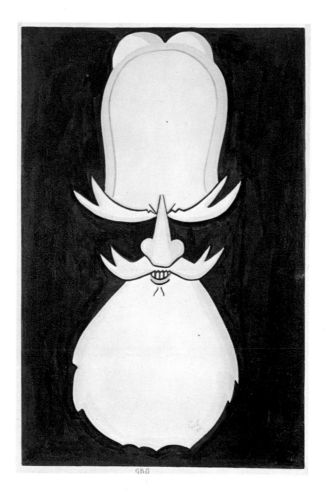

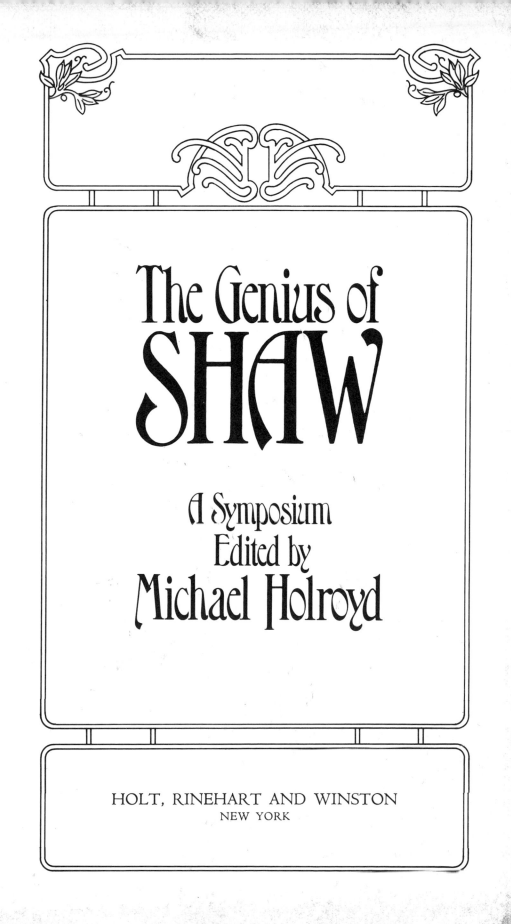

The Genius of SHAW

A Symposium
Edited by
Michael Holroyd

HOLT, RINEHART AND WINSTON
NEW YORK

Copyright © 1979 by George Rainbird Limited

Published by Holt, Rinehart and Winston,
583 Madison Avenue, New York,
New York 10017.

Published simultaneously in Canada by Holt, Rinehart and
Winston of Canada, Limited.

Library of Congress Cataloging in Publication Data

Main entry under title:
The Genius of Shaw
1. Shaw, George Bernard, 1856–1950 – Congresses.
2. Dramatists, English – 20th century – Biography –
Congresses. I. Holroyd, Michael.
PR5366.G4   1979   822'.9'12   78–31306
ISBN 0–03–043541–2

First American Edition: 1979
House Editors: Felicity Luard and Elizabeth Blair
Designer and Picture Researcher: Patrick Yapp
Indexer: Penelope Miller
Production Controllers: Jane Collins and Elizabeth Winder

Printed in Great Britain

Copyright © The Bernard Shaw Estate texts 1979
The Trustees of The British Museum, the Governors and
Guardians of the National Gallery of Ireland, and
Royal Academy of Dramatic Art.

Women and the Body Politic © Michael Holroyd 1979
The First Twenty Years © John O'Donovan 1979
An Irishman Abroad © Terence de Vere White 1979
In the Picture Galleries © Stanley Weintraub 1979
The Music Critic © Charles Osborne 1979
The Way of No Flesh © Brigid Brophy 1979
Bernard Shaw and Religion © John Stewart Collis 1979
The Fabian Ethic © Robert Skidelsky 1979
The Critic's Critic © Hilary Spurling 1979
The Plays © Irving Wardle 1979
A Funny Man © Benny Green 1979
Man of Letters © Barbara Smoker 1979
A Personal View © Colin Wilson 1979

The text was set and printed and the books
bound by Morrison & Gibb Limited, Edinburgh

Contents

Acknowledgments

I would like to thank the Shaw Estate and the Society of Authors for their approbation and encouragement. At Rainbird, I particularly wish to acknowledge the help of Felicity Luard and Elizabeth Blair, Patrick Yapp and Michael O'Mara. The first two edited with tact and skill the editor's work and prepared the book for the printer; the third allowed him to collaborate freely over the choice of illustrations; and the last, by vigorously suggesting another book, put into his head the notion of this one.

Among others who have assisted with this book are Mr Dan H. Laurence and Sir James Pitman; the University of Bath and the Humanities Research Center at the University of Texas.

Color Plates

Note: *The page numbers given are those opposite the colour plates, or, in the case of a double-page spread, those either side of the plate.*

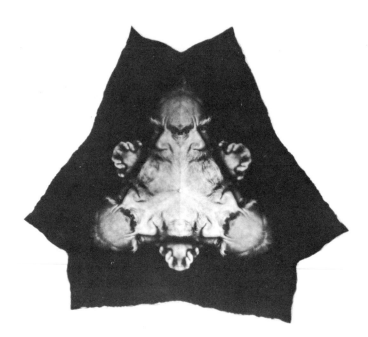

If I am not a genius, I am not worth a biography.

Shaw to St John Ervine (31 October 1942)

. . . for Heaven's sake remember that there are plenty of geniuses about.

Shaw to James Elroy Flecker (6 March 1911)

There are two sorts of genius in this world. One is produced by the breed throwing forward to the godlike man, exactly as it sometimes throws backward to the apelike. The other is the mere monster produced by an accidental excess of some faculty – musical, muscular, sexual even. A giant belongs properly to this category: he has a genius for altitude. Now the second order of genius requires no education: he (or she) does at once and without effort his feat, whatever it may be, and scoffs at laborious practice. The first order finds it far otherwise. It is immature at thirty, and though desperately in need of education . . . can find nothing but misleading until it laboriously teaches itself. I am a genius of the first order . . . but I know my order and the price I must pay for excellence. . . .

Shaw to Florence Farr (28 January 1892)

INTRODUCTION

Shaw is a particularly apt subject for a symposium because he was a man of so many reputations. He claimed, at various times, to be the victim of twelve or fifteen of them, all hopelessly insulated from one another. By 'breadwinning profession' he was of course a playwright; but he was also a professional journalist, in particular a critic of the fine arts – literature, music, pictures and the theatre. 'I am an economist and a biologist,' he explained, '. . . By religion I am a Creative-Evolutionist.' He had been a novelist too and was to become well known as an Ibsenite, a Shelleyan atheist, a street-corner, tract-waving Fabian, a vegetarian and non-tea-drinking tee-totaller, a funny man, a dangerous man, alarming bicyclist, terrific vestryman and 'Heaven knows what else besides'. In his prime he successfully confused almost everyone within earshot. 'I am not altogether,' he admitted, 'what is called an orthodox man.'

There was such a diversity within his multitudinous personality that few people seemed able to acknowledge that these apparent contradictions were aspects of the same 'artist-philosopher'. He had several publics living in separate compartments that never communicated except, of course, paradoxically: that is, politicians, embarrassed by aspects of his politics, paying extravagant tributes to his literary achievements; and men-of-letters, numbed by his Niagara of words, happy to praise his socialism and leave it at that. 'Have you ever considered,' GBS asked Edith Nesbit Bland, '. . . how utterly impossible it is that Shaw of Dublin could have written his wonderful plays . . . Shaw was an utterly ignorant man. His father was an unsuccessful business man always on the verge of bankruptcy, just like old Shakespear . . . He was a disgrace to his school, where he acquired little Latin & less Greek. He got no secondary education & came to London an unknown & obscure provincial. And this is the man to whom people attribute the omniscience, the knowledge of public affairs, of law, of medicine, of navigation &c&c&c which informs the plays & prefaces of GBS. Absurd! [Sidney] Webb, the L.L.B., the man who carried all before him in examinations . . . was clearly the man.'

While dramatizing the variety of his Shavian roles, Shaw sought a synthesis between them. He believed that he had inherited from his parents qualities that, though incompatible in their lives to the extent of driving them to inhabit different countries, he must reconcile within himself. He looked to biographers and critics to help effect this synthesis for the public by making him a recognized individual where formerly he had been not even a species, only a collection of fabulous and fantastic odds and ends.

Composite portrait by Sasha
(page 6)

George Bernard Shaw by Fredrick H. Evans, 1905
(opposite)

The first book about Shaw was published in 1905. It had been written by H. L. Mencken whose aim was to bring all Shaw's commentators together upon the common ground of admitted fact. Such a purpose was to grow increasingly difficult as the facts and commentators multiplied. Over the next fifty years there followed an extraordinary procession of Shavian volumes. Everyone, from G. K. Chesterton to Frank Harris and Professor Joad, had a book in them about Shaw. This period, which culminated in 1956 (the centenary of Shaw's birth), was largely dominated by biographical studies in many of which Shaw himself had a hand, and the most famous of which were written by a British ex-actor, an Irish ex-playwright and an American ex-mathematician. The diversity of his life was being faithfully reproduced.

Even before his death at the age of ninety-four in 1950, infinitely more had been written about Shaw than about any other modern writer. Eric Bentley described reading through these writings in preparation for his study of Shaw in 1947, as 'a gruelling experience'. Bentley's work – described by Shaw as 'a very clever critical book about me' – started a new era of Shavian scholarship in which Shaw himself could not directly collaborate. In recent years such work has benefited greatly from the publication of Shaw's *Collected Letters*, beautifully edited by Dan H. Laurence, which, as it appears, enables scholars to approach ever nearer to the truth by relying more on what Shaw wrote at the time than on what he said afterwards, and so by comparing the two versions to chart his development with more subtlety.

Although there have been exceptions (among them T. F. Evans, Margery M. Morgan, Mander and Mitchenson, and J. I. M. Stewart), most of the valuable Shaw work of the last thirty years has come from America. Since Shaw's death there have been, in six languages, over one-hundred-and-thirty full-length books about him: too many. Most of them are academic and the quality of the worst may be conveyed by assigning to them the collective title: *Meditations on the Relevance of G. Bernard Shaw's Punctuation in Cymbeline Refinished*. But the best, expert and perceptive, have contributed crucially to our understanding of him. It is probably a limitation, nevertheless, that Shaw's posthumous 'reputations' should have been juggled so exclusively by the hands of academic writers. Shaw's opinion that 'every professor is an ass' need not be taken too seriously. Yet it is surely inappropriate, for example, that the 'eternal curse' Shaw laid on those who made schoolbooks of his works should be complacently printed as the epigraph to the *Pan Revision Aids* ('Brodie's Notes') to his plays.

The essays that follow, mingling biography with criticism, represent a shift away from university students towards the general readers whom Shaw looked on as his natural audience. The contributors who have been asked to field one or other of Shaw's hard-hitting reputations are as mixed a team as anyone could wish. They come from America, Britain and Ireland. Some are distinguished academics – others definitely are not. A number of the Old Guard of Shavians (commissioned to write on facets of GBS that have not, at such a length, engaged them before) stand next to several new recruits. One or two infiltrated into these ranks are anti-Shavians – or at least notoriously neutral – for this is not hagiography on which we are engaged. All of us have gained enormously from the best of our predecessors. In this respect we may be said partly to have been *permeated* not only by the work of the best-known biographers, Hesketh Pearson, St John Ervine, Archibald Henderson, but also by that of a number of more recent critics (including Louis Crompton, William Irvine, Frederick P. W. McDowell, Martin Meisel, Arthur H. Nethercot, Warren Sylvester Smith, Alfred Turco Jnr., Robert F. Whitman and J. L. Wisenthal) whose writings, well-respected in academic circles, are not widely known to the general reading public. These, and others, are our unseen contributors and we owe them much.

But there is another contributor on whom I am counting: and that is you, the reader. Although I selected the subjects and set lengths to them; although I have been able to supply in some places unpublished information quarried out during my research for a Life of Shaw, and have superintended this troupe of authors so that one does not stand too painfully on the feet of another, I have not tried to impose an artificial unity on the book. By making a catholic choice of contributors (and had money been unlimited I would have liked to widen it still further) I hoped to emphasize the variety of Shaw's reputations. My chief editorial instruction to all the writers has been to take no notice of their editor: and they responded magnificently. The contradictions that flourish between these covers are reflections of the contradictions in Shaw's own nature: and it is the reader's job, as it was once Shaw's, to reconcile them.

One example: Barbara Smoker identifies Henry Sweet as the 'primary model' for *Pygmalion*'s Professor Higgins; John O'Donovan argues that Higgins was a 'full length portrait' of the remarkable Vandeleur Lee; and Irving Wardle tells us that in Higgins we see a lucid Shavian self-portrait. Has the editor therefore not done his work? Has he fallen asleep? Surely the reader should be informed who is right. The answer is no. All three are right and it is the reader's, not the editor's, business to reconcile these aspects of the truth. It is in this sense that I look on the reader as our final contributor. The reading of books is, to adapt a phrase of Henry Green's, a long intimacy between strangers. This is specially appropriate in the case of Shaw, who claimed to have put the best part of himself into his books and who knew little intimacy except upon the page.

Let those who may complain that it was all on paper remember that only on paper has humanity yet achieved glory, beauty, truth, knowledge, virtue, and abiding love.

The editor and the multitudinous personality of GBS: John Jensen

John O'Donovan

THE FIRST TWENTY YEARS

Drinking, dancing, dinner-partying, card playing, hunting, racegoing, whoring and arguing about religion and politics were the staple of Dublin's social life when Shaw was born there in 1856. The city had no opera house, no professional orchestra, and could not muster enough support for drama to repair the leaking roof of its principal theatre. Thanks to the public spirit of an unusual entrepreneur and a no less unusual Irish viscount, together with a couple of other adventurous spirits, Dublin had been provided with a National Gallery in the 1860s. Shaw hardly exaggerated when he declared that apart from the attendants he was the only Irishman of his time ever to have crossed its threshold.

Shaw's dislike of his native Dublin, a dislike that on occasion touched hatred, may not form a major theme in his work; nevertheless it remained active in him until he attained the apathetic mellowness of old age and could bestow a compliment or two upon the place. Every man over forty is a scoundrel, he had said. Every man over sixty is a hypocrite he could have added, for at ninety he put on his courtliest air when accepting the Freedom of Dublin from a deputation of city fathers to his home at Ayot St Lawrence, murmuring that Dublin alone had the right to affirm he had not disgraced her.

In earlier years he summarized his dislike of his native city by pointing out that no man prefers the city which has conquered him to the city he has conquered. The implication is that during his life in Dublin, his first twenty years, he had in some way taken on Dublin in a hand-to-hand contest over art. No evidence has surfaced, documented or hearsay, that he ever did so. His later boast that things didn't happen to him, he happened to things, is certainly not true of his Dublin period or indeed of his early London period. In Dublin he allowed his life to be shaped by circumstances, which were of course shaped by other people. What might appear to be his first really decisive action, his emigrating to London in April 1876 just three months short of his twentieth birthday, was itself forced on him as we shall see presently.

Much has been made of his oft-quoted outburst in a letter (11 June 1897) to Ellen Terry: 'Oh, a devil of a childhood, Ellen, rich only in dreams, frightful and loveless in realities.' However when Chesterton in his biography of Shaw accepted the devilish childhood as a fact, the consequence of an upbringing in a narrow Puritan home, he was rapped on the knuckles in GBS's review of the book:

> He concludes that, in my joyless Puritan home (oh! my father oh! my mother) I never melted lead on 'Holi-eve', never hid rings in pancakes, never did all those dreary, silly Christmas things, until human nature rebelled against them and they were swept out of

Sackville Street, Dublin, 1864

our domestic existence, like the exchanging of birthday presents and the rest of the incul-
cated tribal superstitions of the kitchen . . .

Moreover in old age Shaw was fond of repeating that the happiest moment of his
life was when his mother told him (he was ten) that they were going to live in a
cottage on Torca hill in Dalkey, overlooking the whole sweep of Dublin Bay, a view
which on a summer's day one is tempted to believe is indeed comparable to the Bay
of Naples.

The truth seems to be that as Victorian childhoods went, GBS's was not all that
bad. On the credit side he was subjected neither at home nor at school to the merci-
less beatings many another boy had to endure, pedagogical flagellomania being as
much an Irish as an English vice; nor did he ever go hungry or in rags. His home was
filled with music, which he loved; outings to the theatre and the concert hall were
frequent and there was no shortage of interesting friends and relatives. Life was
seldom dull at the Shaws'. The summer months were spent in his beloved Dalkey
where there was gorse to be set on fire on the common (which was duly done by him,
another lad being let take the blame), and where there was the sea to swim in as often
as he wished ('the only element I am really at home in').

On the debit side there was the lack of enough income to support the Shaw family
pretensions, which were enormous even by Dublin standards, but then insufficient
income has always been one of Ireland's national diseases. There was the agonizing
compulsion on him to sit quietly through boring Sunday services at the Molyneux
Church in Upper Leeson Street, and there were the few months' attendance at a
predominantly tradesman-class Catholic school, a traumatic episode for the son of a
Protestant gentleman-wholesaler who like all Ascendency Protestants despised the
Roman Catholic majority as inferior creatures, predestined for Hell, with whom
friendship or indeed any social contact was unthinkable. There was his father's
alcoholism (strongly denied by other members of the family); and his belief that his
mother didn't like him, the specific maternal affection having been aroused in her
only by her younger daughter Agnes. Finally there was, as he matured and became
curious about sexual matters, his unease about the nature of the relationship between
his mother and George Vandeleur Lee, the Other Man in what GBS later described
with dogged persistence as an 'innocent' *ménage à trois*, thus returning a perverse
verdict against the evidence he had himself cited. One can only suppose that the
balance between the amount of happiness or unhappiness generated by these various
causes sometimes weighed one way in GBS's consciousness, sometimes the other: so
that like most of us he often enjoyed himself as a child and sometimes didn't.

Besides his upbringing in a *ménage à trois*, Shaw claimed the advantage of three
fathers: the natural one, George Carr Shaw; the Other Man, Vandeleur Lee; and
the Rabelaisian maternal uncle, Walter John Gurly. From what he said about them
one gathers that he didn't care much for his regulation father but admired Lee to
the point of worship, and while having little respect for the Rabelaisian uncle nevertheless entertained a certain affection for him. In making it plain that Lee had the
deepest and most lasting influence of the three upon him, GBS was being not only
accurate but probably more accurate than he realized. I have pointed out elsewhere[1]
that although GBS assured one biographer (O'Bolger) that he hadn't 'one trait even
remotely resembling any of Lee's', yet by stringing together his descriptions of Lee
you get what amounts to a Shavian self-sketch:

> Heterodox and original . . . a man of mesmeric vitality and force . . . impetuous enterprise
> and magnetism . . . an active volcano . . . completely sceptical about lawyers and professions

(Left) *George Carr Shaw*

(Right) *Lucinda Elizabeth Shaw*

generally . . . a fine ear and fastidious taste . . . a moderate liver in all respects . . . interesting . . . always a man apart.

THE ANCESTORS

Shaw's own account of his mother's and his father's families, which naturally forms the basis of what biographers have to say on the matter, is misleading. The odd thing is that the lively anecdotes which are so hard not to regard as tall stories seem to be true enough: it is the sober, factual-sounding statements that are off the mark. People who knew his mother and his sister Lucy flatly contradict his sketches of them, declaring that his mother, far from being the stern, humourless, unmaternal parent he made her out to be, a woman upon whom misfortunes broke like waves on granite, was in fact full of fun and normal human feeling. Lucy, whom he accused of being antagonistic and jealous and described as a person whom everyone loved but who loved no one, appeared to others an affectionate and loyal friend, and proud of her brother's fame, although like her mother she could be irritated by the excessive adulation of his fans. An Australian cousin, Charles McMahon Shaw, rejected out of hand Shaw's allegation that his father was a hopeless drunkard.

There has been a tendency, where Shaw's character sketches of his family differ sharply from those of outsiders, to discount his version as unreliable. But surely this is not to allow for the obvious fact that the viewpoint of a son and brother taken from within the home is necessarily different from the outside viewpoint. The old warning has not been heeded: if you want to know me, come and live with me. Having myself learned with astonishment after my father's death that he who had been so taciturn, careworn and despondent at his own fireside, was the embodiment of talkative gaiety at other people's, I am the less disposed to accuse Shaw of being a faulty or a too biased portrayer. Yet there is no gainsaying that his recollections of people and of incidents varied over the years (whose don't?) and his memory had a trick of tele-scoping events either by contracting an interval of many months to a few days or weeks, or by expanding days into a matter of a year or more. Above all, while seeming to be totally, almost naively candid, he could suppress inconvenient facts when he believed documentary evidence of them no longer existed. Indeed one wonders whether his repeated exhortations to biographers to keep away from the newspaper files and what he scornfully called 'the documents' sprang from fear of what these might reveal or were really a 'dare' to go to them, Shaw being convinced that the only surviving documents would confirm his accuracy. Whichever is the correct view, the checker-up is surprised to find, not that Shaw knew so little about his ante-cedents and their doings before he was born or was old enough to take notice, but that he knew so much. He was his own genealogist from the start. Among his literary remains in the British Museum is a notebook dating from the 1870s in which he jotted down what he had learned of his father's early career. It is by no means an adventurous tale, being just a recital of the clerical jobs the old gentleman had before becoming a corn merchant in a small way. What is significant is that the teenage Shaw already felt self-important enough to record such details so carefully.

It may now be asked why Shaw, having made so many family skeletons dance to entertain us, need have worried about a few more bony additions to the cast. The answer is that he had the usual author's vanity of wishing no hand but his own to limn the family portraits, while the embarrassment of the *ménage à trois* made him desire no deductions to be drawn concerning his mother's relationship with her singing teacher save those he chose to publish himself. Does not history show that the most successful gods are those who write the books themselves? All that we need know about his early life, he announced, 'has been told, and very well told, by myself'.

THE GURLYS

His mother's people, the Gurlys, were not really the minor landed gentry he believed them to be. They are recorded at one time as possessing sixteen acres (valuation £15.15s.0d) but for the most part their property consisted of buildings in or around Carlow, a town in the south-eastern corner of Ireland. The first purchases were made in the eighteenth century by Thomas Gurly, an attorney, whose son, another Thomas (GBS's great-grandfather) followed him into the profession. The variety and scattered nature of the property suggests that the attorneys, like others of their kind, picked it up bit by bit for a song in the course of dealing with clients' business.

The Gurlys' only hope of financial salvation lay in marrying money and this Walter Bagnall Gurly (GBS's grandfather) did. His bride, Lucinda Elizabeth Whit-croft, was the daughter of John Whitcroft, a pawnbroker in the slums of Dublin with at least three premises, the profits of which enabled him to acquire a large amount of property in the city area, establish himself in a small country house in the Dublin foothills, and make his eldest son a barrister who in turn became possessed of some 2267 acres of land and the status of a Kilkenny squire. The pawnbroker, believed by Shaw to have been the illegitimate son of a Somebody, settled about £4000 on the bride and on any children she might have, though 'power of appoint-

St Patrick's Close, Dublin, by Walter Osborne

CÆSAR AND
CLEOPATRA
BY
SHAWKSPEARE

ALICK P.F. RITCHIE

ment' was given to Gurly. It was Shaw's mother's share of the pawnbroker's money, some £1500, which enabled her to keep a roof over his head in his penniless early London period, and to preserve him from absolute starvation.

The marriage between Walter Bagnall Gurly and the pawnbroker's daughter took place in Dublin in 1829, the bride at twenty-seven being old by the standards of the time, which suggests that no more eligible offer than Gurly's had come her way. Shaw's mother, named Lucinda Elizabeth after her own mother, was born the following year. After ten years of marriage Mrs Gurly died, leaving the widower with a nine-year-old daughter on his hands and a son of about four. It seems that the girl was handed over to the care of her mother's youngest sister, the humpbacked great-aunt Ellen Whitcroft of the Shaw saga, who was then probably living with her pawnbroker father at his country seat. The little boy would have gone to her too, although later he seems to have been taken over by the Kilkenny squire. Both children were educated to a standard far beyond what their ne'er-do-well father could afford. Walter was sent to Kilkenny College ('the Eton of Ireland' said GBS with some justification) where as the smallest boy in the school he used to squeeze out under the locked gates to make assignations on behalf of the senior lads with the Kilkenny whores. In due course Walter entered Trinity College, Dublin, from which he 'retired' (GBS's word) without a degree in order to recover from the effects of debauchery. He later qualified as a physician, taking a post as ship's surgeon with the Inman Line and staying with the Shaws in Dublin between voyages until in middle age he gave up the sea, married an English widow, and settled down to private practice at Grange Park Road, Leyton, Essex.

From all that the outsider can gather about Uncle Walter he seems to have been a chip off the old block, a jovial blackguard with an inexhaustible store of limericks and dirty jokes and little respect for idealist attitudes and noble aspirations.

> He was a most exhilarating person, because he had, like my mother, though without her dignity, a youthfulness that no dissipation could exhaust, and was robust and fullblooded. His profanity and obscenity in conversation were of Rabelaisian exuberance; and as to the *maxima reverentia* due to my tender years, he had rather less of it, if possible, than Falstaff had for Prince Hal.

Lucinda Elizabeth Gurly, known in the family as Bessie, would have been taught either by her aunt or, more probably, by a governess. To obtain the musical accomplishments then a social necessity for young ladies she was sent to the most fashionable Dublin teacher, Johann Bernhard Logier, a German immigrant who had invented the chiroplast, an abominable contraption for holding a pupil's hands rigidly in position as they travelled up and down the keyboard. According to GBS she was unable to play the piano with any great skill or feeling, which would hardly have recommended her later on to the fastidious and finely eared Vandeleur Lee. But Bessie had one ability that made her most useful to Lee. Logier had grounded her in the basic principles of harmony (he was the author of a *Thoroughbass*, said to have been Wagner's first textbook) and she could therefore vamp accompaniments and improvise missing orchestral parts. Bessie looked back with hatred on her upbringing by Aunt Ellen. In her late teens she seems to have rebelled and gone to live with her father, or at any rate to have paid lengthy visits to him. Gurly at this period had apartments in a house called Parson's Green in Kilmacud, Stillorgan, now a South Dublin suburb but then a small village with surroundings affording plenty of opportunities to the sportsman. He still kept in touch with his Carlow friends, with two corn merchants in particular, Samuel Haughton and Simeon Clarke.

GBS by Alick P. F. Ritchie

Walter John Gurly

Shaw tells us that Gurly

> . . . most unexpectedly married again: this time the penniless daughter of an old friend of his whose bills he had backed with ruinous consequences. The alliance did not please the family of his first wife, especially his brother-in-law, a Kilkenny squire to whom he owed money, and from whom he concealed his intention to marry again.
>
> Unfortunately my mother innocently let out the secret to her uncle. The consequence was that my grandfather going out on his wedding morning to buy a pair of gloves, was arrested for debt at the suit of his brother-in-law. One can hardly blame him for being furious. But this fury carried him beyond reason. He believed that my mother had betrayed him deliberately so as to stop the marriage by his arrest.

Gurly in fact had little choice in the matter of marrying. His was a shotgun wedding. It took place on 25 May 1852 in Dublin, just two months after the birth in Carlow of the first of the couple's six daughters (some of whom, with their progeny, formed the doleful corps of poor relations whom Shaw helped to support in his prosperous days). Shaw never mentioned the shotgun aspect of his grandfather's marriage and none of his biographers discovered it. Yet he must have known something about it for it is extremely unlikely that the communicative Bessie remained silent about a titbit so discreditable to the father she disliked. It also does much to explain Gurly's furious reaction to the attempt to frustrate his wedding plans, if indeed his fury has any need to be explained away. Shaw tells us that Bessie now found herself obliged to choose between life with a stepmother and an enraged father or a return to the home of the tyrannous Aunt Ellen. 'It was at this moment,' says Shaw, 'that some devil, perhaps commissioned by the Life Force to bring me into the world, prompted my father to propose marriage to Miss Bessie Gurly.' How that devil set about his task we are not told. My guess is that while Bessie was living at Parson's Green before her father's second marriage, the Life-Force devil arranged for her to meet some of her father's Carlow corn merchant friends. Some of the meetings were bound to have taken place at Haughton's country home, a mile or so from Parson's Green. And Haughton's senior clerk in the Dublin office was a well-connected and gentlemanly bachelor nearing forty, whose name was George Carr Shaw.

THE SHAWS

The Shaws, although a considerable cut above the Gurlys in almost every respect, were still not quite as 'county' as GBS claimed. The common ancestor of both branches of the family, the dramatist's and the titled, was an eighteenth century Shaw, Robert of Sandpits, Co. Kilkenny. It seems likely that Robert Shaw was a sand and gravel merchant rather than the landed gentleman implied by his title. If so, it was no bad trade for him to be in because the second part of the eighteenth century saw a great building boom in Ireland. No matter what the source of his income was, Robert of the Sandpits commanded enough money to give his sons a fairly good start in life. The eldest, who succeeded him at the Sandpits, was able to give *his* an even better start, for one became Rector of Kilkenny, and the youngest an attorney and notary public in Kilkenny. The attorney had married the daughter of the Reverend Edward Carr, a Co. Waterford rector, and reputedly sired fourteen children of whom eleven survived infancy. The third son was George Carr Shaw, GBS's father.

THE SHAW BANKER-BARONET

Meanwhile founding father Robert's fifth son, another Robert, had gone up to Dublin with enough capital to start as a merchant and enough political pull to become in 1784 Comptroller of the Sorting at the Post Office there. This Robert, whom we shall call Robert II, was able to invest £5000 in the newly established Bank of Ireland and was elected a director in 1796, the year he died. Earlier that year his son Robert III had married the daughter and sole heiress of a rich Dublin silk merchant, another original subscriber to the bank. It was this girl who brought Bushy Park, Terenure, Co. Dublin into the Shaw family, the mansion they were to make their official country seat. Robert III never became a Bank of Ireland director. He became a partner in a private bank and spent a great deal of time and energy on politics, both local and national. He was elected Lord Mayor of Dublin (1815–1816) and in August 1821 received a baronetcy from George IV. The baronetcy was neither a personal tribute nor a reward for public work. It was engineered by the local big-wigs as one of a number of gestures of reassurance to the Protestant minority, alarmed by the growing power of the Catholics, that their social and political supremacy would be officially maintained. For Robert III was one of the great Protestant champions of his time.

We know little about George Carr Shaw's early life. He was born on 30 December 1814, presumably in Kilkenny, and was twelve when his father died. Some time after this the banker-baronet provided the widow and her children with a cottage in Roundtown, then a very small suburb of Dublin and on the baronet's Bushy Park estate.

We learn from one of Shaw's notebooks in the British Museum that George Carr Shaw took an office job in 1838 with Todhunters the merchants, and after seven years there transferred to a clerical post in the Law Courts (known in Dublin as the Four Courts), almost certainly procured for him through the influence of the baronet's younger brother Frederick, Recorder of Dublin. He retired from this in 1851 on a pension of £44 a year and took a job with Haughtons for about six months, transferring to Wilson's, a wholesale ironmongers, 'for a shorter period', finally moving for a little while to McMullen, Shaw & Co., corn merchants, the Shaw being his younger brother, Henry. He now sold his pension to Joseph Henry O'Brien, later Henry's executor, for £500 and used the money to enter into a partnership with Henry's former associate, George Clibborn. This was his final business venture. The firm Clibborn & Shaw was to provide him with a living of sorts until his death. It was around this time that he became the straw Bessie clutched at when faced with her own domestic trouble. Shaw's account of their courtship is:

She had heard that he had a pension of £60 [sic] a year; and to her, who had never been allowed to have more than pocket money nor to housekeep, £60 seemed an enormous and inexhaustible sum. She calmly announced her engagement, dropping the bombshell as unconcernedly as if it were a coloured glass ball from her solitaire board. People played solitaire in those days.

Finding it impossible to make her see the gravity of the pecuniary situation, or to induce her to cancel her engagement on such a ground, her people played another card. They told her that George Carr Shaw was a drunkard. She indignantly refused to believe them, reminding them that they had never objected to him before. When they persisted, she went to him straightforwardly and asked him was it true. He assured her most solemnly that he was a convinced and lifelong teetotaller. And she believed him and married him. But it was true. He drank.

Without attempting to defend my father for telling this whopper, I must explain that he really was in principle a convinced teetotaller. Unfortunately it was the horror of his own experience as an occasional dipsomaniac that gave him this conviction, which he was miserably unable to carry into practice.

I can only imagine the hell into which my mother descended when she found out what shabby-genteel poverty with a drunken husband is like. She once told me that when they were honeymooning in Liverpool (of all places) she opened her bridegroom's wardrobe and found it full of empty bottles. In the first shock of discovery she ran away to the docks to get employed as a stewardess and be taken out of the country. But on the way she was molested by some rough docklanders and had to run back again.

Otherwise the marriage followed the usual Victorian pattern. Bessie bore a daughter, Lucinda Frances (Lucy), on 29 March 1853 in her home in Synge Street, another daughter, Elinor Agnes ('Yuppy' or Aggie), some time in 1855; and on 26 July 1856, George Bernard Shaw (Sonny). There may have been another child who either died in infancy (unlikely, as we would surely have heard about it) or miscarried, because in the summer after GBS's birth Bessie did a most unusual thing

Shaw's two sisters: 'Yuppy' (left) and Lucinda (right)

for a Dublin wife in her social and domestic circumstances: she went off alone on a six-week visit to her father, then staying at Kinlough, a small village in sporting country in Co. Leitrim.

For a city girl who remained the urban type all her life, a longish holiday in a remote Irish village does not look the kind of thing that would have an overwhelming attraction for Bessie. Any suspicion that she had 'gone home to father' can be ruled out because of the existence of a series of serenely affectionate letters from her husband, carrying no hint of worry about their personal relationship or of domestic trouble. The letters are, on the contrary, the most eloquent testimony we could have that the couple were rubbing along quite comfortably. The reasonable inference from the letters is that the Gurly-Whitcroft squabbles of 1852 had blown over, that Bessie was on visiting terms with her father and at least on speaking terms with her aunt, and that in the summer of 1857 she needed a country holiday. There is nothing to suggest that George Carr Shaw was not at this time the 'sole chief' (as GBS put it) of the Synge Street household and not in possession of as much of Bessie's affection as he ever enjoyed. Clearly the cuckoo whose take-over of the nest so acutely embarrassed his son later on did not yet threaten his domestic peace.

GEORGE VANDELEUR LEE

But if George Vandeleur Lee[2] was not yet dominantly established in the Shaw household, he was established a couple of hundred yards away as a singing teacher in No 48 Harrington Street. His mother lived with him here, likewise his beloved younger brother who was plain William in the school register but had now effloresced into Harcourt William Nassau Lee. Even less is known of Vandeleur Lee's early life than of George Carr Shaw's. Officially he was the son of Eliza and Robert Lee, a coal merchant in a small way, but he let intimates know that his true father was a colonel of militia, Crofton Moore Vandeleur, MP, JP, of Kilrush House, Co. Clare, head of an ancient family of landed gentry and owner of 20,206 acres, a person obviously higher in the social scale than either the Shaws or the Gurlys. It is impossible at this time of day to verify Lee's claim. He stated in his return to the 1881 Census that he had been born in Kilrush. When nearly twenty years ago I went there to look up the parish registers I found that the pages which recorded births and marriages for the relevant period had been carefully removed. My guess is that some indignant Vandeleur did a little censoring in 1872 or thereabouts when the death of Crofton Vandeleur's wife may have made George John Lee feel he could replace the John with Vandeleur without wounding a lady's feelings.

In view of the *ménage à trois* with Lee it was naturally important to Shaw to establish that he himself had been born a respectable time before Lee came on the scene. He recalled the first time he met Lee. The meeting was imprinted on his memory because Lee took him on his lap and painted moustachios on him with burnt cork. The incident could hardly have occurred before 1860 when Shaw was four, thus excluding Lee as a parent. But the trouble is that Lee had been living at No 48 Harrington Street, around the corner from Bessie, since 1853, some three years before Shaw was born, and for a while during that year had also taken an apartment in No 11 Harrington Street, presumably for teaching and rehearsing. No 11 was then only three houses away from Bessie, fewer than a hundred paces.

In Frank Harris's biography of Shaw (mostly written by Shaw himself) there is a description of Lee which derives from Shaw's letters to earlier biographers:

> He had fallen downstairs in his childhood and walked with a limp for the rest of his life, one of his legs being considerably shorter than the other. . . . His upper lip and chin were close-shaved. His face was framed with pirate black whiskers. In his infancy babies wore enormous nightcaps, which occasionally caught fire. Lee's did; and for ever after his glossy black hair grew on his forehead like the 'join' as actors call it, of a wig. He was never carelessly or ill dressed; and he had personal style, physical adroitness, and the art of seeming to succeed in everything he attempted.

When Bessie first met Lee or when she began to take lessons from him we do not know. It is unlikely she would not have noticed from the start so unusual-looking a near neighbour. On the other hand Lee's very noticeability would have drawn attention to any specially close relationship between him and Bessie prior to Shaw's birth, in which case the tone of the 1857 letters from George Carr Shaw to his wife would scarcely have been so untroubled. In short, there was no good reason for Shaw to worry about his legitimacy. But there is plenty of evidence that he did worry about it.

If I were asked to guess the likeliest date for the beginning of Bessie's encounter with Lee I should say 1858, their relationship being merely that of pupil and singing teacher. Time would have hung heavy on her hands. She had finished child bearing, she had one, perhaps two, £8-a-year servants to look after her small house for her, she was only twenty-eight; and there was a mesmeric and inexpensive singing teacher nearby, the inventor of a fascinating method of voice development. Presumably

Bessie underwent the better part of Lee's 'arduous training', said to have taken between two and three years, before she was promoted from chorus member to prima donna of his musical society.

Lee's Amateur Musical Society, if not prominently active in Dublin before 1858, was at least doing something. In that year it gave a concert in aid of the Royal Irish Academy of Music, founded a few years previously by two of Lee's musician colleagues, R. M. Levey and Joseph Robinson. The Academy got £5 from the proceeds. The following year it got £25. But the Amateur Musical Society did not really get going until the 1860s. It had been giving regular concerts, which were not really public, sometimes as the Amateur Musical sometimes as the Collegiate Musical Society, but its first big affair was a choral and orchestral concert held in connection with the Shakespeare Tercentenary celebrations in 1864. This concert was the making of Lee.

So it came about that Sonny Shaw grew up in a house of music. The Shavian experience was of live music, directed by a mesmeric conductor. No other boy in the Dublin of that time enjoyed such an advantage, and few other boys would have had the Shavian capacity to make the most of it. The drawback was that virtually all the musicians were Catholics, from the leading tenor, Charles Cummins, to Peter Hamlet Thompson who afterwards became celebrated for his cockcrowing solo in *Hamlet*. Shaw acknowledges that this fact served to cut him and his family off from his Protestant relations. It would certainly have ended invitations to the Synge Street Shaws from the baronet at Bushy Park, although Shaw insists that the sole reason for this was his father's drinking. (The drinking uncles were not banned from Bushy Park.)

But Shaw did not tell the whole truth about the Amateur Musical Society Catholics. What he suppressed then, and later on in his revelation in *Sixteen Self Sketches* that he had attended what was virtually a Catholic school, was that Lee himself was a Catholic. It may seem incredible to Shaw's admirers nowadays that Lee's Catholicism should have mattered a jot to the lofty prophet of the Life Force. But what was the 'shame and wounded snobbery' caused by enforced association with the sons of Catholic tradesmen during the day compared with the humiliation of having to live in a *ménage à trois* dominated by a Catholic. For around 1865 Lee and the Shaws set up a joint household in No 1 Hatch Street. It was a better address than either had previously enjoyed and in the matter of economy, domestic convenience and social standing it was a commonsense move. To Lee it was the outward and visible sign of his rising professional status, and it solved his bachelor housekeeping problem. It was no less a leg up for George Carr Shaw, being his best-ever address and far beyond his unaided means. To Bessie it solved the problem posed by two teenage daughters and a ten-year-old son in the two-bedroomed Synge Street home, with the added advantage of enabling her to live in perfect respectability under the same roof as the man who had replaced her husband as her chief male interest.

Moreover Lee soon provided them all with a holiday home, the little six-roomed Torca Cottage at Dalkey. St John Ervine quotes a letter from Shaw to a lady in 1907 in which he admits that in other eyes Dalkey might appear no more than a quite ordinary and insipid seaside place, but to him it was wonderland. Without this clue you may well be puzzled as to what exactly he meant when he boasted, 'I am a product of Dalkey's outlook'. To Sonny Shaw, Dalkey meant personal freedom: the freedom to roam around at will, to burn the gorse on the Common, to bathe at White Rock below, and best of all, no Sunday church. The family gave up churchgoing when they went to Dalkey and did not resume it on returning to Hatch Street.

(Top) *Torca Cottage, Dalkey. Shaw was born in Synge Street* (inset) *but in 1865 the family moved to Hatch Street* (below) *with Vandeleur Lee*

Indeed Bessie's spiritual interests had shifted to spiritualism and she had acquired a planchette board.

While at Dalkey Sonny was sent to a private school run by William Halpin in Lawson's Terrace, Sandycove, a couple of miles from Torca Cottage and a couple of hundred yards from the Martello fortification later to become famous in the literary world as James Joyce's Tower. On the family's return to town after the 1867 season, Sonny was transferred to the Wesleyan Connexional School in St Stephen's Green. There was no significance about this selection of a Methodist school, it simply happened to be the nearest Protestant one, being only a couple of hundred yards from the Hatch Street house. Shaw said he learned nothing there that was to be of the slightest use to him, adding that he was 'generally near or at the bottom of the class'. It was left to Lee to make the next move. Lee happened to know the drawing master at the Central Model School in Marlborough Street, who assured him the teaching was more efficient there. So Bessie, apparently undaunted by the religious and social implications, allowed Sonny to be sent to Marlborough Street. It was yet another humiliation – 'my snob tragedy', he called it.

> It was an enormous place, with huge unscaleable railings and gates on which for me might well have been inscribed 'All hope abandon, ye who enter here': for that the son of a Protestant merchant-gentleman and feudal downstart should pass those bars or associate in any way with its hosts of lower middle class Catholic children, sons of petty shopkeepers and tradesmen, was inconceivable from the Shaw point of view.

After seven months of humiliation behind the unscaleable railings and under the shadow of Dublin's Catholic Pro-Cathedral, Sonny Shaw rebelled and refused to go back. His father, understandably as ashamed of the association as Sonny, roused

(Left) *An early photograph of Shaw's mother (left) and his father (right) with George John Vandeleur Lee in the middle*

(Right) *The earliest photograph of GBS with Matthew Edward McNulty in 1874*

himself enough to insist on a change. The change was to the other extreme with a vengeance. Sonny was transferred to his final school, a day school run by the Incorporated Society for Promoting English Protestant Schools in Ireland and provocatively situated in Aungier Street opposite the long-established church and schools of the Discalced Carmelite Friars. It was here he met Matthew Edward McNulty, later a novelist and writer of farces in his spare time from bank managing. McNulty became his intimate friend for the rest of his time in Dublin, and although the intimacy naturally languished after Shaw emigrated, the friendship survived after a fashion until death did them part.

McNulty wrote at least two pieces about his boyhood friendship with Shaw. The longer version has remained unpublished but the shorter was published in *The Candid Friend* in 1901. A copy was annotated by Shaw who, needless to say, disputed McNulty's recollections, especially of his having presented himself at the Aungier Street School in 'an Eton jacket, knickerbockers, long stockings and laced-up boots'. McNulty also complained that while playing schoolyard cricket with Shaw, Shaw deliberately bowled him a ball that on being hit flashed backwards and broke a stained-glass window in the church across the way. Whereupon Shaw threw himself on the ground and rolled around screaming with glee.

At that time it was the custom of day pupils to attend school only during the morning, which meant that Sonny could be hanging around the house for the rest of the day. It may have been that Bessie wanted to get from under her feet a boy passing through the damned nuisance stage, or that she was particularly hard pressed for money at the time, but she allowed her son, not yet fourteen, to be interviewed for a job by the clothing firm of Scott, Spain & Rooney. The junior partner was prepared to take him on but the senior partner turned him down as too young and too unfitted for the work. However at fifteen he was again put out to work, and appears to have been willing enough to go for the independence it would bring.

There seems to have been no question that he would enter his father's business. Doubtless there was little enough money in it for the father as it was, and moreover he and his father disliked each other at this period. (McNulty alleges GBS 'hated' him.) Nor was a berth found for him in any of his Shavian uncles' firms. However Uncle Richard Frederick Shaw, chief clerk in the Valuation Office, pulled the string that got Sonny taken on as office boy in a land agent's office in Molesworth Street at eighteen shillings a month. The head of this firm was Charles Uniacke Townshend, a pillar of the church, the Royal Dublin Society and, as Shaw remarked, everything else that was pillarable in Dublin.

He discussed religion in the office with such freedom that Townshend overheard him with considerable shock and exacted a promise that Shaw would never again mention the subject to his colleagues. That promise, weakly given, troubled Shaw's conscience all his life. His duties in Molesworth Street obliged him to sally out at intervals to make payments on behalf of clients at certain shops, but he had enough leisure to organize his colleagues, *à la* Vandeleur Lee, in improvised operatic performances.

After a year or so in Molesworth Street Shaw received an unexpected promotion. The cashier was found out in a fiddle and dismissed. Townshend made the sixteen-year-old Shaw the stopgap cashier but found him so efficient that he doubled his salary and left him in the post for nearly four years. The promotion not only confirmed GBS's good opinion of himself but also marked the beginning of his self-disciplined work routine. The ledgers also disciplined his handwriting, changing it from a sloping scrawl to an upright, easily legible, elegant script, modelled on that of his predecessor.

As well as going to Lee's concerts he was also going to the theatre. He saw Henry Irving, but he did not impress Shaw as favourably as Barry Sullivan who, with Lee, was to be later deified in Shaw's rose-coloured retrospections.

Meanwhile, Lee and Bessie went from strength to strength. The operas and choral works which Shaw was now able to whistle from beginning to end were no longer being performed for charity but on a semi-professional basis. Bessie had become the complete career woman, Lee's indispensable right hand. She got him to train Lucy's voice according to the Method to enable Lucy to go on the stage professionally, thus freeing her from the obligation to make a living as a wife. Marriage, Bessie was fond of repeating, was Dead Sea fruit. The operas were brought on tour to Cork and to Limerick for a Munster Fair, and no Dublin Exhibition was complete without a Lee concert. Lee had also published at the end of 1869 a handsomely turned-out treatise: *The Voice: Its Artistic Production, Development, and Preservation.*

How the *ménage à trois* would have fared eventually is hard to say. Outwardly the relation between Bessie and Lee was as close as ever, and although McNulty declares that at one time George Carr Shaw initiated legal proceedings over that relationship but then dropped them, the two men were still living under the same roof. Another thing: Shaw *père* had been felled on his own doorstep by a mild fit, which frightened him into putting his ideal of teetotalism into practice. But although the skies seemed clear enough a storm could have blown up at any moment, for Lee was taking more than a musical interest in the teenage Lucy.

According to a Dublin friend Lucy had a bad figure but a lovely face and great charm. She also had at this time the powerful attraction of youth and Lee, at forty, was at a notoriously dangerous age. Shaw always insisted that Lucy disliked Lee from childhood, when he had given her piano lessons. She may have done so, and put up with any approaches he may have made for the sake of his usefulness in furthering her career. But whatever (if anything) went on between Lee and Lucy it appears to have gone unnoticed by Bessie, who wouldn't be the first mother to be strangely unobservant of what was happening under her own nose. The immediate cause of the break-up of the *ménage*, however, was not the relationship between Lee and Lucy but between Lee and Sir Robert Prescott Stewart, C.V. Stanford's early teacher, Professor of Music at Trinity College, Dublin, organist of Dublin's two Protestant cathedrals, and of the Chapel Royal at Dublin Castle, Composer-in-Ordinary to the Viceroy, Professor of Harmony and Composition at the Royal Irish Academy of Music: in short, Dublin's most influential musician.

Stewart probably ignored Lee as beneath notice in the early 1860s when the Amateur Musical Society was still only a group of singers and players performing in aid of charity but chiefly for their own pleasure, trained by a man with no academic qualifications and a highly suspect ability in score-reading and conducting technique. But as Lee's raids into territory normally lorded over by men like Stewart began to be a success with the public, Stewart took hostile action. He secured unwelcome publicity in the Protestant newspapers for disputes in the Amateur Musical Society concerning the society's aims, disputes which Stewart himself had fomented. As a result the society was reorganized and a more active committee elected. Lee accommodated himself to the changes, making a few of his own as well. He renamed the society the New Philharmonic Society and formed a branch called the National Institute of Music. Stewart's counter attack was to insist on conducting his own ode, composed for performance by the society for the opening of the 1873 Dublin

Exhibition. During rehearsals he completely undermined Lee's position in the society by exposing Lee's many technical weaknesses as a conductor. Lee could not bear such humiliation. He fled not only from the society but from Ireland. 'I unmasked one arrant impostor,' crowed Stewart, 'and drove him from Dublin.'[3]

Within a few days Lee had packed his bags and left Dublin, and there is no record of his ever having set foot in Ireland again. He had not intended to go so soon, if at all, for only eighteen months previously he had renewed for a long term his tenancy of Torca Cottage and now abandoned his plans for another concert. What was to be such an embarrassment to Shaw was that before a month had passed his mother had packed her bags too, and with her daughters followed Lee to London. She chose an odd day to desert her husband and her son: 17 June 1873, her twenty-first wedding anniversary.

Shaw insisted that an interval of a year or more passed between Lee's and Bessie's departures. He pointed out that Bessie's departure was an economic necessity, that without Lee the Hatch Street house could not be maintained, let alone Torca Cottage; that her husband's ever-dwindling income from the corn business was not enough to support a wife and two daughters and to subsidize a lowly-paid son; that she had hopes of getting Lucy launched as a professional on the London stage; and that in any event Lee would have had to go over well in advance to prepare the ground. But the evidence of the mail boat's passenger lists shows that Bessie and her daughters had hot-footed it after Lee – 'her man', as Shaw described him in a candid moment.

All the same Shaw need not stand accused of total falsehood. Bessie's following of Lee on 17 June might have been to coax him back to Dublin for economic as well as personal reasons, her decision to make London her future home being taken only when she found he had resolved not to return. Nor is there any need to doubt Shaw's account of how, before she finally settled in London, she tidied up her household affairs in Dublin, ended the Hatch Street tenancy, sold the furniture and saw her husband and her son established in 'comfortable bachelor lodgings' in No 61 Harcourt Street which, with unintended symbolism, stood half a mile or so both from the Hatch Street house and their old home in Synge Street.

There had now occurred a sudden and enormous change in the seventeen-year-old Shaw's domestic circumstances. Gone were the big house and the Dalkey summer cottage, for Lee presently disposed of his interest in it. Gone were his sisters, his mother, and his admired Lee. Gone was the musicmaking that had become a daily necessity of life to him, the exciting bustle of rehearsals, the prestige of being one of the inner circle at gala concerts patronized by the Viceroy. But he seems to have adjusted to the new situation. The friendship with McNulty ripened into close intimacy, and another friendship was started with a fellow lodger in Harcourt Street, Chichester Bell, a cousin of the Bell who invented the telephone. In *Sixteen Self Sketches* he acknowledges how useful Bell's friendship was.

> We studied Italian together: and though I did not learn Italian, I learned a good deal else, mostly about physics and pathology. I read Tyndall and Trousseau's Clinical Lectures. And it was Bell who made me take Wagner seriously. . . . When I found Bell regarded Wagner as a great composer, I bought a vocal score of Lohengrin: the only sample to be had at the Dublin music shops. The first few bars completely converted me.

A few years previously that vocal score would not have been of much use to him because he neither knew his notes nor could play the piano, although he spent a lot of time at the keyboard picking out tunes with one finger. Bessie's refusal to teach a so obviously musical son, or even to have him taught, is eloquent proof of the neglect

he so bitterly reproached her for. However she had spared the family piano when selling off the furniture, so Shaw now taught himself to play by propping the overture to *Don Giovanni* in front of him and stabbing at the notes until he succeeded in reproducing the familiar sounds.

If, as McNulty declared, he had hated his father, the hatred was not deep enough to prevent them from living peaceably together in the Harcourt Street lodging. His life was passed in cashiering for Uniacke Townshend, writing almost daily letters to McNulty who was now working in a North of Ireland branch of the bank; and taking lessons in a drawing school – for his great ambition now was to become a painter. There were also lessons in cornet playing from George Kennedy, a member of the Theatre Royal band who used also to play in Lee's concerts. The visit to Dublin of the popular preaching duo, Moody and Sankey, provoked a satirical letter from him to *Public Opinion* in April 1875, his first appearance in print, which to the scandal of the churchgoing Shaw relatives was a public profession of atheism. All the signs were that he was already subject to his lifelong tendency to remain wherever he happened to be put. He seemed set to live out his life in Dublin, in due course following his father into the family grave in Mount Jerome. Then Fate intervened through the medium of Death and of Charles Uniacke Townshend.

Early in 1876 Townshend brought his nephew into the firm. Possibly perturbed

(Left) *GBS with John Thomas Gibbings, 1876*

(Right) *GBS at the piano with Robert Moore Fishbourne, 1876*

by recollections of the letter in *Public Opinion* and deciding that it would be less risky to disoblige that influential uncle in the Valuation Office than offend the suscepti-bilities of his militantly Protestant clientele by harbouring an atheist in his office, Townshend made his nephew cashier, leaving Shaw with no more than nominal duties. It was clear that there was little future for Shaw in Molesworth Street. This was to be the final humiliation inflicted on him in Dublin. There is no mistaking the wounded pride in the letter written to Townshend on 29 February 1876:

Dear Sir

I beg to give you notice that at the end of next month, I shall leave your office.

My reason is, that I object to receive a salary for which I give no adequate value. Not having enough to do, it follows that the little I have is not well done. When I ceased to act as Cashier I anticipated this, and have since become satisfied that I was right.

Under these circumstances I prefer to discontinue my services & remain

very truly yours

G. B. Shaw

Before the month was out his sister Yuppy had died from tuberculosis at Ventnor in the Isle of Wight. Her death altered the situation with regard to the Whitcroft bequest, a circumstance which would not have escaped the vigilantly businesslike eye of the ex-cashier. Aged just twenty and with little in the way of bright prospects or domestic ties to bind him to Dublin, he packed a carpet bag and left the city which had conquered him, arriving some twenty-two hours later on a beautiful spring day in London, the city which after much dogged labour he would conquer.

He took with him a contemptuously accurate memory of Dublin's less attractive aspects, his only sentimental feelings for it being centred on Dalkey and on the operatic and theatrical performances which had rejoiced his boyhood. He was forti-fied by an intimacy with great music and behind-the-scenes knowledge of its prepara-tion for public performance uncommon in a youth of his circumstances, but was disabled by a keener awareness of his shortcomings as a musician and as a draughts-man than of his strength as an author and critic. He carried the wounds of an inse-cure, unloved childhood and the beginnings of a belief in the virtue of supermen who seemed to succeed in all they undertook. He was to hold so firmly to the certitudes of his youth that when he later observed how people no longer conformed to his Dublin notions of them, he concluded that they had altered, not that his own judg-ment had been faulty. He carried away with him many names of acquaintances and neighbours he would use for characters, especially in the early, more realistic plays: McComas, Dubedat, Warren, Crampton, Hill, and so on. Several of his girl char-acters would embody his vision of Lucy as the person everybody loved but who loved nobody. His father, the ineffective futile male, would keep cropping up, and it is hard not to believe that his mother would be much in his mind as he created Mrs Clandon. He would draw what appears to be a full-length portrait of the most remarkable member of his Dublin circle, Professor Vandeleur Lee, calling him Pro-fessor Higgins who, like Lee, invented a Method and took a woman in hand, trans-forming her by that Method and giving her a 'Cause and a Creed to live for'. Professor Higgins would be another confirmed bachelor 'with no time for sex', and would have a bossy housekeeper like Lee's tyrant in Harrington Street. Higgins, too, would be vituperatively scornful of rivals. His Galatea would even have the same first name, Eliza, who would duly fall in love with her Pygmalion but not marry him. Eliza Doolittle would threaten to do at the moment of parting what Bessie Shaw in fact did in London: teach others the Method she had herself been taught. But both Elizas would end up, like Shaw, more lenient to the husband than to the hero.

AN IRISHMAN ABROAD

Yeats said there were two Shaws, the one who wrote letters to the newspapers and gave public interviews and the Shaw who created. The first kept a close eye on Ireland from the time he left it in his twentieth year and had something to say at each moment of crisis. He was always detached, never mean, and sometimes magnanimous.

In later years as a world celebrity and a rich man it cost him nothing to oppose current trends, but when he defended Parnell and criticized Gladstone's sexual moral standards and the prevailing marriage laws his career had not properly begun; it took even more courage and disinterestedness to defend Wilde; and his attempts to assist Casement, on trial for his life, was, in the temper of the time, quixotic.

To the British public these were typically Shavian stances ('he only does it to annoy because he knows it teases'), but there is no evidence that nationalist Ireland was ever grateful to Shaw, and as his advice was never taken, there was something gratuitous about his interventions; his gallantry went for nothing; his facetiousness was resented, and his habit of running on after he had made his point to drag in a joke or in pursuit of a red herring tended to discount the sincerity that had prompted his intervention.

Shaw left his Dublin office, he said, and went to London because it was the literary centre of the English language (in which he proposed to be king), as every Irishman 'who felt that his business in life was on the higher plains of the cultural professions' left Ireland. There was no Gaelic League then, no sense that 'Ireland had in herself the seed of culture'. If there had been, he speculated on another occasion, might he not have stayed at home and become a poet like Yeats and Synge? This sounds naive. Shaw was probably not taking care. How else could he couple Synge and Yeats as *poets*? The fact that he could make the remark discloses the essentially unpoetic nature of Shaw's genius.

'Personally I like Englishmen better than Irishmen.' Thus Shaw began his examination of the temperaments of the two peoples; but he added that he never thought of an Englishman as his countryman. Yeats would never have made the first remark and the second would have seemed a truism.

Shaw prefixed these observations to a singularly flighty section of his preface to *John Bull's Other Island*. Having accused Macaulay of annexing Swift as an Englishman, he went on to say that there was no Irish race but an Irish climate, which 'will stamp an immigrant more deeply and durably in two years than will the English climate in two hundred'. This is so patently absurd that it hardly seems worth

(Far left) *Oscar Wilde;* (top) *W. B. Yeats;* (centre) *Charles Parnell;* (below) *J. M. Synge* following the argument based on it: the Englishman, according to Shaw, is at the mercy of his imagination having no sense of reality to check it. 'The Irishman, with a far subtler and more fastidious imagination, has one eye on things as they are.'

The difference between the Irishman and the Englishman is illustrated by Nelson and the Duke of Wellington. This then is the rabbit that Shaw was waiting to produce while he was talking through his hat. The emotionalism and gush of Nelson ('Kiss me, Hardy') is contrasted with the 'intensely Irish' Wellington ('Sir, don't be a damn fool'). On the shaky premise that this brace of heroes were nationally representative, Shaw concludes:

> The value of the illustration lies in the fact that Nelson and Wellington were in the highest degree incompatible with one another on any other footing than one of independence. The government of Nelson by Wellington or of Wellington by Nelson is felt at once to be a dishonorable outrage to the governed and a finally impossible task for the governor.

Shaw then passes on to the English preference for stupid leaders because they associate brightness with dissoluteness, and to illustrate this he drags in Thackeray's admiration for sentimental stupidity, impossible for an Irish novelist. This was the prelude to a staggering claim: that the Irish expect their leaders to be clever and humbug-proof, while the English prefer their generals to have 'abilities that would not suffice to save a cabman from having his licence marked' and Prime Ministers 'with the outlook on life of a sporting country solicitor educated by a private governess'; the Irish overlooked 'fluent imbeciles with majestic presences' and were compelled to follow 'a supercilious, unpopular, tongue-tied, aristocratic Protestant Parnell'. He had been succeeded by Redmond, a better speaker; and at this point the reader is mesmerized by a superb paragraph which tells us that if once Redmond behaved in the way that would secure an English politician a permanent place on the front bench, he would lose his leadership immediately. If Shaw's thesis were to be taken seriously, then Parnell was obviously Wellington's successor as the archetypal Irishman, neither of them having a drop of Irish blood in their veins, unless Parnell inherited some from his American mother. Redmond's depressing end, his misguided reliance on English good faith, the romantic chivalry that made him pledge Irish aid to Britain faced by the German enemy without one concession in return – it all makes Shaw's sermon sound hollow; and he was to live to see a British premier outmanoeuvre Ireland's leaders, Griffith and Collins. He would have got himself out of that impasse by pointing out that Lloyd George was a Welshman.

However, it seems churlish to make heavy weather out of a frolic, especially when we know the origin of it.

In 1900 Yeats wrote to Lady Gregory to tell her that Shaw had an idea for a play contrasting English and Irish character. Yeats thought the idea was amusing. Two years later he writes from London: Shaw was talking about the play again. 'Certainly it will be a great thing for our company if he will do us an Irish play.' Another two years later, when Miss Horniman had agreed to subsidize the Abbey Theatre, Yeats commissioned the long-gestating play.

Since the idea of national contrasts had entertained Shaw's mind, the measure known as 'Wyndham's Act' had been passed by Parliament; it enabled some Irish tenants to purchase their holdings from their landlords: the money was provided by the Exchequer, and repayments were made in annuities. Shaw disapproved of the measure for socialistic reasons; it created a hundred petty landlords for every great one it removed. His objection is now better understood by Irish politicians; small farmers are one of the most reactionary elements in the economic life of the country;

Granville Barker as Keegan in John Bull's Other Island, *the Royal Court, 1905*

(Opposite) *A special performance of* John Bull's Other Island *at 10 Downing Street in 1911*

many contrive to keep a 'firm grip on their homesteads' while drawing unemployment assistance in addition.

In writing the play Shaw had to jettison his persiflage about Nelson and the Duke of Wellington. This was to find a home in the preface he wrote two years later. It was the work of the Shaw who wrote letters to the newspapers and gave public interviews – the non-stop debating society – not the 'Shaw who creates'. That one wrote *John Bull's Other Island*, and, if a caveat is entered for the one-act wartime comedy *O'Flaherty V.C.,* this was the only occasion when the creative Shaw took Ireland as his theme. Instead of staging an amusing debate he created God's Englishman, Tom Broadbent, and, as his antagonist, Larry Doyle, an Irish bachelor who has

made a success in England. 'Larry Shaw', he might have been called without misleading anybody. The character of the unfrocked priest, Father Peter Keegan, represents what one might call Shaw's super-ego. Larry is working-day Shaw; Peter Keegan is the Shaw of the rare faintly purple passages who would someday write *St Joan*.

The Land Act as a play theme might well have led to arid wastes if Shaw, the public figure, had been in the ascendant; fortunately he was not. In Matt Haffigan he drew a funny-true representative of the peasant driven to near lunacy by his lifelong struggle to grow seeds on stony ground. If Father Keegan, priest turned Buddhist, is Shaw *in excelsis,* Father Dempsey, the other priest in the play, is a very model of the old-style country parish priest.

James Joyce

Broadbent was created to show the Irish that 'the loudest laugh they could raise at the expense of the absurdest Englishman was not really a laugh on their side; that he would succeed where they would fail. . . .' Broadbent steals the show, whether the play is acted in Ireland or in England. But one must also consider the Irishman that Shaw set up as a contrast to Broadbent. Not in the least like the Duke of Wellington, but very like a lacklustre Shaw. Larry gives tongue to the wretchedness he escaped from when he went to England, not only 'the dreaming! the dreaming! the torturing, heart-scalding, never-satisfying dreaming', but the 'horrible, senseless, mischievous laughter' and the 'eternal derision, eternal envy, eternal folly, eternal fouling and starving and degrading.'

It is all very close to Joyce's picture of Dublin in *Ulysses*; the chief difference is that Joyce himself is part of that dreary landscape. On running away Shaw wanted to forget it, but Joyce brought it all in his luggage.

That Larry Doyle/Shaw meant what he said is proved by Shaw's sharp reaction to Sylvia Beach's request that he should buy a copy of the first edition of *Ulysses*. The picture Joyce painted of Dublin was, Shaw agreed, a truthful one. He (Shaw) would like to put a cordon round Dublin and compel every male inside it between the ages of fifteen and thirty to read it. He knew it all; this was not art but reality, and proved that the conversations he had heard and taken part in and escaped from in 1876 – that 'slack-jawed blackguardism' – was still going on.

The moanings of Larry Doyle were not what made *John Bull's Other Island* Shaw's first commercially successful play. He said elsewhere that the irrepressible clown in him insisted on appearing at those moments when he was about to be grand and tragic; it was his comic genius that brought the public to the Royal Court Theatre under the auspices of Harley Granville-Barker and J. E. Vedrenne. In its second season of matinées the author put a page into the programme asking the audience not to laugh so much during performances. Balfour, then Prime Minister, came four times to the play, bringing with him, on different occasions, Campbell-Bannerman and Asquith, who were to succeed him in office. King Edward commanded a special performance.

It was Shaw's breakthrough; his talent was at its liveliest. In the same season five of his plays were produced. The way had been made easy by the Irish play. But it was not seen in Ireland until 1916. The Abbey's directors excused themselves for not performing it on the ground that it was beyond their resources at the time. Shaw accepted the refusal good-humouredly. 'It was,' he wrote later in the preface, 'uncongenial to the whole spirit of the neo-Gaelic movement, which is bent on creating a new Ireland after its own ideal, whereas my play is a very uncompromising presentation of the real old Ireland.'

Shaw, without Irish touchiness, bore no ill-will. Yeats, the dominant figure in the Abbey, did not like the play. He said everything he could muster in its favour when writing to Shaw.

I thought in reading the first act that you had forgotten Ireland, but I found in the other acts that it is the only subject on which you are entirely serious. . . . You have said things in this play which are entirely true about Ireland, things which nobody has said before. . . . It astonishes me that you should have been so long in London and yet have remembered so much. . . .

'Fundamentally ugly and shapeless, but certainly keeps everybody amused,' was Yeats' verdict after seeing the play in London. 'I don't really like it,' he told Lady Gregory. In this he was not alone. A. B. Walkley, the drama critic, a friend of Shaw

ROYAL COURT THEATRE
Sloane Square, S.W.

Sole Lessee and Manager.
Mr. J. H. LEIGH.

VEDRENNE-BARKER
MATINEES.

Every Tuesday, Thursday and Friday,
at 2.30.

(Left) *Publicity for the*
Vedrenne-Barker Matinées

(Right) *H. Granville Barker:*
E. O. Hoppé

who had been used to some extent as a model for Broadbent in the play, called it a 'Shavian farrago', and accused Shaw of 'throwing all attempt at construction overboard'. Shaw defended himself in an interview with a journalist from *The Tatler*. How was he to get all England and Ireland into three hours and a quarter? He couldn't of course, and what he left out overflowed into the preface.

Shaw was never able to influence opinion over Ireland; the detachment that made *John Bull's Other Island* so amusing on the stage defeated its purpose when used in public statements. Shaw had an abundance of moral courage, but on most occasions he seemed more concerned with the argument than the outcome. He joked about matters of passionate concern to many people; above all he went on too long. In Dublin, as in London, his influence was nil. If he had come back to live in Ireland matters might have been worse; he belonged to a larger world. And he talked too much; Dublin simply didn't have the acoustics for that performance.

If Yeats be taken as representative of the new Ireland that Shaw saw at work behind the refusal of his play, he pitted himself against Shaw as one of 'the rooted against the rootless people'. He described Shaw to AE (the Ulster poet, George Russell) as an atheist 'trembling in the haunted corridor' . . . 'haunted by the mystery he flouts'.

To Florence Farr, who had made love to both men, Yeats said Shaw was 'a barbarian of the barricades'; and when there were preparations on foot to found an English Academy in 1910, Yeats, writing to Gosse, called Shaw 'the Joseph who had brought his brethren into captivity'. (He was referring to the conquest of the spirit of literature 'by the spirit of the press, of hurry, of immediate interests'.) In his best-known criticism of Shaw, Yeats described him as 'a sewing machine that clicked and shone, but the incredible thing was the machine smiled, smiled perpetually'. In the same paragraph Yeats admits that he delighted in Shaw 'the formidable man' who could hit out at 'my enemies and the enemies of all I loved, as I could never hit, or no living author that was dear to me could ever hit'.

The other Shaw, the Shaw who wrote to the newspapers, who, in Yeats' opinion, wrote *The Apple Cart*, hit often and hard for Ireland. The first time was when the British Government, by diplomatic pressure, persuaded Pope Leo XIII on 23 April 1888 to condemn boycotting, a practice which got its name from a Captain Boycott, a landlord's agent; anybody who bought property from which a tenant had been evicted was 'boycotted'. Shaw's Irish Protestant blood approximately boiled to hear that 'the liberties of Ireland have been sacrificed to a base Tory intrigue'. He was writing an unsigned leading article for *The Star*.

Shaw was born in a decade when Irish nationalist hopes were at their lowest. O'Connell was dead, and the 'Young Irelanders' who had attempted to stir a hungry and reluctant peasantry into revolt in 1848 were in exile. But in the 'sixties some of them launched from America the Fenian conspiracy. Shaw decided that he was a Fenian, but he joined no organization. It was merely an expression. In later years he might have described himself as an Irish Protestant federalist Fenian landlord. He dismissed Parnell as politically behind the times and the Gaelic revival as 'a quaint little off-shoot of English Pre-Raphaelitism'; nor did he lend his support to the Irish parliamentary party, led by Redmond, working for Home Rule, nor to Sinn Fein, established by Arthur Griffith in 1905, to which Yeats belonged for a time. The unionists (loyalists) did not get Shaw's support either. He wanted Ireland to be self-governing within a federation (under Socialism), but he did not associate himself with James Connolly, the only Marxist among the leaders of the Easter Rising in 1916. He had appeared on a London platform with Connolly, AE, and James Larkin during the 1913 Strike in Dublin.

When the Home Rule Bill was at its second reading in the same year, Shaw informed himself of its contents – he was more thorough than many professional politicians – and wrote an unsigned article in the *New Statesman* on the subject. Ulster, he declared, required 'a little more consideration than it is receiving at present'. If she wanted the *status quo*, she couldn't have it, but she would have to be left out of the Home Rule arrangement if she insisted.

> We must also bear in mind that political opinion is not a matter of talk and bluff as it is in England. . . . The Ulster man . . . has thrown stones, and been hit by them. . . . Give him a machine gun, and he will not recoil in horror from the idea of mowing down his fellow townsmen with it. . . . It is possible that the Ulsterman should be exterminated as an untolerable, unamiable, unneighborly, unsocial, unclubbable person; but as that is a job no English Government is prepared to undertake, the alternative seems to be to comply with his demands short of exterminating all the Catholics, which, though it is what he would like, is also impractable.

Let her become an ultra-Protestant enclave of England. This was Shaw's advice in 1913.

On future occasions, Shaw predicted that whatever the outcome, the inevitable growth of socialism among workers in the industrial north would eventually drive the capitalist employers into seeking accommodation with Catholics in the agricultural south. Socialism, one of Shaw's religions, gave him a blind spot where his political vision was otherwise clear.

He urged the Ulster leaders to seize the opportunity of the Home Rule Bill in another unsigned article in the *New Statesman*, but when the Convention was set up in 1917 to arrive at an agreed solution to the Irish problem, he published a long article in the *Daily Express*, rich in suggestions. There must be a federal parliament, he insisted, in addition to national parliaments for the constituent members of a new federation, and the Empire should be managed by a conference. As for Ireland, she would have a voice in the national parliament, the federal parliament, and the imperial conference. Separation was impossible, Ireland had too much to gain by pooling services, and a separatist Ireland was at England's mercy.

Shaw was to strike this note again during the Second World War. He urged de Valera to bring Ireland into the war; he had prophesied that, in the event of war, Britain would have to occupy Ireland. For this he was reproved by de Valera, for putting such an idea into the hearts of the British: there is an historic dislike in Ireland for what used to be called 'felon-setting'.

Shaw wanted Ireland to engage in both World Wars. In November 1914, he telegraphed to AE asking for his and Horace Plunkett's advice: should he write a letter to the newspaper urging Ireland to support the French Republic in arms? They agreed, and he published an appeal to Irishmen in the *Freeman's Journal* (the chief nationalist paper) to remember their debt to France, forget British tyranny, and help the French Republic to shatter the Prussian military machine. Ideally, the Irish should form an 'Irish Brigade'.

Eamon de Valera

Half-a-dozen Irish historians might have seen Shaw's point (as H. G. Wells said that he did), but even at the time it must have sounded phoney. In 1915, Nathan,

the Irish Under-Secretary, asked Shaw to assist in the recruiting campaign. Shaw responded with *O'Flaherty V.C.*, a one-act play, highly unsuitable for its purpose, but full of shrewd fun. It was not performed until the war was safely over. As well he prepared a long poster text which was never used.

Shaw had insisted in an article in the *New York Times* in April 1916 that 'Ireland as a nation cannot keep out of the present conflict', and later in the month heard of the fighting in Dublin. Unaware of the fact that some of the leaders had been executed, he wrote a defence of the Irish action for the *New Statesman*. He was elated. 'All the slain men and women of the Sinn Fein Volunteers fought and died for their country as sincerely as any soldier in Flanders has fought and died for his.' But then he destroyed the effect by seeming levity;

> Let us grieve, not over the fragment of Dublin city that is knocked down, but over at least three-quarters of what has been preserved. How I wish I had been in command of the British artillery on that fatal field! How I should have improved my native city!

After he heard about the executions, he wrote to the *Daily News*: 'My own view – which I should not intrude on you had you not concluded that it does not exist – is that the men who were shot in cold blood after their capture or surrender were prisoners of war, and that it was, therefore, entirely incorrect to slaughter them . . .' Admirable, but again he went on to spoil the effect of his protest by lecturing on the pre-Rising situation, disclosing in the process an inadequate briefing.

He went to very considerable trouble to help Roger Casement who fell into British hands after a German submarine landed him in Kerry. Ironically, he had come to try to stop the Rising, German help not being available. Shaw drafted his defence (not used) and a petition for his release, which he didn't sign 'because my name might have frightened off some of the more useful signatures'. A Captain Fryatt was shot by the Germans for trying to ram a submarine. Shaw took this as an opportunity to write to the *Daily News* with an eleventh-hour appeal for Casement: 'If we miss it, and miss it in cold blood, we must not expect America or France or any other country to draw that distinction between the merciful and magnanimous Briton and the cruel and ruthless Hun, which most of us, I hope, would like to see realized in deeds as well as in printer's ink.' Shaw wrote as a member of the British public, not as an Irishman, the stance he took on less tragic occasions.

It was uphill work, and in the temper of the time – when the war was going badly – to argue successfully that Casement was justified in opening negotiations with the Germans if he believed they were going to win the war was asking for a greater degree of impartiality than could have been expected. He agreed that Casement had had a fair trial. 'In Ireland he will be regarded as a national hero if he is executed, and quite possibly as a spy if he is not.' But even on this occasion Shaw could not resist throwing in what might have sounded effective in one of his plays but in the circumstances looked like stark insensitivity.

> There need be no hesitation to carry out the sentence if it should appear, on reflection, a sensible one. Indeed, with a view to extricating the discussion completely from the sentimental vein, I will go so far as to confess that there is a great deal to be said for hanging all public men at the age of fifty-two, though under such a regulation I should myself have perished eight years ago.

His facetiousness deprived Shaw of political influence and a place in the hearts of his countrymen. Nobody believed Shaw cared, and his later fatuities about the Dictators, no less than his unerring capacity to be wrong in his tireless appearances as a prophet, did nothing to alter this impression. He had convinced himself that the death of many was no more tragic than the death of one because the measure of suffering is what any one individual endures. The more, if not the merrier, is not the sadder either. It must explain why he came to talk so casually about Stalin's mass liquidations, a strange aberrancy in a man who was generous, charitable and humane, incapable personally of cruelty to man or beast. His maternal inheritance may also help to explain it: that unloving, unhating, gentle-mannered mother.

In later years he is found describing himself as a member of the landlord class. He mentioned to Ellen Terry that he had inherited his uncle's insolvent estate in County Carlow. He made it solvent at his own expense and held on to it for many years before having the Irish parliament pass a special Act to municipalize the property shortly before his death. Had he a trace of the Irish snobbery he noticed with disapproval in Wilde, that he included among the oddities of his hopeless father? He

Charlotte, photographed by Shaw shortly after their marriage

hid for most of his life the fact that he had attended a Model School with Roman Catholics. Did the 'millionairess with the green eyes' who married him owe his surrender to her cousinship with the senior partner in the land agency Shaw joined at fifteen?

Edith Somerville, writing to her brother about the match, said, 'Charlotte is now Mrs Bernard Shaw and I hope she likes it. . . . He began as an office boy in Townshend French's agency office in Dublin, and now he is distinctly somebody in a literary way, but he can't be a gentleman. . . .' The joint creator of the 'Irish R.M.' was agreeably surprised on meeting him to find Shaw sane and affable. In his choice of a wife and in many other respects Shaw was, and was always to remain, an old-fashioned Irish gentleman. He fled Dublin because he wanted to escape from poverty and obscurity. In his own phrase a full life has to be 'cleared out every day by the housemaid of forgetfulness'.

Shaw confided in Lady Gregory on one occasion that Miss Somerville had sent him 'a dreadful play to criticise . . . She ought to have given up that old opinion of the Irish upper classes that the peasant was ridiculous, that there was something ridiculous in poverty, in dishonesty, in dirt.' Nowhere does Shaw appear to better effect than in Lady Gregory's *Journals*. Staying with the Shaws, she read *St Joan* in draft; when Shaw, on the day he wrote it, read her the scene where the wind changes, she said that she would have made the boy sneeze. Shaw put the sneeze in.

She won his support eventually for her campaign to obtain her nephew Hugh Lane's pictures for Dublin. Shaw at first expressed the view that London, where people went to look, was 'the right place for them, whereas the Dublin National Gallery is a silent desert.' But in the same breath he told her that his 'whole life was influenced by the Dublin National Gallery, for I spent many days of my boyhood wandering through it and so learned to care for Art.'

Some of his good things were recorded in that tireless woman's *Journals*: Shaw told her that 'a man who is a failure is always popular' and 'the worst of victims is that

Coole Park, the home of Lady Gregory

they always let you down.' For all his affectionate approval, he eluded her sometimes, when she wanted him to come to Coole to check Black-and-Tan outrages, when she asked him to lecture for her theatre fund; she sighed because he did not do more work for Ireland; but he responded handsomely when Richard Hayes, Director of the Irish National Library, wrote him a note suggesting that the Library was the most suitable home for his papers. 'Your invitation as national librarian is in the nature of a command' – he gave without stint.

When it came to the matter of his will, his chief, eccentric beneficiary was his 40-letter phonetic alphabet: that was disposed of by payment of an agreed sum. The residue was divided between the British Museum, where he had found his books, the Royal Academy of Dramatic Art – he owed his fortune to the stage – and the National Gallery of Ireland.

National Gallery of Ireland with the statue of GBS by Paul Troubetskoy standing outside

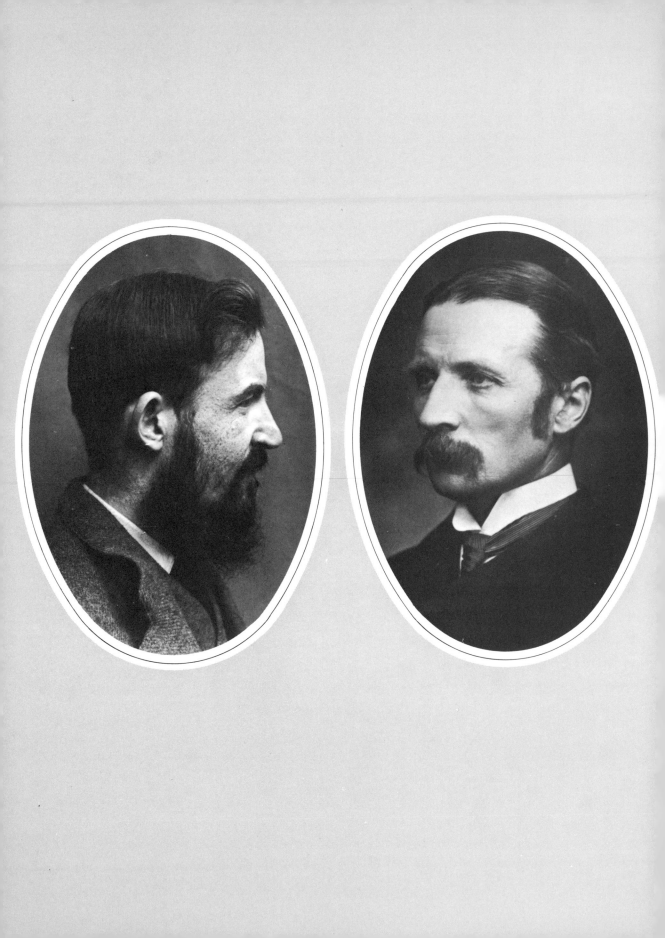

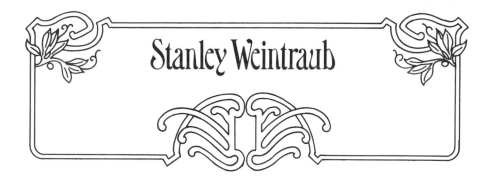

IN THE PICTURE GALLERIES

In the days of Bernard Shaw's boyhood, when English painting was suffering from the blight of the sentimental academic subject picture, and Ireland lagged culturally at least a generation behind, the young Shaw could have been guaranteed a surfeit of such paintings in Dublin. When he left for London at twenty, in 1876, the art which English galleries found salable, despite the inroads of Pre-Raphaelitism, was still much the same. An index of the situation was the fate of Whistler's 'Mother' – the *Arrangement in Grey and Black, No. 1,* which had been exhibited in London in 1874 and, being unsold and unnoticed, spent most of the following eighteen years in pawn until the Government of France purchased it for the Luxembourg Museum, for living painters the 'vestibule to the Louvre'.

The later years of the portrait's purgatory were Shaw's years as an art critic in London. It was an unanticipated career. His friend, William Archer, who was dramatic critic of *The World* in 1885, had found himself suddenly compelled to double as art critic. He invited Shaw to accompany him to the galleries. Shaw had written two unsalable novels in which art played a major role, *Immaturity* and *Love Among the Artists*, where the artists of some worth had been influenced by Pre-Raphaelitism and Whistler, and the philistine painters believed in society portraits, anecdotal pictures and making money. Wandering the galleries and offering comments as he went was not work to Shaw, who was surprised when Archer sent him a cheque for £1.6s.8d. – half the fee. He returned it; Archer sent it back; Shaw then 're-returned' it on 14 December 1885, claiming that he had been under no 'external compulsion' to go, while Archer had been under the orders of his editor, Edmund Yates. Shaw explained:

> I have the advantage of seeing the galleries for nothing without the drudgery of writing the articles. I do not like to lose the record of the art life, and yet going to a gallery by myself bores me so much that I let the [Royal] Academy itself slip last year, and should have done so this year but for your bearing me thither. . . .[1]

Archer solved the problem by persuading Yates to name his friend as art critic, a post Shaw held, often concurrently with half-a-dozen other responsibilities, from February 1886 until January 1890. Although Shaw's novels were uncommercial, as a critic, he boasted, 'I came to the top irresistibly, whilst contemporary well-schooled literary beginners, brought up in artless British homes, could make no such mark.' He had a critical strategy, he claimed:

> I was capable of looking at a picture then, and, if it displeased me, immediately considering whether the figures formed a pyramid, so that, if they did not, I could prove the

picture defective because the composition was wrong. And if I saw a picture of a man foreshortened at me in such a way that I could see nothing but the soles of his feet and his eyes looking out between his toes, I marvelled at it and almost revered the painter, though veneration was at no time one of my strong points. . . . I can only thank my stars that my sense of what was real in works of art somehow did survive my burst of interest in irrelevant critical conventions and the pretensions of this or that technical method to be absolute. . . .[2]

One of his earliest campaigns as a critic was fought in a war that had already ended. Pre-Raphaelite painting had already made an impact upon contemporary art and had itself either faded into commercialism or been transmuted into new conventions. Still, Shaw (to the end a follower of Ruskin) regularly praised Dante Gabriel Rossetti, who had died in 1882, but he tempered his appreciation of Rossetti's later work by noting that although he had dazzled with his 'wealth of colour and poetic conception', 'our eyes are now used to the sun; and . . . Rossetti's want of thoroughness as a draughtsman, and the extent to which his favourite types of beauty at last began to reappear as mere . . . conventions, with impossible lips and mechanically designed eyebrows, came as something of a shock upon many who had previously fancied him almost flawless.'[3] He also continued to admire the earlier art of Rossetti's *confrères* Millais, Hunt and Burne-Jones – all of whom had long since done their best work. The sheer labour they evidenced, of which Ruskin would have approved, led Shaw – ever the social critic – into observing that intended didacticism often had an improving effect, if not the one which the artist may have intended. Of an exhibition of Holman Hunt's work, he wrote:

> Mr Holman Hunt, the catalogue tells us (it is a mine of instruction and amusement, that catalogue), painted *The Hireling Shepherd* 'in rebuke of the sectarian vital negligences of the nation'. The seriousness of the painter's aim probably did not bring a single Sandemanian into the fold of the Established Church, or induce one woman of fashion to give up tight-lacing (the most familiar form of 'vital negligence'); but it is the secret of the perseverance and conscientiousness which has made this small picture one of the most extraordinary units of a collection that does not contain one square inch of commonplace handiwork.

Spencer Stanhope, he wrote in *The World* in 1886, 'has imitated Mr Burne-Jones quite long enough. If he would imitate Hogarth for a season or two, and then look out of the window and imitate Nature, we might gain some adequate return from his praiseworthy industry.' Conscientious industry was not enough, nor imitation of Burne-Jones, although Edward Burne-Jones remained to Shaw the giant of his art-critic decade, with 'the power to change the character of an entire exhibition by contributing or withholding his work'. It was not that he was more technically gifted, Shaw thought, but that he had more imagination, while others who displayed similar wares in Bond Street were 'venal, ambitious, time-serving and vulgar'. Of the P.R.B. survivors he found least to admire in John Millais, who was making more money and less art than ever before. His *Forlorn*, Shaw thought, reviewing an 1888 exhibition, 'ought surely to have been called *Abandoned*. She is an arrant pot-boiler as ever was painted: her upper lip dripping vermillion, and her ill-made flaunting theatrical red sleeves, are intolerable to contemplate.'

Whistler, once a P.R.B. crony, years later was still on the outside, as uncommercial as ever; and if only as rebel and wit he was bound to receive Shavian support. Yet Shaw praised Whistler's art while warning imitators against it, and when he felt that Whistler was showing work not up to his abilities, as in the cleverly-mounted Dowdeswell show of Venice etchings in 1886, he hoped – with scepticism – for more formidable future results:

Mr Whistler's Notes, Harmonies, and Nocturnes are arranged in brown and gold, in a brown and gold room, beneath a brown and gold velarium, in charge of a brown and gold porter. It cannot be said of Mr Whistler, as of Mr Sparkler's ideal mistress,* that he has no nonsense about him. . . . The 'Chelsea Fish Shop', the Hoxton street scene, the Dutch seaside sketch, are a few out of many examples of accurate and methodical note-taking, which is just the reverse of what the rasher spectators suppose them to be. As Mr Whistler presumably takes notes with a view to subsequent pictures, it is to be hoped that something will soon come of them.

Shaw was never to be satisfied, as literary critic, art critic, music critic or theatre critic, with the work of an artist who was performing at less than his potential. As he put it in a music column in 1890,

> . . . A criticism written without personal feeling is not worth reading. It is the capacity for making good or bad art a personal matter that makes a man a critic. The artist who accounts for my disparagement by alleging personal animosity on my part is quite right: when people do less than their best, and do that less at once badly and self-complacently, I hate them, loathe them, detest them, long to tear them limb from limb. . . .

Finding himself once, in *The World*, speaking 'contemptuously' of the 'elderly school', he confessed as much, and then went on to observe that it was

> not a time to be just to it. Its principle of giving a precise pictorial account of what it knew to be before it, led it to paint a great deal that it did not see, and to omit a great deal that it did see. It is now getting a tremendous lesson from the men [of the impressionist school] who are trying to paint no more and no less than they see; and I am more disposed to help to rub that lesson in than to make untimely excuses for people who for many years outraged my taste for nature until I positively hated the sight of an ordinary picture.

As a result, although he could not reconcile himself 'to the occasional prevalence of a ghastly lilac-coloured fog,' still, 'looking at the more elderly British wall-ornaments . . ., it is hard to admit that such airless, lightless, sunless crudities, coloured in the taste of a third-rate toymaker, and full of absurd shadows put in *a priori* as a matter of applied physics, could ever have seemed satisfactory pictures.'

Shaw's concern, he wrote later in *The Sanity of Art*, was that when 'Whistler and his party' forced the dealers and art societies to exhibit their work, and by doing so, to accustom the public to tolerate, if not appreciate, what at first appeared to be absurdities,

> the door was necessarily opened to real absurdities. Artists of doubtful or incomplete vocation find it difficult to draw or paint well; but it is easy for them to smudge paper or canvas so as to suggest a picture just as the stains on an old ceiling or the dark spots in a glowing coal-fire do. Plenty of rubbish of this kind was exhibited, and tolerated at the time when people could not see the difference between any daub in which there were aniline shadows and a landscape by Monet. Not that they thought the daub as good as the Monet: they thought the Monet as ridiculous as the daub; but they were afraid to say so. . . .

Among the early impressionists Claude Monet was a particular hero of Shaw's picture-gallery period. Shaw regularly attempted to separate the daubers from such new masters, and also responded coolly to innovation which seemed to him not fraudulent but to lack range. As to the 'New English Art' reformers, he had his doubts as to where the newness would lead: 'These gentlemen are painting short-sightedly in more senses than one. The trick of drawing and colouring badly as if you did it on purpose is easily acquired; and the market will be swamped with "new English art", and the public tired of it, in a year or two.'

* Edmund Sparkler appears in Dickens's *Little Dorrit*.

The artistic direction which Shaw saw as most hopeful was one to which he had been converted first by Ruskin and then by William Morris, who had put his theories of decorative art to use well beyond the fresco and the frame.

> It has been for a long time past evident that the first step towards making our picture-galleries endurable is to get rid of the pictures – the detestable pictures – the silly British pictures, the vicious foreign pictures, the venal popular pictures, the pigheaded academic pictures, signboards all of them of the wasted talent and perverted ambition of men who might have been passably useful as architects, engineers, potters, cabinet-makers, smiths, or book-binders. But there comes an end to all things; and perhaps the beginning of the end of the easel-picture despotism is the appearance in the New Gallery of the handicraftsman with his pots and pans, textiles and fictiles, and things in general that have some other use than to hang on a nail and collect bacteria. Here, for instance, is Mr Cobden Sanderson, a gentleman of artistic instincts. Does Mr Cobden Sanderson paint wooden portraits of his female relatives, and label them Juliet or Ophelia, according to the colour of their hair? No: he binds books, and makes them pleasant to look at, pleasant to handle, pleasant to open and shut, pleasant to possess, and as much of a delight as the outside of a book can be. Among the books he has bound are illuminated manuscripts written by William Morris. . . . The smaller unbound pages in the same case show better what Mr Morris can do with his valuable time in his serious moments, when he is not diverting himself with wall-decoration, epic story-telling, revolutionary journalism and oratory, fishing and other frivolities of genius. From his factory he sends specimens of the familiar wall-papers and carpets; but the highest point in a decorative manufacture is reached in his 'arras' tapestries, and in a magical piece of stained glass. . . .

What Shaw was then preaching with missionary zeal has now become a fact of the art marketplace.

As season followed season, he continued to turn out his columns on art, at the same time writing book reviews for the *Pall Mall Gazette*, music reviews (as Corno di Bassetto, beginning in 1888) for *The Star*, and political and economic journalism for the myriad radical publications in London. However his loyalty to the picture galleries, he confessed, was giving way to more pressing personal interests. Winding down his commentary on art for *The World* he wrote in the issue of 23 October 1889, 'I cannot guarantee my very favourable impression of the Hanover Gallery, as I only saw it by gaslight. This was the fault of Sarasate, who played the Ancient Mariner with me. He fixed me with his violin on my way to Bond Street, and though, like the wedding guest, I tried my best, I could not choose but to hear.' The concert hall was winning out.

Shaw was already trying his hand at playwriting, beginning, and then discarding or putting aside, a number of experiments for the stage. Eventually painting had to pall, although his on-the-job art education was useful later as a working playwright in ways he could never have anticipated. The experience had also convinced him of the effectiveness of art as an instrument of culture, a subject he wrote about explicitly in the influential *The Sanity of Art* (1895, expanded 1908) and in such prefaces as those to *Misalliance* and *Back to Methuselah*, and implicitly wherever he put his pen to paper. 'We all grow stupid and mad,' he concluded in the *Misalliance* preface, 'to just the extent to which we have not been artistically educated.'

Shaw's early dramatic settings could not help but be influenced, even when he intended to use a scene ironically, by what English eyes were accustomed to encountering in art. In his earliest plays, one can visualize what Shaw himself saw, as he tramped through Bond Street and Burlington House and the art clubs and societies in the 'eighties. In the final stage directions in *Candida* (1894), for example, young Marchbanks, spurned, turns to Candida and her husband for the last time, and '*She* takes his face in her hands; and as he divines her intention and falls on his knees, she kisses his forehead'. In his tableau Shaw was parodying the sentimental Victorian anecdote in painting, although his first audiences, unaware of his satirical intent, took it straight. In *The Devil's Disciple*, the first act includes a Reading of the Will – an obvious grouping of people for a Royal Academy set piece. In the last act the scene of Dick Dudgeon mounting the scaffold owes much, as Shaw confessed, to dramatizations of Dickens' *A Tale of Two Cities*, but perhaps even more to Frederick Barnard's popular painting, *Sydney Carton, 'A Tale of Two Cities'*, exhibited at the Royal Academy in 1882 and much reproduced.[4] Yet Shaw's painterly images were

From Fredrick Barnard's popular painting Sydney Carton, 'A Tale of Two Cities', *exhibited at the Royal Academy in 1882*

not necessarily ironic. Putting the case for realistic theatre in a *Saturday Review* column (17 July 1897), he declared, 'The most advanced audiences today, taught by Wagner and Ibsen (not to mention Ford Madox Brown), cannot stand the drop back into decoration after the moment of earnest life. They want realistic drama of complete brainy passional texture all through, and will not have any pictorial stuff or roulade at all. . . .' He intended to provide the intellectual realism.

GBS always did his homework before writing a scene, even researching American Civil War memoirs as preparation for a play in which war would have a part, *Arms and the Man*. He was thus quick to respond to his critic-friend William Archer, who reviewed the play unfavourably, 'Do you think war is any less terrible & heroic in its reality – on its seamy side, as you would say – than it is in the visions of Raina & of the critics who know it from the engravings of Elizabeth Thompson's pictures in the Regent St shop windows?'[5] Elizabeth Thompson (Lady Butler) was famous for her obsessively detailed paintings of British feats of arms during the Napoleonic and Crimean wars: Shaw's play was at least in part a response to her sentimental pictures, one of which, *The Roll Call* (1874), was purchased by Queen Victoria.

Candida was a much more complex response to art. Shaw called it his 'modern Pre-Raphaelite play', and intended it on one of its many levels as an analogue to medieval religious painting. Even its curious subtitle, 'A Mystery', suggests medieval associations. In the sitting-room of the comfortable London parsonage in which the play is set, a single picture is seen on the wall, described in Shaw's opening stage directions as '*a large autotype of the chief figure in Titian's Assumption of the Virgin*' (the upper half, showing Mary ascending into the clouds). But *Candida*, he wanted to make plain by a recognizable work of art, was an ironic Shavian mystery play about Madonna and Child, with the heroine of the title the Holy Mother. At Candida's first entrance Shaw's stage directions muse, '*A wise-hearted observer, looking at her, would at once guess that whoever had placed the Virgin of the Assumption over her hearth did so because he fancied some spiritual resemblance between them, and yet would not suspect either her husband or herself of any such idea, or indeed of any concern with the art of Titian.*' The reproduction is the gift of the eighteen-year-old Eugene Marchbanks, the sensitive and emotional young poet the Rev James Morell and his wife have befriended. The resemblance he perceives will vanish through the play, and with it his idealism.

In letters to Ellen Terry, Shaw confided that Candida was 'the Virgin Mother and nobody else', and that he had written 'THE Mother Play'. To Janet Achurch, for whom he had written it, he suggested that she make herself up for the role by recourse to examples in art, having been horrified by the idea that she would play his Madonna in frizzed, bleached-blond hair.

> Send to a photograph shop for a picture of some Roman bust – say that of Julia, daughter of Augustus and wife of Agrippa, from the Uffizi in Florence – and take that as your model, or rather as your point of departure. You must part your hair in the middle, and be sweet, sensible, comely, dignified, and Madonna-like. If you condescend to the vulgarity of being a pretty woman, much less a flashy one . . . you are lost.[6]

The Shavian play in which critics have begun to explore the impact of the visual arts is *Caesar and Cleopatra*, written in 1898. As Shaw insisted to his German translator Siegfried Trebitsch, in sending him crude sketches for the play,

> Barbarous as my drawings of the scenery are, a great deal depends on them. Even an ordinary modern play like *Es Lebe das Leben*, with drawing room scenes throughout, depends a good deal on the author writing his dialogue with a clear plan of stage action in his head; but in a play like Caesar it is absolutely necessary: the staging is just as much a part of the

Detail of Assumption of the Virgin *by Titian*

(Top right) *Janet Achurch;*
(centre and below) *Scenes
from* Candida *from the
Hamer-Pearson 'Candida'
Company's Continental Tour,*
1908–9

play as the dialogue. It will not do to let a scenepainter & a sculptor loose on the play without a specification of the conditions with which their scenery must comply. Will you therefore tell the Neues manager that we will supply sketches. I will not inflict my own draughtsmanship on him; but I will engage a capable artist to make presentable pictures.[7]

Shaw was taking no chances. Ancient Egypt had tremendous appeal for a pre-cinematic, Bible-familiar public, and cheap colour lithographs were a popular commodity. Society painter Edward Poynter (later President of the Royal Academy) even achieved his first successes with enormous scenes from the times of the pharaohs, one crowded and carefully researched ten-foot panorama, *Israel in Egypt* (1867), being typical of the genre.

At least two paintings seem to have inspired specific scenes in *Caesar and Cleopatra*. Martin Meisel points to Luc Olivier Merson's 1879 painting, *Répos en Egypte*, citing a Shaw letter to Hesketh Pearson in 1918 which establishes the source of the famous tableau:

> The Sphinx scene was suggested by a French painter of the Flight Into Egypt. I never can remember the painter's name, but the engraving, which I saw in a shop window when I was a boy, of the Virgin and child asleep in the lap of a colossal Sphinx staring over a desert, so intensely still that the smoke of Joseph's fire close by went straight up like a stick, remained in the rummage basket of my memory for thirty years before I took it out and exploited it on the stage.

The 'relevance of the new god in the arms of the old' is implicit in the scene whether or not the influence of the Merson painting is known, but the suggestive relevance is more than a matter of scenery, for knowledge of the artistic source of the scene opens up a new avenue of interpretation. Shaw places Caesar in the Sphinx's lap, the position occupied by Christ and the Virgin in the Merson painting. Thus, as Meisel suggests, Caesar 'explicitly equates himself with his successor, the unborn Christ'.[8] Likewise, the young and barely nubile Cleopatra is equated with the Virgin, already a familiar figure in Shaw.

(Below) Israel in Egypt *by Edward Poynter*
Répos en Egypte *by Luc Oliver Merson (below right) suggested the famous sphinx scene in* Caesar and Cleopatra *to Shaw (top)*

The so-called 'rug scene', in Act III of *Caesar and Cleopatra*, in which Cleopatra, wrapped in a rug, is delivered to Caesar, has also been traced to a painting. The incident itself is described in Plutarch's life of Caesar, but as George W. Whiting asserts, Jean-Léon Gérôme's painting, *Cleopatre Apportée à Caesar dans un Tapis* (1866), may have influenced Shaw's rendering of the scene.[9] The picture focuses upon a more mature Cleopatra than Shaw's child-woman, standing amid the folds of the carpet from which she has just emerged, and turning toward Caesar, who is seated at a table. An apprehensive Apollodorus (having just unwound the rug) kneels behind her, and several male Romans in the background look on curiously. Gérôme's Caesar is younger and less bald than Shaw's and history's; also, the details differ from Shaw's exterior conception of the scene, yet Gérôme's conception is one of its rare evocations in art, and Shaw declared in a letter to Trebitsch (15 December 1898) that his handling of the incident would give considerable pause to the French painters who were so fond of her. Shaw's, presumably, was to be a more relevant Cleopatra.

Man and Superman (written 1901–02) owes at least one element both to popular nineteenth-century art and to a favourite and archetypal eighteenth-century image – that of the collector in his gallery or study surrounded by the acquisitions which reflect the personality he wanted to evoke. Thus Johann Zoffany painted his famous *Charles Townley in his Gallery* (1782) in the sanctum of Townley's house in Westminster, amid a clutter of the works of art – from paintings to portrait busts – which were to establish his client's neoclassic tastes. The canvas remained well known in Shaw's day.

Roebuck Ramsden's study, described in the opening scene of *Man and Superman*, might be another Zoffany. It contains, in addition to busts and portraits of famous contemporaries, '*autotypes of allegories by Mr G. F. Watts . . . and an impression of Dupont's engraving of Delaroche's Beaux Arts hemicycle, representing the great men of all ages*'. Shaw's selection of the works he describes helps to establish both the atmosphere of the scene and Ramsden's personality. George Frederick Watts, the fashionable Victorian painter, painted portraits, classical scenes, and Biblical settings, in addition to his allegorical works, but it is significant that Shaw chose the latter category with which to decorate Ramsden's study. Allegorical representations, such as Watts' 'Time, Death, and Judgment', 'Love and Death', and 'Hope', possess a very literal, uncomplicated quality; and they would appeal to the relatively unimaginative mind – to Ramsden's conservative point of view, for example, for he 'believes in the fine arts with all the earnestness of a man who does not understand them', according to Shaw's description of him. Paul Delaroche's *Hemicycle* (1837–41) is a comment on the pompous Ramsden. So named because it occupies the semi-circular frieze of the Palais de Beaux Arts amphitheatre, it depicts Appelles, enthroned within the portico of an Ionic temple, flanked by Ictinus and Phidias. Near them are five allegorical figures (reminiscent of Watts' allegories in Ramsden's study), Fame, Greek Art, Gothic Art, Roman Art, and Renaissance Art. At each side of this ideal group sit and stand seventy-five colossal figures of the great artists of the world – a complement to Ramsden's own miniature collection of Victorian celebrities. Ramsden's study, then, is, in effect, a 'Hemicycle' in miniature.

Little of Shaw's description of Ramsden's crowded study is perceptible to the audience, only the reader thus being 'in' on Shaw's satirical treatment of the ultrarespectable, well-to-do Englishman of liberal persuasion whose views have not changed in a generation. But the clutter is itself Victorian, and the suggestion that change has passed Ramsden by is thus palpable to people in the furthermost seats.

When Shaw came to *The Doctor's Dilemma* (1906), a number of artistic temptations affected his dramaturgy. His scamp of a hero, who dies operatically with an artist's credo on his lips, must evoke the tensions of ambiguity about his supposed genius in order to leave the weight of guilt at his death unresolved. 'I believe in Michael Angelo, Velasquez, and Rembrandt,' he declares; 'in the might of design, the mystery of colour, the redemption of all things by Beauty everlasting, and the message of Art that has made these hands blessed. Amen. Amen.' But the chief believers in his genius – aside from his ultra-loyal wife – are a group of physicians who buy his work and bicker about his treatment; and Shaw notes early in the play, as he works his spell upon his doctors, that *'his artist's power of appealing to the imagination gains him credit for all sorts of qualities and powers whether he possesses them or not'*. Based upon Aubrey Beardsley, from whom he inherited his mortal disease, and Dante Gabriel Rossetti, from whom he acquired his unscrupulousness in mulcting patrons, Louis Dubedat (his surname suggestive of double-dealing) is seen sketching during the play, although none of his drawings are seen by the audience. But in the fifth act – an epilogue following Dubedat's death – Shaw succumbs to a self-defeating dramatic device: he portrays a posthumous show of the artist's work, and displays the art itself.

Stage directions for Act V note that the setting is *'one of the smaller Bond Street Picture Galleries . . . the walls . . . are covered with Dubedat's works. Two screens, also covered with drawings, stand near the corners right and left of the entrance.'* For the first production at the Court Theatre Shaw borrowed representative contemporary drawings from Robert Ross's Carfax Gallery, compounding his failure to leave the problem of the artist's genius to audience imagination, for the gallery attendant asks the widow, 'Have you seen the notices in *Brush and Crayon* and in the *Easel*?' 'Yes,' says Jennifer Dubedat indignantly; 'most disgraceful. They write quite patronizingly, as if they were Mr Dubedat's superiors. After all the cigars and sandwiches they had from us on press day, and all they drank, I really think it infamous that they should write like that.' But the drawings on display are by Beardsley, William Rothenstein, Augustus John, Charles Ricketts and Charles Shannon, creating not ambiguity, but confusion. The ex-art critic in Shaw had pressed himself too convincingly upon the playwright. As Max Beerbohm (who doubled as artist himself) observed in *The Saturday Review* dramatic column he had inherited from Shaw,

Scene from Act IV of The Doctor's Dilemma *at the Royal Court, 1906*

Dubedat seems to have caught, in his brief lifetime, the various styles of *all* the young lions of the Carfax Gallery*. . . . We are asked to accept him as a soon-to-be-recognised master.

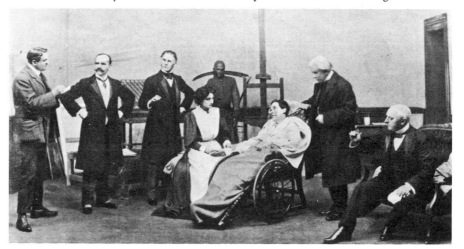

* Shaw owned shares in the Carfax Gallery.

Of course, it is not Mr Shaw's fault that the proper proofs are not forthcoming. But it certainly is a fault in Mr Shaw that he wished proper proofs to forthcome. He ought to have known that even if actual masterpieces by one unknown man could have been collected by the property-master, we should yet have wondered whether Dubedat was so remarkable after all. Masterpieces of painting must be left to an audience's imagination. And Mr Shaw's infringement of so obvious a rule is the sign of a certain radical lack of sensitiveness in matters of art. Only by suggestion can these masterpieces be made real to us.

Shaw might have countered that it was safer to portray artistic genius in the pages of a novel, but he never again attempted to do so onstage. His next several plays eschewed the arts altogether; however in *Pygmalion* (1914) he returned to a less hazardous formula. As with Roebuck Ramsden's study in *Man and Superman*, the art in Mrs Higgins' Chelsea drawingroom in the third act of *Pygmalion* helps to establish her personality both to readers of the printed play and the theatre audience:

Mrs Higgins was brought up on Morris and Burne Jones; and her room, which is very unlike her son's room in Wimpole Street, is not crowded with furniture and little tables and nicknacks. In the middle of the room there is a big ottoman; and this, with the carpet, the Morris wall-paper, and the Morris chintz window curtains and brocade covers of the ottoman and its cushions, supply all the ornament, and are much too handsome to be hidden by odds and ends of useless things. A few good oil-paintings from the exhibitions in the Grosvenor Gallery thirty years ago (the Burne Jones, not the Whistler side of them) are on the walls. The only landscape is a Cecil Lawson on the scale of a Rubens. There is a portrait of Mrs Higgins as she was when she defied the fashion in her youth in one of the beautiful Rossettian costumes which, when caricatured by people who did not understand, led to the absurdities of popular aestheticism in the eighteen-seventies.

Again the once-advanced taste of the occupant is immediately apparent, although the Cecil Lawson landscape is a private Shavian tribute to a long-dead young friend.

The movement from which came Lawson and Whistler and Burne-Jones also inspired a scene in Shaw's next major play, *Heartbreak House* (written in 1916–17),

From Act III of Pygmalion *at His Majesty's Theatre, 1914*

although it was many years later that he revealed his indebtedness. In his 1949 puppet play, *Shakes versus Shav*, written when Shaw was ninety-three, 'Shakespear' taunts the puppet GBS, 'Where is thy Hamlet? Couldst thou write King Lear?' Shav encounters, 'Aye, with his daughters all complete. Couldst thou have written *Heartbreak House*? Behold my Lear.' And in Shaw's stage directions, '*A transparency is suddenly lit up, shewing Captain Shotover seated, as in Millais' picture called North-West Passage, with a young woman of Virginal beauty.*' The Captain raises his hand and intones lines from Act II of *Heartbreak House,* and the young woman responds with lines of Ellie Dunn's after which the Captain warns, 'Enough. Enough. Let the heart break in silence.' The picture then vanishes. But the revelation is clear.

John Millais' 1874 painting parallels Shaw's scene in other respects than the two seated figures, for the setting is a room with a nautical flavour, as is Shotover's house, and visible are a log-book, flags, maps and telescopes. The young woman in *North-west Passage* is more idealized than Shaw's Ellie, whom life's insecurities only too quickly cause to become hard; but her youth and beauty and affection for the old captain make the scene a dramatic representation of Millais' once-famous work. Pre-Raphaelite art and that of the Aesthetic Movement which emerged from it clearly had a profound and continuing impact upon Shaw the playwright.

A brief and literally pre-Raphael reference in Shaw's long dramatic cycle *Back to Methuselah* (written 1918–20) suggests a more familiar use of art in Shaw. Savvy, in *The Gospel of the Brothers Barnabas,* the second play, is described as a '*vigorous sunburnt young lady with hazel hair cut to the level of her neck, like an Italian youth in a Gozzoli picture.*' Thus the fifteenth-century Italian master is utilized to provide a more precise image of Shaw's character. But later in the cycle, in the futuristic parable *As Far as Thought Can Reach,* the scorn of art ('pretty-pretty confectionery' and 'vapid emptiness') by the inhabitants of the world of AD 31,920 is utilized to reflect the coldness and soullessness of an earth in which the physical body and its needs have been

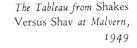

The Tableau from Shakes Versus Shav *at Malvern,* 1949

reduced to an ever-diminishing minimum, and the pleasures of intellect take precedence, intimating a condition in which the body might eventually disappear altogether. People quickly outgrow an adolescence which is the only period of life in which the business of art is thought to be the creation of beauty. Only the reflection of 'intensity of mind' – a super-realism – is important thereafter, and art is condemned as 'dead' because only the creation of life (or pseudo-life, as in the inventor Pygmalion's stimulus-responding human substitutes) has practical value.

The writing of *Back to Methuselah* exhausted Shaw. He saw no likelihood of another play. Yet in 1913, when he was touring what he referred to as 'the Joan of Arc country', he had seen at Orleans a bust 'of a helmeted young woman with a face that is unique in art [of the period] in point of being evidently not an ideal face but a portrait, and yet so uncommon as to be unlike any real woman one has ever seen.' It was 'yet stranger in its impressiveness and the spacing of its features than any ideal head, that it can be accounted for only as an image of a very singular woman; and no other such woman than Joan is discoverable.'[11] The discovery was a slow-burning fuse, but from Orleans Shaw did write to Mrs Patrick Campbell – his Eliza in *Pygmalion* – that he would do a Joan play 'some day',[12] and he described his proposed Epilogue for it, complete to English soldier rewarded in heaven for the two sticks he tied together and gave Joan for a cross as she went to the stake. Ten years later he wrote the play which was the preface to that Epilogue.

The helmeted head, once in the Church of St Maurice, and attributed to the fifteenth century, is surmised to have been inspired by Joan. According to tradition, when Joan entered Orleans in triumph with the relieving force, a sculptor modelled the head of his statue of St Maurice from Joan herself. When the church was demolished in 1850, the head of the statue was preserved. After Shaw saw it he declared that although no proof existed, 'those extraordinarily spaced eyes raised so powerfully the question "if this woman be not Joan, who is she?" that I dispense with further evidence, and challenge those who disagree with me to prove a negative.'[13] The eyes do cast a spell: one can imagine the woman beneath them as capable of Joan's visionary uniqueness.

Joan's legend has always invited artistic representation but most of the events in which she is depicted defy stage dramatization – the panoply of the coronation at Reims, the sieges and battles, her capture and her burning. Shaw handled each of these on stage indirectly, but his indebtedness to the visual art of Joan's period is strong nevertheless. His description of the immature twenty-six-year-old Dauphin is memorable. The future Charles VII is '*a poor creature physically; and the current fashion of shaving closely and hiding carefully every scrap of hair under the head covering or head-dress . . . makes the worst of his appearance. He has little narrow eyes, near together, a long and pendulous nose that droops over his thick short upper lip, and the expression of a young dog accustomed to be kicked, yet incorrigible and irrepressible.*' That the Dauphin seems to have been imagined from the Jean Fouquet portrait on wood of Charles VII now in the Louvre is unquestionable, as Shaw's description is exact, from the Dauphin's glum expression to the shaven rim of skull which emerges from under a large and ugly hat. That Shaw knew Fouquet's work is clear indeed. In the Epilogue to the play, Charles is discovered in bed reading – or rather looking at the pictures – in a Fouquet-illustrated Boccaccio.

Shaw's only wartime visit to France came four years after his exploration of Lorraine. He kept mentally busy on a dull stretch of road between Calais and Boulogne 'on an evening stretch of the journey', he reported in a newspaper account in 1917, 'by inventing a play on the Rodin theme of The Burgesses of Calais, which like the play about the Reims Virgin, I have never written down, and perhaps never will.'[14]

(Opposite) Shakes versus Shav: *a Lanchester Marionette*

(Overleaf left) *GBS by Bernard Partridge*

(Overleaf right) '*Abenobarbus at Rehearsal*' by Bernard Partridge, 1914

Bernard Partridge.

But he did, although it was not until 1934 that he consulted Froissart's *Chronicles* and brought the sculpture to life in a short play. Rodin's *Les Bourgeois de Calais* (1884–86) and Shaw's *The Six of Calais* depict an event which occurred in 1346–7 when, for eleven months, Calais was besieged by the English under Edward III. Edward agreed to lift the siege on the starving city if six hostages, wearing sackcloth and halters, and carrying keys, would surrender themselves at his camp outside Calais. Rodin's work commemorates the bravery and selflessness – and misery – of the six burgesses who submitted themselves to Edward's humiliating conditions, and immortalizes the wretched men, half-naked and wearing halters at the moment of their surrender. The play dramatizes the statue, but not with strict exactitude.[15] Shaw was not playing Pygmalion and seeking to bring a statue directly to life, but perhaps no one else in drama brought so many actual statues to life on the stage as Bernard Shaw.

The rest is epilogue. To the end of his life Shaw found mental pictures for his dramatic concepts from his encounters with painting and sculpture. *In Good King Charles's Golden Days*, written when he was eighty-three, included – anachronistically by two generations – the court painter Geoffrey Kneller, as Shaw was unable to find a significant artist of Isaac Newton's own time to parallel the physicist. (He had wanted to use Hogarth.) Yet Kneller is more a debating opponent to Newton than portraitist, insisting – with the ample charms of a Royal mistress to point to as microcosm of an Einsteinean curvilinear universe – that because space is curved, 'the line of beauty is a curve. My hand will not draw a straight line'. But all the figures of the play were oft-painted, and the play can be visualized in one sense almost as a three-dimensional composite of seventeenth-century royal portraiture.

A comedy completed when Shaw was ninety, *Buoyant Billions* (1947), had been begun some years before, but the third act, the germinal one about which the others were integrated, found its shape when Shaw, visiting a neighbour, saw a print of Leonardo's *The Last Supper*.[16] He then conceived a 'last supper' for a wealthy old man who had brought his guests together to solicit their advice on how to dispose of his money. When he wrote the scene, however, he had old Bill Buoyant invite his children instead, and through his solicitor warn them of the difficult future which will await them when he dies and the Buoyant billions revert largely to the State via death duties and charitable bequests. But a picture had been its impetus. And in his last year, in *Shakes versus Shav*, he summoned up for the stage his recollection of the Millais painting that had inspired the *Lear*-like scene in *Heartbreak House*. To the end, the art of his own formative years remained a catalyst for his playwriting, and his encounters with the visual arts added an unique dimension to his plays.

The last side of Shaw's involvement with art exists off stage. From his earliest public years his striking features – first set off by red hair, jutting beard and Mephistophelean eyebrows, and later metamorphosed into white-maned, white-bearded Old Testament sage – captivated artists. His vanity teased by such interest, Shaw encouraged the practice, in some cases assuming that he was engaging in art patronage rather than self-indulgence. As a result, his flats at Adelphi Terrace, and then Whitehall Court, and his study at Ayot St Lawrence were narcissistic art galleries, always including a number of Shavian portraits and busts.

More than most public figures outside politics, he was also the subject of caricaturists and cartoonists, worked over by such masters as 'Ruth' in *Vanity Fair*, Partridge (Bernard Gould) in the *Sketch*, 'Max' (Beerbohm) in myriad publications, Low in the *New Statesman*. As early as the 'nineties he was painted by Chelsea artist Bertha Newcombe as a platform spellbinder. It was, Shaw said as an old man, 'the

Sketches for the costumes of In Good King Charles's Golden Days: Paul Shelving

*Bertha Newcombe's painting
of GBS*

(Opposite) *Shaw in the pose
of Rodin's* The Thinker:
Alvin Langdon Coburn

best vision of me at that period', and it may have been the artist's best work because she – a fellow Fabian – was in love with Shaw, and her rapture gave new impetus to her brush.

The best photographers of the day vied for the opportunity to take his portrait, not only Evans, Sarony, Coburn, and Elliott & Fry in Shaw's earlier years, but Karsh in Shaw's last years. Alvin Langdon Coburn's nude study of Shaw in the pose of Rodin's *Thinker* is the most striking and seemingly most narcissistic of all, but his subject explained that most portraits were only masks of one's reputation – in fact, disguises.

The result is that we have hardly any portraits of men and women. We have no portraits of their legs and shoulders; only of their skirts and trousers and blouses and coats. Nobody knows what Dickens was like, or what Queen Victoria was like, though their wardrobes are on record. Many people fancy they know their faces; but they are deceived: we know only the fashion mask of the distinguished novelist and of the queen. And the mask defies the camera. When Mr Alvin Langdon Coburn wanted to exhibit a full-length photographic portrait of me, I secured a faithful representation up to the neck by the trite expedient of sitting to him one morning as I got out of my bath. The portrait was duly hung before a stupefied public as a first step towards the realization of Carlyle's antidote of political idolatry: a naked parliament. But though the body was my body, the face was the face of my reputation. So much so, in fact, that the critics concluded that Mr Coburn had faked his photograph and stuck my head on somebody else's shoulders. . . .[17]

The Rodin pose resulted from Shaw's interest in having the man he regarded as 'the greatest sculptor of his epoch' do his bust. To Shaw, Rodin was akin to a 'river god turned plasterer', and the three busts he accomplished – in bronze, plaster, and marble – would 'outlive plays'. A thousand years hence, he suggested, he would be certain of a place in the biographical dictionaries as 'Shaw, Bernard: subject of a bust by Rodin: otherwise unknown'.[18]

Few of the many portraits and busts Shaw commissioned, or encouraged, resulted from anything like modesty. The playwright was offering a friend a viable subject, enabling a young artist to make his mark with a picture likely to attract notice, or feeding his vanity by having a famous creative personality paint or sculpt him. 'A man's interest in the world,' Shaw had a character in *Heartbreak House* say, frankly, 'is only the overflow from his interest in himself,' and after Rodin he permitted, or abetted, busts of himself by Kathleen Bruce (afterwards Lady Scott), Jacob Epstein, Jo Davidson and such fashionable Continental sculptors, in their time, as the Russian Prince Paul Troubetskoy, the Yugoslav Sava Botzaris and the Hungarian Sigismond de Strobl, provoking H. G. Wells' remark that it was impossible to move in Europe without being confronted by an effigy of Shaw.

Only Epstein's bust resulted in a troublesome aftermath for the sitter. Shaw had been an outspoken champion of the American expatriate's work in days when the artistic establishment had attempted to shut the sculptor out. The sitting had even been arranged because Shaw thought that Epstein could 'benefit materially'[19] from it, and he praised the sculptor's primitivism and his rejection of classicism, admiring the way he 'broke up the brassy surfaces of his busts in his determination to make them flesh.'[20] But the striking, prophetic head was not sedate enough for Charlotte Shaw who, GBS wrote to Epstein, 'said that if that bust came into our house she would walk out of it.'[21] Privately, he defended his wife's tastelessness – while admitting that Epstein's 'atavism' was part of his appeal as a sculptor – by describing the work as 'Neanderthal Shaw, not a XX century one'.[22] Perhaps the most powerful image inspired by Shaw's person, it was never to reside at a Shavian address.

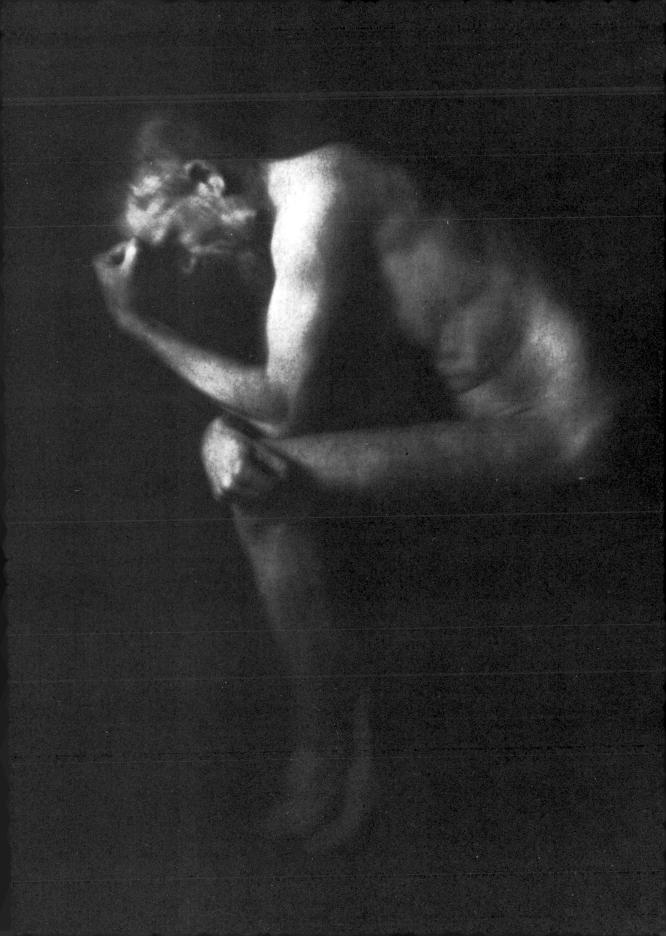

(Right) *GBS modelled by Jacob Epstein*

(Opposite) '*The original and the copy of a famous countenance: GBS' as he poses for a portrait by the American sculptor, Jo Davidson*

(Below right) *GBS modelled by Paul Troubetskoy*

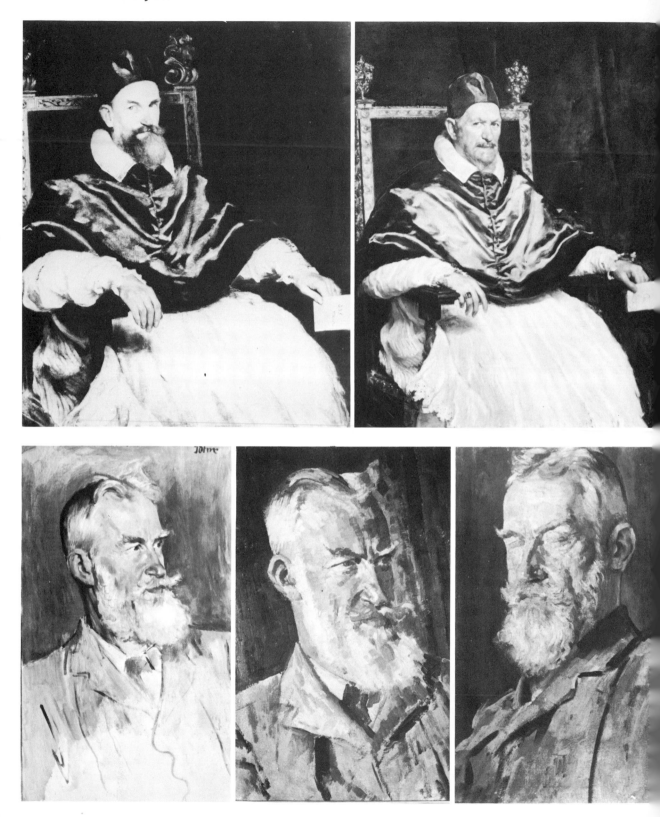

Shavian portraits abound, ranging from the curious one by the third Earl of Lytton in 1905, showing a robed GBS on a golden throne, orb in one hand and red skull cap on his head, like some mysterious pope, and the quizzical one by John Collier strangely rejected by the Royal Academy Hanging Committee, to more conventional pictures like the benign canvas by Dame Laura Knight, the puckish drawings of Feliks Topolski, and the celebrity likeness by Augustus John. Invited to Lady Gregory's home at Coole Park in 1915 specifically to do Shaw's portrait, John produced three – actually six, Shaw suggested, but 'as he kept painting them on top of one another until our protests became overwhelming, only three portraits have survived.' One showed the subject with eyes closed, apparently asleep, which he described to Mrs Patrick Campbell as 'Shaw Listening to Someone Else Talking'. He purchased the two more vigorous representations (the Queen Mother now owns the third), giving one to the Fitzwilliam Museum and keeping the other at Ayot St Lawrence, where he described the breezy, posterish picture as 'the portrait of my great reputation'.[23]

In one way or another, all the drawings, paintings and busts he commissioned or inspired *were* portraits of his reputation. When Sir Harold Nicolson travelled to Ayot the month after Shaw's death to assess the property's possibilities for the National Trust, he noted in his diary with amazement, 'The pictures, apart from one of Samuel Butler and two of Stalin and one of Gandhi, are exclusively of himself. Even the door-knocker is an image of himself.'[24] (He was wrong: there was also a large pastel portrait of Charlotte as a young woman.) But Shaw would have seen nothing wrong in art as a celebration of self. As is written in Ecclesiastes, a book he knew well, 'Wherefore I perceive that there is nothing better, than that a man should rejoice in his own works; for that is his portion: for who shall bring him to see what shall be after him?'

(Opposite, top left) *Shaw as Pope in imitation of Velasquez and* (top right) Pope Innocent X *by Velasquez*

(Below left) *Three paintings of Shaw by Augustus John*

(Above) *The brass door knocker at Shaw's Corner depicting Shaw with the inscription* Man and Superman

(Right) *Shaw looking at the pastel of Charlotte at Shaw's Corner*

Charles Osborne

THE MUSIC CRITIC

One of the most endearing (to some) and exasperating (to others) aspects of Shaw is his inability to limit himself to the task in hand. The playwright embraces philosophy, the political orator expounds aesthetics, the drama critic discusses economics and sociology, while the music critic reaches out to embrace the whole of human life, and always in the least prosy, most musical prose, and with a life-enhancing wit and gaiety that at times bubble over into downright clowning.

Wit, gaiety, clowning? Is the man, then, never serious? On the contrary, he is never *not* serious. But the truth is no less true when spoken with a smile, and it is with a responding smile that I contemplate Shaw's music criticism. I first read it in the Collected Edition more than thirty years ago with a mounting excitement and delight, and I have returned to it frequently, for sheer enjoyment, as one returns to the cool irony of Jane Austen or the energetic force of Dickens. A more suitable analogy, perhaps, would be with one of the great essayists; but, precisely because Shaw never attempted to separate his creative and critical faculties, precisely because the plays are both creation and criticism, and the critical essays and reviews frequently adopt the methods of the imaginative novelist, it is with his peers in imaginative literature that one tends to compare Shaw, even when the subject under discussion is not his dramatic oeuvre but his criticism.

Looking back nearly half a century later on his days as a music critic, Shaw wrote: 'For two years I sparkled every week in *The Star* under this ridiculous name, and in a manner so absolutely unlike the conventional musical criticism of the time that all the journalists believed that the affair was a huge joke, the point of which was that I knew nothing whatever about music.' With an engagingly characteristic immodesty he went on to explain that, in fact, he was 'one of the few critics of that time who really knew their business'. He had, at first, intended to call himself Count di Luna (the baritone villain of Verdi's *Il Trovatore*, an opera for which Shaw had a great affection), but this initial thought led him on to the more fantastic Corno di Bassetto, which is simply Italian for basset horn. Shaw was thirty-two years old, a free-lance book reviewer, political writer and street-corner orator, when the Irish MP and journalist, T. P. O'Connor, founded a London evening newspaper, *The Star*, in 1888. Shaw was at first taken on by *The Star* as a leader writer; his version of the events leading to the birth of Corno di Bassetto is that his leaders were far too Marxist in tone and content to be printed, and that the kind-hearted O'Connor, rather than sack Shaw, allowed him instead to contribute a musical column two or three times a week. In fact, after a few weeks as a member of the editorial staff of *The Star*, Shaw resigned because his pieces were not being printed. For some months, however, he

Shaw at the piano at Maybury, Knoll, 1905

contributed occasional articles to *The Star* as a free-lance journalist, and then agreed to act as second-string critic to the paper's existing music critic, 'Musigena', a pseudonym masking the identity of E. Belfort Bax, uncle of Arnold Bax. For nine months Shaw expatiated anonymously on concerts in St James's Hall, the Crystal Palace and the Albert Hall, and opera at Covent Garden, before replacing Bax completely and inventing the persona of Corno di Bassetto in February, 1889.

Shaw's early pieces are, it must be admitted, frequently brash, for the inexperienced critic is attempting to brandish a confident manner without, as yet, having acquired or earned a real confidence. Parry's oratorio, *Judith*, is ferociously attacked with heavier weapons than were necessary to despatch it:

> There is not a rhythm in it, not a progression, not a modulation that brings a breath of freshness with it. The pretentious choruses are made up of phrases mechanically repeated on ascending degrees of the scale, or of hackneyed scraps of fugato and pedal point. . . . The instrumentation is conventional to the sleepiest degree: tromboned solemnities, sentimentalities for solo horn with tremolo accompaniment, nervous excitement fiddled *in excelsis*, drum points as invented by Beethoven, and the rest of the worn-out novelties of modern scoring. . . .

And Brahms is dismissed with a fervent Wagnerian contempt:

> Brahms's music is at bottom only a prodigiously elaborated compound of incoherent reminiscences, and it is quite possible for a young lady with one of those wonderful 'techniques', which are freely manufactured at Leipzig and other places, to struggle with his music for an hour at a stretch without giving such an insight to her higher powers as half a dozen bars of a sonata by Mozart.

Shaw admitted, indeed boasted, of having read a literary magazine throughout a performance by the Bach Choir, in order to lighten 'the intolerable tedium of sitting unoccupied whilst the Bachists conscientiously maundered through Brahms' *Requiem*. Mind,' he continued, 'I do not deny that the *Requiem* is a solid piece of musical manufacture. You feel at once that it could only have come from the establishment of a first-class undertaker.' He went on to dismiss the *Requiem* with a side-swipe at the writer of the programme notes.

At the age of eighty, Shaw was to make generous amends to Brahms, though not to the writers of boring or silly programme notes. No one who has ploughed through such jargon in concert programmes as 'The principal subject, hitherto only heard in the treble, is transferred to the bass (ex. 28), the violins playing a new counterpoint to it. . . .' can fail to respond to what Corno di Bassetto calls his celebrated analysis of Hamlet's soliloquy on suicide, 'To be, or not to be':

> Shakespeare, dispensing with the customary exordium, announces his subject at once in the infinitive, in which mood it is presently repeated after a short connecting passage in which, brief as it is, we recognize the alternative and negative forms on which so much of the significance of repetition depends. Here we reach a colon; and a pointed repository phrase, in which the accent falls decisively on the relative pronoun, brings us to the first full stop.

'I break off here,' says Bassetto, 'because, to confess the truth, my grammar is giving out.'

Two of the great Shavian qualities, common sense and humour, are already clearly present in these early sallies of Bassetto, and equally apparent in his weekly column is his determination not to confine himself narrowly to musical composition and performance. On one occasion, for instance, he discusses a conflict between the Bishop of London and a lesser clergyman on the subject of the godliness, or otherwise,

Adelina Patti: William Barraud, 1889

of dancing. Shaw, of course, takes the side of the clergyman who apparently wanted to brighten up church services, and castigates the Puritan notion of a church as a singularly joyless place 'where ladies are trained in the English art of sitting in rows for hours, dumb, expressionless, and with the elbows uncomfortably turned in'. Again, common sense comes to the fore: Shaw does not, he says, want to see Westminster Abbey turned into a ballroom, but if some enterprising clergyman of a working-class parish were to put a sign over his church door, offering the building for dancing on Fridays, music on Saturdays, prayer on Sundays, discussion of public affairs 'without molestation from the police' on Mondays, amateur theatricals on Tuesdays, children's games on Wednesdays and then 'volunteer for a thorough scrubbing down of the place' on Thursdays, 'well, it would be all very shocking, no doubt; but after all, it would not interfere with the Bishop of London's salary'. The humanity of the voice is as refreshing as its humour. The humour, though frequently malicious, is never devoid of humanity, and a justly famous example of it is Corno di Bassetto's hilarious description of a concert appearance by the famous soprano Adelina Patti:

Madame Patti kissed hands last night, in her artless way, to a prodigious audience come to bid her farewell before her trip to South America. The unnecessary unpleasantness of the most useful of Mr Louis Stevenson's novels makes it impossible to say that there is in Madame Patti an Adelina Jekyll and an Adelina Hyde; but there are certainly two very different sides to her public character. There is Patti the great singer . . . who sang *Bel raggio* and *Comin' thro' the Rye* incomparably. *With Verdure Clad* would also have been perfect but that the intonation of the orchestra got wrong and spoiled it. But there is another Patti: a Patti who cleverly sang and sang again some pretty nonsense from Delibes' *Lakmé*. Great was the applause, even after it had been repeated; and then the comedy began. . . . Mr Ganz, whilst the house was shouting and clapping uproariously, deliberately took up his *baton* and started Moszkowski's *Serenata in D*. The audience took its cue at once, and would not have Moszkowski. After a prolonged struggle, Mr Ganz gave up in despair; and out tripped the *diva*, bowing her acknowledgements in the character of a petted and delighted child. When she vanished there was more cheering than ever. Mr Ganz threatened the serenata again; but in vain. He appealed to the sentinels of the greenroom; and these shook their heads, amidst roars of protest from the audience, and at last, with elaborate gesture, conveyed in dumb show that they dare not, could not, would not, must not, venture to approach Patti again. Mr Ganz, with well-acted desolation, went on with the serenata, not one note of which was heard. Again he appealed to the sentinels; and this time they waved their hands expansively in the direction of South America, to indicate that the prima donna was already on her way thither. On this the audience showed such sudden and unexpected signs of giving in that the *diva* tripped out again, bowing, wafting kisses, and successfully courting fresh thunders of applause. . . .

A masterly piece of scene-painting. His reaction to the music that Patti sang is interesting. 'Bel raggio' from Rossini's *Semiramide* he accepts as a fit vehicle for the prima donna's art, whereas the aria from Delibes' *Lakmé* (probably the Bell Song, 'Ou va la jeune Hindoue?') is dismissed as 'pretty nonsense'. He sees nothing wrong in the juxtaposition of 'Bel raggio' and 'Comin' thro' the Rye' which, until the recent arrival of Rita Hunter upon the concert scene, would have been thought to be in impossibly poor taste by today's more strait-laced artists and audiences. Most critics, certainly most newspaper reviewers, tend to keep cautiously abreast of the taste of their time, and thus in a sense become victims of it. Shaw, however, began with an independence of mind which he retained throughout his long life. He was the victim only of his own temperament, a bondage none of us can or ought to avoid, though we can alleviate its restrictions by broadening our tastes to as great an extent as remains consonant with our temperament, and this too was Shaw's method.

In the fifth edition (1954) of Grove's *Dictionary of Music and Musicians*, the article on Shaw begins by describing him as 'one of the most brilliant critics, not only of the drama but also of music, who have ever worked in London, or indeed anywhere'. In the same dictionary the long article on Criticism lists and discusses eight qualities required of the ideal music critic and ends by referring to Shaw ('one of the few really outstanding music critics') as the only critic possessing in abundant measure all eight qualities, 'with the possible exception of the second'. They are: (i) a knowledge of the technical and theoretical principles of music; (ii) a knowledge of musical history and scholarship; (iii) a wide general education, covering as many as possible of the subjects with which music can be shown to have a point of direct contact; (iv) the ability to think straight and to write in a clear and stimulating manner; (v) an insight into the workings of the creative imagination; (vi) an integrated philosophy of life; (vii) an enduring inquisitiveness and willingness to learn; (viii) an acceptance of his own limitations, both individual and generic.

To these qualities Shaw added his own social concern and his distinctly uncommon common sense. Not only did he possess an insight into the workings of the creative imagination, he was himself a creative artist of the highest order. He received very little formal education in music, or in anything else for that matter, so where did his musical knowledge come from? It came, first, by inheritance from his mother who played the piano and was a mezzo-soprano of apparently high amateur standard, and second, from the family's close relationship with Mrs Shaw's eccentric singing teacher and friend, Vandeleur Lee. Lee used the Shaw house for rehearsals of the concerts and opera performances he mounted in Dublin, and Mrs Shaw, when authentic orchestral parts were not available, would make up orchestral accompaniments of her own from the vocal score. According to Shaw, Lee had never seen a full orchestral score in his life, and had no musical scholarship whatsoever, 'but he could do what Wagner said is the whole duty of a conductor: he could give the right time to the band; and he could pull it out of its amateur difficulties in emergencies by sheer mesmerism'. As a child, Shaw picked up much of the standard operatic repertoire from these scratch performances. By the time he reached his teens he claimed to be able to 'sing and whistle from end to end' most of the major works of Handel, Haydn, Mozart, Beethoven, Rossini, Bellini, Donizetti and Verdi, and also to be saturated with English literature from Shakespeare to Dickens. At the age of fifteen, Shaw began to teach himself to play the piano, with the help of an instruction book and a diagram of the keyboard, and he later took vocal instruction from Vandeleur Lee, developing 'an uninteresting baritone voice of no exceptional range' which he was still using at Ayot St Lawrence in his ninetieth year, playing through unfamiliar operas at the piano and singing all the parts. 'Music has been an indispensable part of my life,' Shaw wrote in his eightieth year: 'and of my art', he could well have added, for the great speeches in *Saint Joan*, *Major Barbara* and *Pygmalion* could not have been written by anyone insensitive to music.

As Shaw pointed out in his Preface to *London Music in 1888–89*, Corno di Bassetto knew all he needed to know about music, but in criticism he was only a beginner. Writing in *The Star*, 'a ha'penny newspaper', he knew he was addressing a popular readership: 'the bicycle clubs and the polytechnics', as he put it, rather than 'the Royal Society of Literature or the Musical Association'. He purposely vulgarized music criticism which, in his view, 'was then refined and academic to the point of being unreadable and often nonsensical'. *Plus ça change* . . . 'I cannot deny that Bassetto was occasionally vulgar,' wrote Shaw in 1935, 'but that does not matter if he makes you laugh. Vulgarity is a necessary part of a complete author's equipment; and the clown is sometimes the best part of the circus.' Bassetto's humour is best indicated in the context of a complete review, for it is endemic in his stance, his attitude, his – to use a word that he would not have used – *Weltanschauung*; but there are also in his reviews quite a large number of what today's show business jargon calls 'one-liners':

In one of the Henry VI chronicle plays which Shakespeare had a hand in, there is a ghost who abruptly closes a conversation by saying 'Have done; for more I hardly can endure'. It was with much the same feeling that I withdrew at the end of the first part . . .

Miss Nordica turned Elsa of Brabant into Elsa of Bond Street, by appearing in a corset.

M. Lestellier left out *Dalla sua pace*, and will, I hope, leave out *Il mio tesoro* next time, unless he will take the trouble to learn the song in the interim.

At Neumarkt an official railway colporteur thrusts into my hand a great red placard inscribed with a WARNUNG! (German spelling is worse than indifferent) against pick-pockets at Bayreuth. This is a nice outcome of Parsifal.

The pack of hounds darted in at the end of the second act evidently full of the mad hope of finding something new going on; and their depression, when they discovered it was *Dorothy* again, was pitiable. The SPCA should interfere. If there is no law to protect men and women from *Dorothy*, there is at least one that can be strained to protect dogs.

. . . prima donna ma ultima cantatrice . . .

More often than not, Corno di Bassetto's humorous sallies are those of a clown, but a clown who, when he wants to, can assume the style of a Lady Bracknell. That aside about German spelling is worthy of Oscar Wilde's engaging monster, whose voice can also be clearly heard in such comments as 'I had also gone to Ramsgate to see a melodrama; but I had to leave the theatre at the eleventh murder, feeling that my moral sense was being blunted by familiarity with crime.' However, in general, Bassetto's thrusts are more robustly acerbic:

I devoted myself to the encouragement of English music at the first Crystal Palace concert of the year on Saturday afternoon by patiently listening to a concert overture 'to the memory of a hero'. The particular hero was not named; but there was some doubt about the consecutiveness of his memory; for I took him to be a musical amateur in whose head the finale of Brahms's violin concerto had got mixed with the overture to *William Tell*, and whose reminiscences of Mendelssohn were adulterated with incongruous scraps of *La Favorita*. Sir George Grove declares that the overture is 'apparently written on a program, though a program which does not obtrude itself'. My opinion of it is also written on a programme, which I, too, refrain from obtruding. Such overtures should be contracted for at so much the dozen.

Thwarted from contributing a political column to *The Star*, Shaw reacted by inserting political point-making into his music reviews whenever he could decently do so, but always with a disconcerting good humour. A socialist, as surely anyone with a social conscience must have been, he was nevertheless no tame acceptor of cant about the 'working classes', for whose native intelligence he maintained a healthy respect:

Young genius has rather a habit, by the way, of writing to my editor to denounce me as flippant and unenlightened, and to demand that I also shall tear round and proclaim the working man as the true knower and seer in art. If I did, the working man would not think any the better of me; for he knows well enough that society is not divided into 'animated clothes-pegs' on the one hand and lovers of Beethoven in ligatured corduroys on the other.

He recognized the truth that, in the innumerable grades of culture and comfort between the millionaire and the casual labourer, a taste for music was likely to erupt anywhere. What we need, he insisted, is not music for the people, 'but bread for the people, rest for the people, immunity from robbery and scorn for the people, hope for them, enjoyment, equal respect and consideration, life and aspiration, instead of drudgery and despair. When we get that I imagine the people will make tolerable music for themselves, even if all Beethoven's scores perish in the interim.'

After his two years of apprenticeship with *The Star*, Shaw resigned when refused an increase on the three guineas a week he was being paid, and immediately contracted to provide a weekly musical column for *The World*, a journal to which he had formerly contributed art criticism as a free-lance. For more than four years, he remained *The World*'s music critic, signing his weekly articles G.B.S. It is in these articles, written weekly between May 1890 and August 1894, that Shaw's mature music criticism is to be found.

To me, Shaw's unique value as a critic of music is due to the fact that he wrote an incomparably fine prose and that he was completely uninfluenced by fashion. He clearly agreed with his beloved Verdi that 'the boring is the worst of all styles'. To us today it may seem incomprehensible that Verdi could ever not have been recognized as a great composer, but in Shaw's day the conventional critical view was that he had only redeemed himself from the crimes of his earlier operas by the works of his old age. As late as 1908, *The Times* could claim that 'Madame Melba is perhaps the only singer who can delude her hearers into believing for a moment that "Traviata" is a work of beauty or of real importance . . . how this is accomplished and how this most tedious of operas reaches in her hands almost the level of real music drama can hardly be guessed. . . .' Shaw, as early as 1891, was asserting that *La Traviata* was 'before its time at Covent Garden, instead of behind it. It is a much more real and powerful work than *Carmen*, for instance, which everybody accepts as typically modern.' But he did not think Verdi beyond reproach: indeed, Shaw castigated Verdi for having, so he claimed, ruined the baritone voice by writing only for the upper fifth of its compass. Wagner, he thought, was the only modern composer to

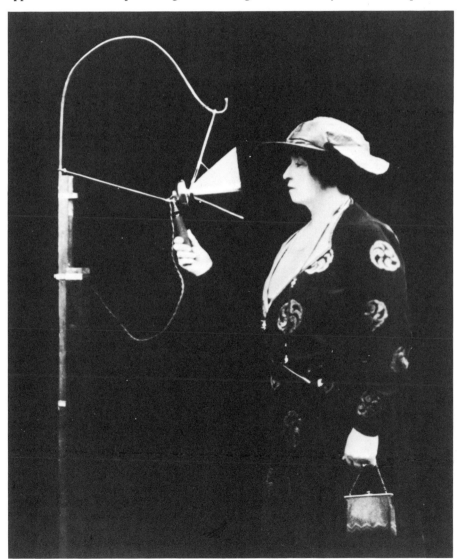

Dame Nellie Melba, 1920

write for the voice with the skill of Handel. But Shaw understood the genius of Verdi, and he understood, as none of his colleagues appeared to, that it was completely uninfluenced by Wagner. He argues very strongly his contention – which I endorse – that there is no evidence in *Aida, Otello* or *Falstaff* that Verdi ever heard a note of Wagner's music. (We know, in fact, though Shaw at the time probably did not, that Verdi attended the first performance in Italy of *Lohengrin*.) Shaw contributed a long and moving obituary of Verdi to the *Anglo Saxon Review* in March 1901, some years after he had ceased to practice music criticism. It is an article full of critical insights as valid today as when they were written; but, more important than this, it is the response of one great creator to another. Shaw is especially perceptive about the Verdi–Boito collaboration on *Otello* and *Falstaff*, and about Boito's influence on the elderly Verdi. While recognizing that Boito could certainly not have written those operas himself, he notes with the sympathy and understanding of a fellow-artist that 'nothing is more genial in Verdi's character than this docility, this respect for the demands of a younger man, this recognition that the implied rebuke to his taste and his coarseness showed a greater tenderness for his own genius than he had shown to it himself.'

Shaw understood and responded to every aspect of Verdi. He never found it necessary to denigrate the early works in order to praise the mature masterpieces, nor did he make the mistake of finding in those last works nothing but the decline of the earlier 'profuse strains of unpremeditated art'. He was not afraid to proclaim his love for the melodic fertility of the middle-period Verdi while at the same time greeting *Falstaff*, when it was new, as an improvement on Shakespeare. He claimed that Verdi had an easier task with *Otello*, 'for the truth is that instead of *Otello* being an Italian opera written in the style of Shakespeare, *Othello* is a play written by Shakespeare in the style of Italian opera'. To Shaw, the characters in the play are already operatic monsters, Othello's transports of jealousy make sense only as magnificent musical sound, and the plot is that of pure farce, supported as it is on 'an artificially manufactured and desperately precarious trick with a handkerchief which a chance word might upset at any moment'. Verdi's achievement, as Shaw sees it, is that he did not belittle the play as Donizetti would have done, or conventionalize it 'as Rossini actually did' with the same plot, but rose fully to it and occasionally enhanced it. Comparing the choruses in *Otello* with those in *Il Trovatore*, Shaw realizes 'how much Verdi gained by the loss of his power to pour forth *Il balens* and *Ah, che la mortes*'.

'The Perfect Wagnerite', Shaw's major contribution to Wagner literature, is really not to be classified as music criticism for it has little of interest to say about Wagner's music: its concern is with Wagner as dramatist, and in it Shaw interprets the libretto of *The Ring of the Nibelungen* in purely political terms. But, though his view of the meaning of *The Ring* is a partial one, Shaw's essay is remarkable both for the cogency of its argument and for the beauty of its prose. It remains as readable today as when it was written, though no more so than the many reviews Shaw wrote of Wagner performances at Covent Garden and at Bayreuth, from which it is clear that his understanding of Wagner as a composer of opera was acute. He dismisses the notion of Wagner as a reformer of opera and insists that he was the inventor of a virtually new art form. He concedes that, in the earlier operas, Wagner's melody lacks the originality of Weber's, and that, judged by the criteria of pre-Wagnerian opera, the later works make neither musical nor dramatic sense; he then proceeds to demonstrate the astonishing nature of Wagner's vast achievement. Surprisingly – at least, it is surprising to me – Shaw responds warmly to *Parsifal*, but he understands that it is not necessarily a work for all of us. 'To enjoy *Parsifal*,' he says, 'either as a listener or an

(Below) GBS and Charlotte with Dr Hans Richter at Bayreuth, 1908

(Opposite) Autograph Musical Manuscript in Shaw's hand of various leitmotifs of The Ring of the Nibelung's *and of the theme and lyrics of a French song*

executant, one must be either a fanatic or a philosopher. To enjoy *Tristan* it is only necessary to have had one serious love affair.' He thought all other operatic love scenes pallid in comparison with Act II of *Tristan und Isolde*. After a Covent Garden performance of the opera, he writes of 'those supreme moments at which the Wagnerian power sweeps everything before it', even in the face of unimaginative staging and uninteresting singers. The most articulate of nineteenth-century rationalists is so moved by *Parsifal* that he comes away from a performance feeling that 'the theatre is as holy a place as the church and the function of the actor no less sacred than that of the priest'. Perhaps he first heard his own call at that performance of *Parsifal*. His review ends with this sentence: 'And that long kiss of Kundry's from which he learns so much is one of those pregnant simplicities which stare the world in the face for centuries and yet are never pointed out except by great men.'

It was from Mozart that Shaw claimed he learned a lightness of touch, and how to say serious things in a non-ponderous manner; and implicit in everything he writes about Mozart is a reverence for the composer above all others. Scornful of late nineteenth-century performance practice in Mozart, he had occasion to admonish an admired conductor, Mr August Manns, that it was 'useless to try to make the G minor symphony "go" by driving a too heavy body of strings through it with all the splendour and impetuosity of an Edinburgh express'; to inveigh against Covent Garden's habit of performing *Don Giovanni* in *four* acts (I am somewhat fearful of having drawn attention to this, knowing the present management's penchant for long and frequent intervals); and to castigate Marcella Sembrich for having 'altered the exquisite and perfect ending of Mozart's exquisite and perfect song, "Deh, vieni, non tardar".' The singers of the time appeared to find Mozart deficient in providing opportunities for them to display their high notes, and even when they sang the notes as written, they as often as not misunderstood their musical import. In his notice of a concert at which a baritone named Holman Black had sung the Serenade from *Don Giovanni*, Shaw gave the singer some useful advice by pointing out that the effect of the last bar is ruined if the singer emphasizes the high D, in the sequence B,C,D instead of the D an octave lower which immediately follows. 'However,' he concludes philosophically, 'it is better to fail on the low note written by Mozart than to try for a high F sharp, as the fashion once was.'

Shaw's comments on Mozart were sometimes misunderstood, which annoyed him, or at least he pretended it did: 'It is infuriating to be misunderstood in this way,' he once complained in his best Lady Bracknell manner, 'particularly as it is admitted in literary circles that I write the best English in the world.' But there could have been no misunderstanding his attitude to the managements of Covent Garden and Her Majesty's Theatre, and what he regarded as their shameful method of flinging operas onto the stage with no regard for dramatic values. His descriptions of some of the performances he witnessed are wickedly funny, but his concern for opera as an art form is serious and self-evident. Even when he was having fun at the expense of certain singers, he realized that the blame for scratch performances was to be laid firmly at the door of the managements. 'The lyric stage,' he thundered, 'cannot lag a century behind the ordinary theatre.' And so he objected to the 'two ragged holes in a cloth' which represented heaven and hell in Boito's *Mefistofele* at Covent Garden, and the noisy scene-shifting which was so destructive of stage illusion; the inane non-productions of *bel canto* operas which were an insult to Donizetti, Bellini and Rossini; the senseless cuts which he regarded as 'wanton outrages'.

In the concert hall, Shaw was receptive to new music: if he seems to have done less than justice to the English composers of his day, this is mainly due to their propensity to produce oratorios, an art form for whose nineteenth-century productions he conceived an intense dislike. For Shaw, oratorio meant Bach. He heartily detested Mendelssohn's *St Paul*, 'all that dreary fugue manufacture, with its Sunday-school sentimentalities and its Music-school ornamentalities', and was only willing to grant that Mendelssohn was preferable to the English 'organist, the professor, the Mus.Bac., and the Mus.Doc. who were busily churning out oratorios for the provincial music festivals'. I have earlier quoted him on Parry's *Judith*. Parry was a composer whom Shaw respected, but 'when a man takes it upon himself to write an oratorio – perhaps the most gratuitous exploit open to a nineteenth-century Englishman – he must take the consequences.' Parry's *Job* is a dreary ramble 'through the wastes of artistic error'. A long and devastating review of it ends with the hope that the composer 'will burn the score, and throw *Judith* in when the blaze begins to flag'. Shaw was no friend to the oratorio-mongers, but he responded to the Sullivan of the Savoy operas though he was rude to the same composer's *Ivanhoe* ('a good novel turned into the very silliest sort of sham "grand opera" '); and he recognized the genius of Elgar, whom he considered the first English composer of real stature to have emerged since Purcell.

Infinitely preferring the profligacy of Offenbach 'to the decorum of Cellier and the dullness of Stephenson', Shaw warned his readers that 'Offenbach's music is wicked. It is abandoned stuff; every accent in it is a snap of the fingers in the face of moral responsibility: every ripple and sparkle on its surface twits me for my teetotalism.' But he did not mind being twitted for his teetotalism, or for his vegetarianism. When a correspondent sent him a pamphlet proving vegetarianism to be an enfeebling and ultimately fatal practice, the thirty-two-year-old Corno di Bassetto claimed it was confuted by the fact that he had eaten no meat for the past ten years: 'Pamphlet or no pamphlet, a mind of the calibre of mine cannot derive its nutriment from cows.'

In a letter to *The Times* in 1932, congratulating the BBC for having commissioned Elgar's third symphony, a work the composer did not live to complete, Shaw threw in the remark that, in his view, 'the only entirely creditable incident in English history is the sending of £100 to Beethoven on his deathbed by the London Philharmonic Society'. That he loved and revered Beethoven is evident from so many of the articles in *The Star* and *The World*. There is a sensitive, lyrical description of the Norwegian pianist Agathe Backer-Gründahl in a passage in the 'Emperor' Concerto; there is, too, a dismissal of Arditi genially beating his way through the Ninth Symphony ('occasionally he ecstatically rose and sank in his characteristic manner like an animated concertina set on end'). And there is the famous irreverent account of the slow movement of the 'Eroica', likened to the funeral processions in the Dublin of Shaw's childhood. Shaw's religion was Beethoven's. The agnostic socialist responded to the secular, humanitarian note of the choral finale of the Ninth Symphony, and of Mozart's *Zauberflöte*, though he praised Sarastro's music in *Die Zauberflöte* by saying that it was the only music one could imagine, without blasphemy, as issuing from the voice of God.

Some critics are sound on composers but not to be trusted on performers, or *vice versa*. Shaw's descriptions of the pianists, violinists, singers and conductors of the 1880s and '90s are convincing, and when one is able to check them with gramophone records they are generally found to be accurate as well. Some of the performers died or retired too early to have recorded, so we shall never know whether, at the end of her career, Ilma de Murska's voice 'was not unjustly compared to an old tin kettle', or whether Tamberlik had 'certain traditional phrasings which the old-fashioned training used to knock into singers, usually knocking the voice out of them at the same time'. But Shaw is fully appreciative of the purely vocal qualities of Adelina

Patti, though he regrets that she never cared to play any other part than that of Adelina, the spoiled child with the adorable voice. When he first heard the young Melba, in Gounod's *Romeo et Juliette,* he liked her 'fresh bright voice and generally safe intonation' and thought that, at one or two moments in the balcony scene, she sang with genuine feeling. Three or four years later he found her transformed, singing with heart as well as head, and with her intonation even more impressive. It was then, in 1894, that he was able to say 'you never realize how wide a gap there is between the ordinary singer who simply avoids the fault of singing obviously out of tune and the singer who sings really and truly in tune, except when Melba is singing'. That this remained true of Melba at her best is clear from her gramophone records, the earliest of them made ten years later in 1904, though there are also records of Melba in which the intonation is careless, occasionally disastrously so.

There are only snippets on record of two of the original cast of Verdi's *Otello*. Shaw heard them at the Lyceum Theatre, under Faccio, the conductor of the première, and tells us that Tamagno's Otello was shrill and nasal, and Maurel's Iago woolly and tremulous. This we can confirm with our own ears, for Tamagno recorded the 'Esultate' and the death scene, and Maurel Iago's rendition of Cassio's dream; but only Shaw's eyes can reveal that Maurel produced striking pictorial effects, or that Tamagno was 'original and real, showing you Othello in vivid flashes'. Can Shaw have had in mind Hazlitt's description of Kean revealing Shakespeare by flashes of lightning?

A young soprano named Adrienne Verity ('a pleasant-faced, well-grown lass, with refreshingly unceremonious ways and a healthy boisterousness which would make her the life and soul of a haymaking') was misguided enough to send Shaw a ticket for her concert. She was rewarded with this description of her person and the advice that she should either study hard with a competent teacher for a couple of years or find a place in the D'Oyly Carte chorus 'and there unskilfully scream her voice away in less than six months. And whoever gives her a more flattering opinion will do her a very cruel kindness.' I wonder what happened to her.

Shaw's period as a professional music critic lasted no longer than six years. But, for the rest of his long life, he retained his love for music. In 1910, when he considered that Ernest Newman was less than fair to Richard Strauss's *Elektra* in the music columns of *The Nation,* the fifty-four-year-old ex-music critic crossed swords with Newman, and a fierce exchange of scurrilities ensued. Ten years later, Shaw contributed a perceptive essay on Elgar to *Music and Letters.* A splendidly scathing letter in *The Daily News* in 1922 castigated London society for not having flocked to hear Elgar's *The Apostles,* 'one of the glories of British music'. His very last article on music which appeared in *Everybody's Magazine* a few days after his death in November, 1950, attacked the idolizing of singers of the past. 'This does not impose on me,' he wrote. 'I have heard them. The extraordinary singers were no better than ours; the average singers were much worse. . . . Let us hear no more of a golden age of *bel canto.* We sing much better than our grandfathers.'

When Corno di Bassetto wrote his last piece in *The Star* in May 1890, he ended with his usual immodesty by asking some indulgence for his successor,

> handicapped as he will be for a time by the inevitable comparison with one whom he can hardly hope to equal, much less to surpass. I say this on my own responsibility, as he has not invited me to make any such appeal on his behalf, perhaps because it is not yet settled who he is to be.

Rest in peace, caro Corno, for it is still not settled.

(Top) *Shaw with Sir Edward Elgar at the first Malvern Festival in 1929*

(Below) *Elgar rehearsing his 'Nursery Suite' in 1931. GBS is on his left and the Duke and Duchess of York (George VI and Queen Elizabeth) on his right. Elgar and Shaw became intimate friends and Elgar's 'Severn Suite' is dedicated to Shaw*

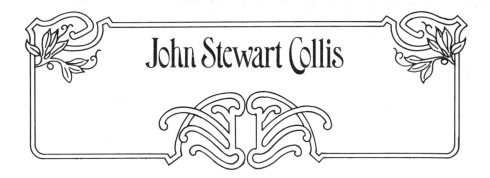

RELIGION AND PHILOSOPHY

I

If we pass in review the total writing of Shaw on religion we are surprised to find how long he continued to force an open door. You remember the conception of God as an elderly gentleman with a white beard and a forbidding expression? That such a conception was held there is no question, for it does not matter how absurd a belief may be, and we know that there were people who believed for centuries in hell where the damned spent eternity in being burnt. Five minutes' reflection would convince anyone that five minutes' burning would demolish the person, but if not, and the burning continued indefinitely, it could not be very painful and might be as pleasant as eating strawberries and cream. But so great is the force of irrational belief, that no such reflections were made.

As Shaw was born in 1856 the elderly gentleman image had overshadowed all his early years, and was so much the official view that Bradlaugh, the atheist, was ejected from the House of Commons; indeed he was actually thrown out of the House with such violence that John Bright was horrified to see him dragged down the stairs by six policemen. It is therefore perhaps explicable that Shaw was fond of recalling his own stand against this conception of deity. He liked giving an account of how, in 1878, he had been at a bachelor party of young men who mentioned an alleged story of how Bradlaugh had once taken out his watch publicly and challenged the Almighty to strike him dead in five minutes if he really existed. As some doubt was thrown upon the authenticity of this, Shaw offered to make the same experiment on the spot – but when he took out his watch all the advanced young men fled from the house.

It makes an amusing story, but Shaw told it over and over again in speeches and essays and finally in the Preface to *Back to Methuselah* when he was sixty-four; and one is surprised at so continuous a dethroning of a deity who had long since lost his seat. Still, he was writing theological history and was concerned to make clear the sort of God who was to be exchanged for Darwinism. It is true that until that conception was dropped altogether the Church's Article which defines deity as 'without body, parts, or passions', was disregarded and the Old Testament Jehovah preferred. At the age of eighty-four Shaw was still troubled by that image – 'a grotesque tribal idol described in the Book of Numbers as God, who resolves to destroy the human race, but is placated by a pleasant smell of roast meat brought to its nostrils by Noah.' Looking back, Shaw adds that the intensity of the revolt against this by thinkers of all kinds can scarcely be imagined nowadays.

As everyone now knows, this revolt came with the advent of Darwinism in the nineteenth century. The idea of evolution was not new, but Darwin's elaborate *Origin*

'I dreamt St Peter sat for his portrait' by Frederick Elwell, R.A., caused much controversy in 1947 because of the likeness of St Peter to GBS

of Species brought it into focus and assured it vast publicity. When evolution was accepted, this Almighty God, who had come to be secretly regarded as an almighty fiend since he was responsible for evil, could be discarded, and the problem of evil interpreted as the failure of the evolutionary force to be completely successful in its endeavour to evolve ever higher forms of life. But the idea of evolution as a meaningful creative force was not generally accepted at first. Civil war broke out among the adherents of the new gospel. Unfortunately, in the course of his book Darwin had used phrases such as 'survival of the fittest', 'natural selection', 'accidental variation', 'reflex action', giving a weighty number of examples to make his point. This aspect of his book made it possible for a 'mechanical' interpretation of life to be advanced; for there are always men, especially clever and able men, who have a strong will to prove that there is no will, men whose whole meaningful endeavour is to show meaninglessness, free men who desire to prove that they are bound. And they are always respected and listened to, for stupidity in the guise of cleverness, and ignorance in the cloak of knowledge, never fail to win support. On the other hand there are always others, people who, taking exception to that view, crave for purpose and meaning and design, and however much they may hate the bogey-man god, wish to replace him with something more to their taste than an accidental, purposeless universe. Shaw recognized that there must inevitably be a good deal of random selection resulting from accidents and the pressures of external circumstance; but he declined to accept this as the norm. 'It was as if someone had shown,' he wrote, 'that the fact that most men's hats fit them, usually accounted for by the belief that they were made on purpose to fit them, could be accounted for on the hypothesis that hats occur in nature like wild strawberries, and that men picking them up discard those that do not fit, and retain and wear those that do.'

Nevertheless the accidental and mechanical view of evolution was favoured at first. But when the real upshot of the theory became evident there was a revolt against it, heralded by the great Henri Bergson in France with his *Elan Vital*, and in England by the ill-mannered Samuel Butler who declared that Darwin had 'banished mind from the universe'. Shaw was so fond of that remark that he repeated it as a kind of incantation throughout his life, but he reserved his most considered attack upon the mechanists until 1920 in the Preface to *Back to Methuselah*. 'When its whole significance dawns on you, your heart sinks into a heap of sand within you. There is a hideous fatalism about it, a ghastly and damnable reduction of beauty and intelligence, of strength and purpose, of honor and aspiration,' he wrote.

> To call this Natural Selection is a blasphemy, possible to many for whom Nature is nothing but a casual aggregation of inert and dead matter, but eternally impossible to the spirits and souls of the righteous. If it be no blasphemy, but a truth of science, then the stars of heaven, the showers and dew, the winter and summer, the fire and heat, the mountains and hills, may no longer be called to exalt the Lord with us by praise: their work is to modify all things by blindly starving and murdering everything that is not lucky enough to survive the universal struggle for hogwash.

Shaw never wrote better than in this Preface because the subject gave full scope to his capacity to throw a controversy into dramatic narrative form enforced by particular incident, and at the same time gave channel to his intensely religious nature. And the tenderness he always felt for animals was outraged by the vivisectionists who carried out awful cruelties in order to prove obvious facts concerning acquired characteristics.

II

In place of random evolution, he put what he called creative evolution. He saw the matter in terms of a force of life, conceived as an invisible will – utterly unexplainable – working itself out through matter in ever more complex forms, culminating just now with Man through whom it attains consciousness of itself, the awakening of a soul in nature. We need a religion very much, he said. The old ones have failed. But we can have a new one – creative evolution. In this he was mistaken.

Creative evolution is not a religion, it is a scientific theory. We might just as well call Marxism a religion, but it is not a religion, it is a sociological theory. We might just as well call humanism a religion, but it is not a religion, it is an ethical scheme. Of course creative evolution is a valuable corrective to the idea of material mechanism. Those who are depressed by it can see evolution as a force of life in which they are taking part, feeling themselves to be, as it were, the hands of God, rather than in God's hands. I think the idea of creative evolution is well summed up by Will Durant who, writing on Bergson, said,

> We were near to thinking of the world as a finished and pre-determined show, in which our initiation was a self-delusion, and our efforts a devilish humour of the gods; after Bergson we come to see the world as the stage and the material of our own originative powers. Before him we were cogs and wheels in a vast and dead machine; now if we wish it, we can help to write our own parts in the drama of creation.

Bergson did not claim that this was a religion. It remains a reasoned scientific theory. It is not something *experienced*: it is not a religious experience.

Bernard Shaw not only claimed that it was a religion but that Superman would follow. But there are no grounds for such a belief. Evolution has never proceeded in a straight line. It has gone in all sorts of different directions – into all sorts of *perfections*. There is surely nothing more perfect than a tiger in its line; or a foxglove in its line; or a beech-tree in its line – take your choice. 'There can never be any more perfection than there is now,' said the mystic, Walt Whitman. 'Paradise is here,' said another mystic, Jacob Boehme, 'but man is not yet in Paradise.' Perfect human beings also keep coming into the world. Few of them remain perfect for long, very few remain whole or holy but are slashed into pieces, because this very consciousness which is such a wonderful thing in terms of contemplative apprehension, is also a terrible thing in terms of practical technology; for the prodigiously rapid growth of the cerebral cortex (a Life Force error of the first magnitude) has allowed our hellish propensities more scope than our heavenly attitudes; so that today every modern prophet is warning us that we stand on the brink of a human holocaust. When Shaw was writing *Man and Superman* in 1902 he sensed the danger, declaring that evolution was the only way out. Superman must make a prompt appearance. And how? He hadn't a clue. After an intolerably long-winded approach in his *Revolutionist's Handbook*, which formed a sort of appendix to *Man and Superman*, he reached the conclusion that the coming of superman was our only salvation. The method by which he could be ushered in, he said, was by selective breeding, as we do with horses and dogs. But after about two pages concerning this he lost heart, his best lofty-assurance manner failed him, and his pen dried up.

However, this did not deter him from writing *Back To Methuselah* which he called a Metabiological Pentateuch. The idea seems to have been to work out in evolutionary terms what Man might accomplish by sheer *willing*. The play starts well with a scene called 'In the Beginning'. A light is cast upon the myth of the Garden of Eden: a slanting ray illuminates the meaning of words and the birth of language; Wicked, Years, Marriage, Fear, Hope, Jealousy, Kill, Death, Strangers – old words lit up as if

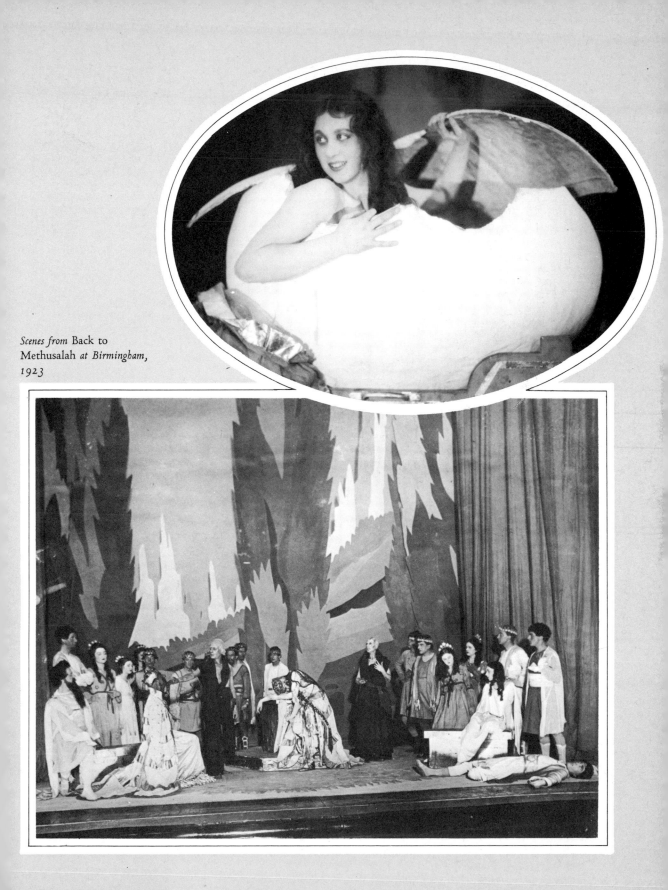

Scenes from Back to
Methusalah *at Birmingham,*
1923

a bulb were switched on. That is true genius, making old things new and worn things shine. This scene is complete in itself. But if we turn at once to the end piece called 'As Far As Thought Can Reach', we come in for a surprise. Lilith (in medieval Jewish folklore, the first wife of Adam, before the creation of Eve) tells how at last men had repented and turned away from their vileness and were redeemed from their sins. We wonder how this had come to pass. It is a supreme moment, in the supreme act, in what the author regarded as his supreme work. This will be something: no vessel of clay but a cup of pure gold filled with pure wine. Why had they repented, where was the road to salvation, and what the revelation that caused them to turn away from their vileness and be redeemed from their sins? We await the answer. It comes: 'They repented – *and lived three hundred years.*' What a let down!

And when we turn to these people given the power to will evolutionary advance we find that they can do no better at first than grow extra heads and arms, and eventually pass into a life of contemplation, just thinking, unaware of external reality and freed from all earthly sorrows and joys. They contemplate nothing, for nothing is worth contemplating. Thus they are prepared to spend hours of eternity. There is no hint of the mystic's capacity to take his eternity in an hour.

The odd thing is that these deplorable Ancients were not organic to Shaw. They were in no way a wish-fulfilment. True, he often spoke of the condition when thought could become an ecstasy – as much an ecstasy, he declared, as the sexual act and more prolonged. But you cannot think to any purpose in the void and alone: for there is then nothing to think about. In any case Shaw was not a Contemplative. He was not a Solitary. He was not a Recluse. A moralist and reformer to the marrow of his bones, he was never happier than when hard at work, *in medias res*, at improving this world which, as Wordsworth said, 'is the world of all of us, – the place where, in the end, we find our happiness or not at all!' Once, on catching sight of Shaw crossing Trafalgar Square, swift, upright, brisk, purposeful, with a quizzical look to right and left as he hurried along, I said to myself, 'There goes a happy man, probably to a committee meeting of some sort to put matters straight.' Impossible to think of him taking things easy, perhaps pausing to sit on a seat and gaze at the ducks in St James's Park. Perish the thought. Had he not fled from Ireland to prevent himself from looking out of the window instead of working? 'If Patrick O'Reilly is found maudlin by the side of Lough Dan,' he said to George Russell, 'have him thrown into it.'

It would not have suited him at all to be like the Ancients in *Back to Methuselah*, living on indefinitely unless an accident occurred. 'The characters in this book are all actual people,' wrote Charles Macmahon Shaw, cousin to GBS, in his book called *Shaw's Brethren*, 'but unfortunately many of them have been long since deceased.' 'Why unfortunately?' wrote Shaw in red ink against this, 'would you have had them live for ever?' Shaw had no love of people. He wanted to improve them out of recognition, out of existence, and see them replaced by a race of long-life intellectual voluptuaries.

Once, during a visit to him at Adelphi Terrace, I asked if he could be a little bit more specific about the likelihood of this longer-living business. He replied, 'I don't know any more about it than you do yourself. I was just turning a philosopher's stone.' Some stone, I reflected, and some gathering of moss. I have formed the impression that once having hit on the idea he was carried away by the luxuriance of his invention, which he admitted proliferated in him unbidden, and (I think) unchecked once he was sure of his audience and free from the disapproval of publishers. But I also think that Shaw really did have a strange *penchant* for the idea of people

(Opposite) *John Farleigh's version of Shaw's suggestion*

(Below) *Shaw's own suggestion to John Farleigh for an illustration in* The Adventures of the Black Girl in her Search for God. *The flying Irishman is Shaw himself*

unimpeded by all fleshly bonds. In 1939 he wrote to Sir James Jeans from Whitehall Court, reminding him how in his reckless youth he had conceived of a stationary universe in which all the heavenly bodies, having been slowed down and finally stopped dead by the braking action of the tides, crashed together like aeroplanes with propellers jammed, with a single world of inconceivable density, to inhabit which life must take inconceivable forms – perhaps bodiless Cartesian vortices. It was a gorgeous vision and he was tempted to incorporate it into his Newtonian play *In Good King Charles's Golden Days*. A gorgeous vision?

It is hard to find much in the way of religion in this Pentateuch. Our search is no more fruitful when we turn to *The Black Girl in Search of God* – which is not surprising since she also was disappointed. She comes upon plenty of theologies and idols and idolatries, for from the beginning men have craved something to *worship*, and even with only a few chance boughs and scattered stones have built altars to the Unknown God of their imagining and bowed before the image. But the Girl sought

the reality and not the idol. She does not find Him – only various personages symbol-
izing Jehovah or Michah or Mahomet or Peter, all of whom disappoint her. In the
course of her search she comes upon a man who symbolizes Jesus. Shaw had already
written about Jesus at length in the Preface to *Androcles and the Lion*, relating him to
the long line of saviours and gods stretching back through history as evidenced by
Frazer's *The Golden Bough*. The Black Girl finds him very congenial and wise, but given
to conjuring tricks. 'Get rid of your miracles and the whole world will fall at the feet
of Christ,' said Rousseau. He had a point. For truly the miracles are a terrible red
herring: to be able to heal people has no theological significance. But when Shaw said
that Jesus did conjuring tricks he offended a more than usual number of people, for
while they don't mind what is said about God they are touchy about what is said of
Jesus. Soon the black girl is confronted with a man standing for Voltaire, and she
tells him what she is seeking. Nothing doing, he says, don't waste your time, better
just to cultivate your garden. In the garden she finds a person resembling Shaw himself
whom she marries. They have many children, and this impedes her search and the
desire to smash idols when she finds them instead of God, while nothing 'would ever
persuade her husband that God was anything more solid and satisfactory than an
eternal but as yet unfulfilled purpose, or that it could ever be fulfilled if the fulfilment
were not made reasonably easy and hopeful by socialism'. And with this scientific and
sociological approach she is obliged to be content.

We turn to *Saint Joan*. It is generally regarded as a very religious play. True, there
are many clergymen in it and a lot of talk about God and much wrangling over
theology, but it is very difficult to understand how Joan of Arc qualified as a saint.
She was a military genius. This is very rare, even among men – can you think of a
military genius during World War I? For an uneducated country girl to have possessed
it is extraordinary indeed. But what has this to do with religion? The French novelist,
Huysmans, has expressed the regret that Joan of Arc ever rose to wrest France from
the Normans who were seeking to preserve her racial and prehistoric unity with
England, and thus handed her over to Charles VII and his southerners. The advantage
of the union of France and England for the world generally would have been incalcul-
able (and incidentally, the Mediterranean population of France and the Mediterranean population of Ireland would have rendered impossible an 'Irish question').
And indeed, anyone today walking across the soil of France between Passchendaele
and the Somme, knowing that beneath his feet lie nearly a million British dead who
were comrades of the French, might well endorse this view. At any rate the claim
seems to me by no means outrageous that when the peasant girl from Lorraine with
her hallucinations galvanized into action the nerveless arms of Charles she inflicted a
blow upon the progress of the modern world which may never have been exceeded.

It is hard to see exactly where her sainthood comes in. She was a martyr, certainly,
to outward cruelty and inward folly. I am fond of the Epilogue because of its splendid
rhetoric. But it is confusing. Near the end the various parties praise Joan. Each in
turn kneels in praise. Indeed they give her a very good hand. But when she asks if
they would like her· to come back to earth, each makes an excuse and discreetly
withdraws. We are supposed to think ill of them for this. But why should they want
her back? She was not a saviour with a gospel of salvation; she was not a philosopher
with a solution to the riddle of the world; she was not a moralist with a message for
mankind. She was a soldier. Why should they want her back unless they had some
military coup in mind? When they have all departed she has the nerve to kneel down
in a holy manner and to ask God how long it must be before this beautiful earth is
ready to receive its saints.

*Saint Joan at the New
Theatre, 1924*

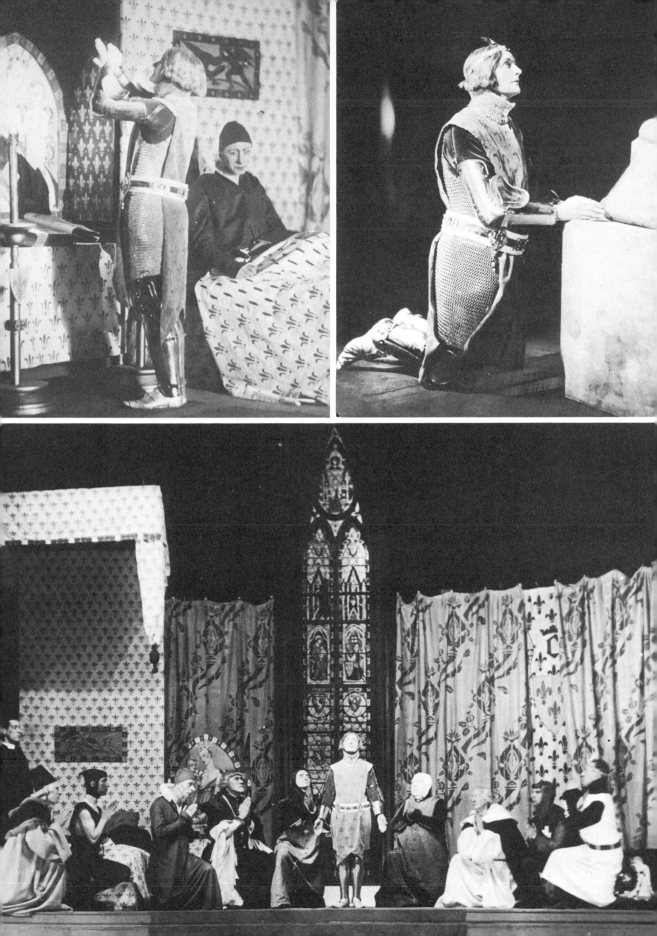

III

In our search for religion in Shaw we are still short of the real article: we have talk about religion rather than religion itself. His mind moved superbly in the field of ethical discussion and theological polemic, but he passes by the actual *experience* of religion. He has used the word inspiration freely in relation to himself, and at intervals has been at pains to refer to himself as a mystic while disassociating himself from the term atheist (which after all only means non-theist), and emphatically repudiating the term agnostic which is so often used by those who, in the guise of having 'an open mind', are really cowards careful to offend no one. But Shaw, though claiming to be a mystic, never mirrors mysticism. He took creeds seriously. 'Creeds must become intellectually honest,' he declared in the Preface to *Major Barbara*. 'At present there is not a single credible established religion in the world. That is perhaps the most stupendous fact in the whole world situation.'

It is not a stupendous fact but a very natural one, which could not be otherwise. A creed, a credo, ('Lord I believe, help thou mine unbelief') rests on faith in the supernatural. It is credible for those who have that assurance, and incredible for those who do not. Nothing can mend this situation. There is conflict between science and creeds. There is no conflict between science and religious experience simply because it *is* an experience unaffected by theory and independent of circumstance. 'This is my third Christmas in a cell' wrote Rosa Luxembourg in prison,

> the sand crunches so hopelessly under the steps of the sentry that all the desolation and futility of existence rings from them in the deep dark night. I lie there quiet, alone, covered in the four-fold black cloth of darkness; weariness; bondage; winter; and at the same time my heart beats with an incomprehensible inner joy, as if I were walking in radiant sunshine over a flowery meadow. And in the darkness I smile at life, as if somehow I knew the magic secret, and that all evil and sorrow lay defeated, changed into clear light and joy. And then I search myself for a reason for this joy, and find nothing, and am compelled to smile at myself again; I believe that the secret is nothing less than life itself; and the deep darkness of night is as beautiful and soft as velvet if only one sees it rightly. And in the crunching of the damp sand under the slow heavy steps of the sentry sings too a lovely little song of life if only one knew how to hear it rightly.

Rosa Luxembourg was an absolutely dedicated socialist, a Marxist, I think, and maybe a creative evolutionist! But her heightened consciousness of Life owed nothing to those theories. 'To hear it rightly' would not come from that quarter. It was a state of grace. It was an experience of religion not subject to creed or theory. It was no solid deduction from fact, but an intimation, a presage, a surmise, an intuition of the excellence of the divine mystery, powerful enough to lift up the mind of one even cast into the cold darkness of a prison cell.

This kind of extraordinary awareness comes in many forms, as witnessed to in William James's *Varieties of Religious Experience*. It comes as a sudden shift in apprehension from one plane of thought to another as, for example, Carlyle turning from what he called 'the Everlasting Nay' to 'the Everlasting Yea'. The turn tends to follow from a period of despairing ratiocination. Thus, Shaw's greatest biographer to date, Hesketh Pearson, in a thoroughly unshavian manner, tells how his problems suddenly vanished on reading (not for the first time) Shakespeare's lyric which begins 'Fear no more the heat o' the sun', after which he 'never worried about the mystery of the universe, the ultimate truth, the nature of God, or any other insoluble problem'. Kenneth Clark tells us how, after perhaps a too extensive reading in the history of religions, suddenly during a tour in Europe, when in the Church of San Lorenzo, his whole being was 'irradiated with a kind of heavenly joy' which lasted for months. He felt bound to recognize this as a state of grace, and as having been touched as it were by the finger of God. These wise men have said no more than that about their experience, recognizing that it is not something that can be preached, nor handed from one person having it to another person not having it. But for all such the problem of religion is overcome. Salvation is not sought, for the experience *is* salvation. The problems are not solved, they are dissolved in beatitude. Conviction of sin is obliterated by conviction of joy. The natural is seen to be as supernatural as the supernatural; for the mystic is not mystified by such terms, any more than he is concerned with occultism, spiritualism, clairvoyance, or second sight – he prefers his own first sight. And he is less interested in the 'survival of the fittest' problem, than astonished at the *arrival* of anything.

None of this appealed to Bernard Shaw, the practical man, the reformer and moralist. It did not come within his field of vision. He would not even consider it when expressed by the poets, as in terms of a rhapsody from Wordsworth or an apophthegm from Keats ('. . . Beauty is Truth . . .'). He thought that William Morris was a better poet than Keats because he was a better socialist. It was Byron as 'a bold and vigorous critic of morals' who held his attention more than anything in Wordsworth. In *Back to Methuselah* the artists are represented as making idle imitations of reality, and the sculptor as passing from the creation of dolls to the study of mathematics! To 'a professional talk maker' – Shaw's own description of himself – the magnificent Dialogue called *The Book of Job* is only a debate in the Shavian manner. He represents Jehovah as saying to the Black Girl, 'I got the best of the argument.' But God did not argue with Job; He did not even give him a new argument; He gave him a new perspective; He pointed out *the intrinsic value of the incomprehensible*; and He did it with such style that Job was cheered up enormously.

Lots of people understand this perspective clearly or vaguely, but the greater masses throughout the world do not and cannot achieve it, they need the creeds and the symbols, the idols and the idolatries, it is all that 'is allowed' in Coleridge's harsh phrase, 'to the poor loveless ever-anxious crowd'. And they should have them. Oh no, said Shaw, they must have a new religion, a credible creed. But there can be no new religion, only this perennial affair of experience. Shaw could only give them his creative evolution. Apart from the fact that you can't really be inspired by Life in that way, you cannot 'hear it rightly' on that plane, the theory may be undercut by some new intellectual conception. What then? You get the Elder in *Too True to Be Good*. He was in a bad way. In very poor shape. Close to hysteria. And why? Because of the Quantum Theory – the discovery that in the deepest fortress of the primal power, in the nucleus within the atom, the electrons were behaving in a capricious manner – they were being thoroughly indeterminate. The Elder was very upset by this. Others have been upset also. But this sort of thing does not worry your mystic. He knows that the universe is *not* capricious; he knows, to use a homely phrase, that it is all right, and that if it were not so, everything would be all wrong, the very stones in the street would rise against us, the moon might crash on the golf links, and our arms or legs perhaps fall off.

Of course the Elder's deplorable state of mind does not represent the mind of Shaw. He was not as confused as all that. The playwright was having his fun. All the same I think that to the end of his life Shaw confused theology with religion. Furthermore, I am convinced that he overestimated the importance of science in this area, and by his literary expertise gave an impression of knowledge which was not justified. Indeed, he knew it was a mask. 'I don't want people to discover,' he told Sir James Jeans, 'that I have remarkable imagination but no brains to speak of, and my ignorance is colossal.' He meant it. 'All of us are humiliated,' said St Bernard of Clairvaux, 'but which of us is humble?' Shaw could be humble. He was humble with Jeans. He was humble with William Morris. He was humble with Elgar. He was humble with Dame Laurentia McLachlan, the Abbess of Stanbrook. Some have thought that his letters to her suggest that he began to entertain doubt about doubt; but I doubt it; he wanted to encourage and to humanize the dear old soul, for he loved her unworldliness. But I think that the findings of the scientists always worried him a good deal. He could never reconcile himself to the fact that the sun is ninety-three million miles away, since a little cloud coming between us and its rays will make us shiver. And in his eighties he was ironically asking Jeans if he was sure that the moon is really more than twenty miles from the earth.

(Left) *William Morris* (right) *Dame Laurentia McLachlan*

IV

When we are confronted with the man himself we fall upon a paradox and are compelled to adjust our view. We have declined his claim to be a mystic. Yet that claim was just. An intense experience of purpose informed his inner life, so much so that in the manner of some mystics he rationalized the experience into a doctrine, in this case the doctrine of the Life Force. He was not just an analyst who could see that if you take a watch to pieces you will not discover the meaning of time. He experienced the knowledge, was obedient to it, and in that service found perfect freedom. 'This is the true joy of life,' he said, 'the being used for a purpose recognised by yourself as a mighty one; the being thoroughly worn out before you are thrown on the scrap heap; the being a force of Nature instead of a feverish selfish little clod of ailments and grievances complaining that the world will not devote itself to making you happy.' And life was a joy to him, and a religious glory; all conceptions are immaculate, he kept declaring, the holy trinity a constant occurrence, life more miraculous than any 'miracle', the transfiguration on the mount open to all. And he *was* worn out when he died, burnt out, the inspired evangelist changing at last into the politically ignorant and disgruntled old man – easily discerned by those graphs of life we call photographs. But need we disparage the ashes of a mighty flame?

Even if we do not grant him the term mystic, many have named him saint. 'He was the last saint sent out from Ireland to save the world', said George Russell (who greatly preferred him to Yeats). He was incorruptible. He never quarrelled. He took no offence. He bore no malice. He was without resentment: 'What have I to do with resentment? Do I resent the wind when it chills me, or the night when it makes me stumble in the darkness?' A Tolstoy will keep a diary, in which he strives against sin, in which he determines to be good. Shaw kept no such diary, and did not strive to be good – for he was good. What with his not drinking or smoking or eating meat or quarrelling; what with his boundless magnanimity of spirit (and act); what with his display of virtue instead of virtuousness, of heroism instead of heroics, of temperament instead of temperaments, of piety instead of piousness, of sentiment instead of sentimentality, he was somewhat daunting. That is what Oscar Wilde meant by calling him 'an excellent man; he has not an enemy in the world, and none of his friends like him'.

In an endeavour to align *You Never Can Tell* with *The Importance of Being Earnest*, Mr Dennis Potter said in the *Sunday Times* that Shaw had not appreciated 'the importance of being unearnest'. Mr Potter had evidently sensed the underlying gravity of the play, for indeed there is much pain in it, and this had troubled him. But earnestness was a categorical imperative in Shaw, giving humanity to his comedy. In general the public only discerned the comedy. He knew it was his own fault: 'I have got the tragedian and I have got the clown in me, and the clown trips me up in the most dreadful way.' He hated senseless laughter. 'And all the time you laugh, laugh, laugh!' cries Larry in *John Bull's Other Island*, 'eternal derision, eternal envy, eternal folly, eternal fouling and staining and degrading . . .' It is one of his most earnest plays. The deepest-felt words come from Father Keegan. They are all roaring with laughter over the death of the pig caused by Broadbent's car. 'I don't know how you can laugh,' says Nora. And Keegan replies with fierce intensity: 'Why not? There is danger, destruction, torment. What more do we want to make us merry? Go on Barney: the last drops of joy are not squeezed from the story yet. Tell us again how our brother was torn asunder.' Yet when this play was first produced at the Court Theatre the management was obliged to distribute a leaflet to each member of the audience, requesting no laughter during the performance, since the amount of it was impeding the actors and holding up the play.

'I shall make a few jokes for you presently, as you seem to expect them from me, but I beg you not to laugh until I come to them,' said Shaw to a meeting at Farringdon Street in 1912 on the subject of Religion; for he had been interrupted by laughter which had greeted all his opening remarks which he had not thought in the least funny. However, it is a notable fact that on these occasions, judging by the remarks of the chairmen, he inspired his audiences by his own inspiration, his earnestness, his sincerity, and his force. A remarkable thing, that Force.

We cannot get a clear ruling from Shaw on any subject, whether religion or ethics or politics. It has been truly said of him, as of Voltaire, that his mind was a chaos of clear ideas. But if we do not go to the polemicist, we may go to the dramatist. What shall we do to be saved?

We turn to *John Bull's Other Island*. Broadbent, who in the popular view is supposed to stand for 'the silly Englishman', in the main represents the principles of the Fabian Society. He stands for 'efficiency' above all else: for industrial planning and fair distribution of wealth; for progressive civilization. He is going to bring happiness to poor old Ireland. 'I shall bring money here,' says Broadbent, 'I shall raise wages. I shall found public institutions, a library, a polytechnic, a cricket club, perhaps an art

"MAJOR BARBARA," BY BERNARD SHAW, AT THE COURT THEATRE.

Mr. Oswald Yorke as Bill Walker.

Miss E. Wynne-Matthison as Mrs. Baines.

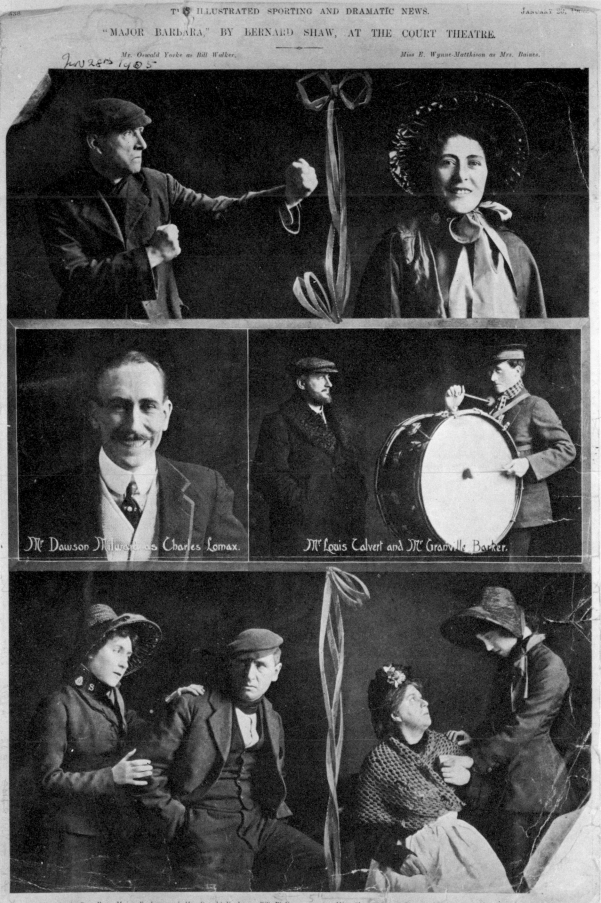

Jan 28th 1905.

Mr. Dawson Milward as Charles Lomax.

Mr. Louis Calvert and Mr. Granville Barker.

Miss Annie Russell as Major Barbara and Mr. Oswald Yorke as Bill Walker.

Miss Clare Greet as Rummy Mitchens and Miss Dorothy Minto as Jenny Hill.

school. I shall make a Garden City of Rosscullen.' To which Keegan replies, 'And our place of torment shall be as clean and orderly as Mountjoy Prison.' Later, Broadbent, the Fabian, is mercilessly lampooned in a sustained harangue from Keegan ending with the words, 'For four wicked centuries the world has dreamed this foolish dream of efficiency; and the end is not yet. But the end will come.' The voice of idealism is raised high above the voice of materialism.

We turn to *Major Barbara*. Here the scales are weighted on the side of efficiency. Undershaft, an arms manufacturer, preaches the gospel of materialism at any price. The making of anything, the doing of anything rather than poverty: thou shalt die ere I die. He shows his daughter round his factory. To her it seems appalling. 'Justify yourself!' she cries, 'show me some light through the darkness of this dreadful place, with its beautiful clean workshops, and respectable workmen, and model homes.' He replies, 'Cleanliness and respectability need no justification, Barbara, they justify themselves.' He has given the men money, therefore he has given them happiness. '*Their souls are hungry because their bodies are full.*' A non-sequitur to end all non-sequiturs. The voice of materialism is raised high above the voice of idealism.

We turn to *Heartbreak House*. Writing of this, Herbert Farjeon said, 'Thought, of which he is the past-master, now, after half a century of struggle, gains the upper hand, soaring to the sky in rocket after rocket and clarifying the dim horizon as the author, delighted and surprised, his beard cleaving the elements, holds madly to the tail of the stick he has released.' Once more the mighty opposites are poised in mortal combat. But now the voice of the one is as strong as the voice of the other. Yet in the end the voice of one is stronger. Ellie Dunn thinks she should marry Mangan because he is rich. In a great dialogue she defends her view convincingly. But at last she concedes to Shotover who says, 'You are looking for a rich husband. At your age I looked for hardship, danger, horror, and death, that I might feel the life in me more abundantly. I did not let the fear of death govern my life; and my reward was that I had my life. You are going to let the fear of poverty govern your life: and your reward will be that you will eat but you will not live'.

The solution could not have been otherwise. The greatest men have the greatest hearts. Materialism could not answer the needs of the man who said, 'Whether it be that I was born mad or a little too sane, my kingdom was not of this world: I was at home only in the realm of my imagination, and at ease only with the mighty dead.'

(Opposite) *Oswald Yorke as Bill, Annie Russell as Barbara, Louis Calvert as Undershaft, Granville Barker as Cusins, Dorothy Minto as Jenny and Clare Greet as Rummy in a 1905 production of* Major Barbara *at the Royal Court Theatre*

(Below) *A photograph of himself that Shaw signed and gave to John Stewart Collis in 1925*

Brigid Brophy

THE WAY OF NO FLESH

ORIGINAL TRAUMA

Shaw was three when Western civilization suffered one of its gravest intellectual traumata: the publication, in November 1859, of Charles Darwin's book *On The Origin of Species By Means of Natural Selection*.

As the adult Shaw tirelessly pointed out, Darwin was not the first naturalist to assert that evolution had taken place. He was, however, the first to put forward so much evidence that there was no dodging the conclusion except by violent and self-destructive contortions of the reasoning faculty; and as a result he was the first evolutionist to be universally heeded and almost universally believed.

Promulgated by Darwin, the news that the human species had ancestors in common with the other animal species was almost universally received, by members of the human species, as an insult. To Edmund Gosse's father, whose career and spirit were broken by his effort to disbelieve Darwin, Darwinism implied the lugubrious question 'What, then, did we come from an orangoutang?' To one of Shaw's uncles in Dublin in the 1870s Darwin was 'the fellow who wants to make out that we all have tails like monkeys'. The message was frequently garbled, but the affront it provoked was constant. Indeed, Sigmund Freud presently (1917) distinguished the theory of evolution as one of the (so far) three severe wounds inflicted by science on 'the general narcissism of man' – the other two being the discovery that the planet man lives on is not the centre of the universe and the discovery, of which Freud himself was the instrument, that man is not entirely master of his own mind, since large and vital areas of it are unconscious to him.

THE EVOLUTIONIST

For Shaw evolution became both major subject matter and personal talisman. First, however, he had to discard the mechanism Darwin attributed to evolution, namely natural selection (or, as Shaw accurately called it, circumstantial selection), which was a matter of blind environmental chance acting on blind genetic chance. (Perhaps the only substantial inaccuracy that Shaw was ever guilty of leaving uncorrected is the second half of his statement, in the Preface to *Back To Methuselah*, that Darwin himself 'did not pretend that' natural selection 'excluded other methods, or that it was the chief method'. Darwin's own declaration is: 'I am convinced that Natural Selection has been the main but not exclusive means of modification.')

For Darwin's mechanism Shaw substituted the earlier and more elastic version of the French naturalist J.B.P.A. de M. de Lamarck. Lamarck's hypothesis, involving the cultivation of habits, could be interpreted as allowing for a measure of at least unconscious will, and it was this will that Shaw enlarged into, and all but personified as, the Life Force.

It was an act that, perhaps to the vindication of Lamarck, ensured the survival of Shaw the artist. The Life Force provided him with a metaphor, not so closely characterized as to be oppressive, for his own sense, which he shared with most true artists, of being only the tool of a power greater than himself. Indeed, the Life Force was Shaw's equivalent of the classical poet's metaphor of merely taking down dictation from a slightly less than personal Muse (whose dictation Shaw took down in, indeed, Pitman's shorthand); and from his interpretation of the instructional voices heard by Saint Joan it seems fair to construe that he understood very well that the Force that directed him dwelt in that area of his mind of which, as Freud remarked, man is not the master.

At the same time, the Life Force saved Shaw from the fate of the fashionable dramatist who merely hits (much as Darwin thought evolution did) on one successful theme after another. Although, since it was not omnipotent but a method of trial and error, it had abolished the 'Problem of Evil', it did not wholly deprive Shaw of the preacher's most resonant weapon, the threat of hellfire, since Homo Sapiens, as the species self-praisingly named itself, could constantly be warned, in the words Shaw gave to Conrad Barnabas, that 'if we turn out to be one of the errors, we shall go the way of the mastodon and the megatherium and all the other scrapped experiments'.

The Life Force provided Shaw with the constant intellectual content that runs, if not always discernibly from one play to the next, certainly from one Preface to the next. Since evolution is a question of breeding and therefore of mating, it allowed him, in 1901, to turn the folklore and Mozartian hero Don Juan (Giovanni) into the hero of 'a dramatic parable of Creative Evolution', adapting F.W. Nietzsche's *Übermensch* (whom Shaw had at first translated as 'the Overman') into the Superman who may relegate Homo Sapiens to the obsolete status of the mastodon; and two decades later it invited him to create his 'metabiological pentateuch' *Back to Methuselah*, where his dramatic imagination swept through man's evolutionary past (to which, Shaw insisted, the myths embodied in the biblical pentateuch were clues no less valid and indicative than the fossil record deciphered by more limited biologists) and on to the year 31,920 AD or 'As Far As Thought Can Reach'.

However, Shaw's first perception on the subject of evolution, which probably came to him between the year 1871 AD, when he was engaged as a clerk in a Dublin land agent's office, and 1876, when he became an emigrant to London, was of a simpler though no less penetrating kind. The anger most Victorians felt on learning they were kin to monkeys was by Shaw directed at Darwin's description of the evolutionary method as devoid of will and intelligence. This left Shaw free to look dispassionately at the kinship itself. What he saw was that the kinship which had so widely been taken as degrading to man could, with equal justice and logic, be read as up-grading the other species.

Having once seen the matter this way about, Shaw (like any other reasonable person who accepts that evolution took place) had no reasonable or moral alternative but to become a vegetarian and an anti-vivisectionist.

THE EGALITARIAN

In writing of the blow Darwin dealt human self-esteem, Freud observed that it is only in sophisticated cultures that humans invent a 'gulf' between human and animal nature. This 'piece of arrogance', as he called it, is foreign to totemistic societies, which consider it no insult to conceive of their very gods in animal form, and likewise foreign to small children, who regularly consider animals as (whether in friendship or rivalry) their equals.

This egalitarianism the child Sonny Shaw shared with the run of children. More unusually, he put up a conscious and successful resistance when adult culture tried to encroach on his egalitarianism by indoctrinating him with its invented gulf. 'Certain doctrines,' he authorized Hesketh Pearson to record in his account of Shaw's childhood, 'aroused his immediate antagonism. For example he was told that the dog and the parrot were not creatures like himself but were brutal while he was reasonable. Being on intimate terms with both of them he rejected the distinction.'

Having rejected it, Shaw grew up not only better placed than most of his contemporaries to swallow the fact of evolution without umbrage but better placed than most scientists to take an unmuddled view of its implications for human morality. As he pointed out in the Preface to *The Doctor's Dilemma*, the vivisector who claims a right to inflict pain on dogs or parrots in the hope (or on the mere off-chance) of thereby improving human knowledge or human medicine is contradicting the science he professes to serve. He is brushing aside the scientific discovery of evolution and choosing instead to adhere to the old theological doctrine that placed an absolute line between man and the beasts, maintaining that the beasts had no rights inasmuch as they had no souls.

Such a belief, Shaw observed, was questionable even from inside the system of Catholic faith. For a post-Darwinian scientist to fall back on it was an act of gross superstition: 'nothing could be more despicably superstitious in the opinion of a vivisector than the notion that science recognizes any such step in evolution as the step from a physical organism to an immortal soul.'

THE ANTI-VIVISECTIONIST

After his ninety-second birthday, Shaw helped the National Anti-Vivisection Society to assemble, under the nominal editorship of G.H. Bowker, a little book (published in 1949) called *Shaw on Vivisection*. (Thus at least the title page. The jacket adds an epitome of his views and reads 'Shaw on Vivisection: Abolish It'.)

The text, linked by editorial matter unmistakeably Shavian in cadence, consists of Shaw's major speeches and writings against vivisection, including his exposure of the scientific as well as the emotional obtusity of Ivan Pavlov, and centres round a (to adopt a technical term Shaw was fond of in its evolutionary context) condensed recapitulation of the argument he advanced in the Preface to *The Doctor's Dilemma*. The (in full) fifteen sections on the subject in that Preface, which Shaw first published in 1908, are the classic statement of the case. The animal liberation movement that took a new lease of life in the 1960s and is now, in the 1970s, expanding fast in moral force and non-violent militancy owes its philosophy to Shaw – whose arguments it has expanded, only to find him reaffirmed at every point.

Once the evidence obliges you to accept the evolutionary kinship of all animals, you find there are certain basic rights (which you may as well list, as Shaw did, as those named in the Declaration of American Independence, the rights to life, liberty and the pursuit of happiness) which you can discover no means of validly denying to certain types of animal that will not let you, just as validly, deny them to any type of animal, including your type – indeed, including you. Of course you can arbitrarily declare that the life (and the freedom from pain and fear) of a guinea pig is valueless to *you*. But that means that you ignore the crucial thing, which is the value of the guinea pig's life to the guinea pig, and in doing so you morally license someone as

The picture used on the jacket of Shaw's anti-vivisection booklet

unscrupulous as yourself to ignore the value of your life to you and vivisect you on the grounds that your life and pursuit of happiness hold no value for *him*. You cannot dissolve the moral obligations of humans to animals of other species without dissolving the moral contract between fellow human animals and replacing it by an anarchy in which anyone who is strong enough has a right to vivisect anyone who is too weak to prevent him.

Evolution, Shaw recognized, exposed as a superstition the notion of a gulf between humans on the one side and all the other animal species on the other. It is a superstition Richard Ryder has recently, in his book *Victims of Science*, named 'speciesism' on the analogy of 'racism'. The supposed gulf could never, of course, be located in a scientifically reputable place. After the attempt failed to locate it in man's supposedly unique possession of a soul, it became fashionable to site it his supposedly unique possession of a faculty for syntactical language, but that attempt too has now collapsed, since chimpanzees have consented to learn and wield human syntax. Meanwhile, Richard Ryder has sharpened the point of Shaw's egalitarianism by asking on which side of the supposed gulf between man and brute a vivisector would place the (perfectly plausible) child of a human and a primate of another species; and John Harris, in his contribution to *Animals, Men and Morals* (the *Revolutionist's Handbook* of the modern animal liberation movement), has translated the evolutionary images of *Man and Superman* into SF terms and asked whether, if 'a group of beings from another planet were to land on Earth, beings who considered themselves as superior to you as you feel yourself to be to other animals', you would concede them the rights over you that you assume over the other animals.

Undeceived by the vivisectors' claim to high-mindedness, Shaw discerned a core of personal, voluptuous sadism in the practice of vivisection, though to the majority of practitioners he ascribed only the dulled sensibility of routine and a quite unscientific submission to the convention that vivisection is the professionally done thing. He added that a routine insensibility to the pain of fellow creatures is the worst credential the medical profession can proffer to its patients.

As a respecter of truth as well as a shrewd debater Shaw was always careful not to deny that additions to knowledge or even occasional medical cures might result from vivisection. He argued correctly that whether vivisection does or does not produce useful results is a question entirely beside both the moral and the scientific point.

Shaw's moral point was simply and forcibly this. To put one's mother on the stove would undoubtedly increase human knowledge of 'how long an adult woman will survive at a temperature of 500° Fahrenheit'; indeed, scientifically interesting results have constantly followed from wars and other catastrophes; but the usefulness of the results cannot be taken as excuses for permitting mother-boiling or for inducing wars. The argument that the possibly useful result justifies the immorality of the experiment would, if it were correct, not merely countenance the vivisecting of humans but, because that is naturally more germane to human medicine than experiments on other animals can be, would make human vivisection 'the first duty of the vivisector'.

Within Shaw's lifetime scientists did undertake what Shaw had said their own logic made their 'first duty'. As Richard Ryder records, the President of the German Red Cross and his assistant carried out a research programme at Ravensbrück, causing and then deliberately infecting wounds, in which some of the victims were animals and others women. The assistant, at his trial, pleaded that his sole motive had been his desire to help the wounded. As Shaw said in one of the headlines in his Preface, the argument that the results may be beneficial is, once admitted, 'An Argument Which Would Defend Any Crime'.

The companion argument, still often advanced by vivisectionists, namely that such-and-such a cure could never have been discovered but for vivisection, Shaw exposed as unscientific nonsense. Cures can result only from methods that are used. If you use only cruel methods and do not bother to seek humane ones, it is only the unthinking you can deceive when you attribute any cures that turn up to the indispensability of cruelty – and even then you would be prudent not to list the cures you have sought by cruel methods and failed to discover. You have no means of knowing, and therefore no grounds for asserting, that the same (or better or more) cures would not have resulted had you spent the same quantity of money and energy on experimenting by humane methods.

Already in 1908 Shaw could cite demonstrations which teachers preferred to make routinely and crudely on frogs, though there was an equally cogent and more elegant painless method available. This situation has come to a massive crux today, when the vivisection method has had more than a century of virtual monopoly in which to produce what results it can, and when the growing-point for the development of the techniques of biological investigation has plainly shifted to the humane area of cell and tissue culture and computer simulation. Yet millions of public and capitalist money continues to be thrown into vivisection, backed up by the self-perpetuating financial interest of the industry that breeds victims for vivisection, while only private charitable subscriptions fund the development – or even the mere dissemination – of humane techniques. Given the imbalance in the deployment of money and energy, it has become impossible to accept even the good faith (it was never good sense) of the vivisector's public protestations. His choice stands more than ever naked as a choice of cruelty, whether for its own sake or for the sake of professional conservatism – whether, that is, through a lack of human or of scientific imagination. Nowadays when an orthodox scientist proposes an experiment that does not involve animals he is liable to be turned down by the orthodox and rich sources of money for experimentation and sometimes has to get his work financed by the poor and charitable humane funds instead.

WHY IT IS A SMALL BOOK

Shaw on Vivisection runs only to sixty-five not very big pages, and would have remained small even had it reprinted all the relevant sections of *The Doctor's Dilemma* Preface. Shaw considered vivisection a gravely important subject but, like everybody who shares his views, he found it a repugnant one. Shavians can detect his prose nerving itself to recount the acts of vivisectors, just as they often have to nerve themselves to read what he wrote. The confession of the mental stress it cost him to attack inhumanity with chapter and verse is recorded in a self-effacing relative clause in the Preface *Killing for Sport* which he wrote in 1914 for a symposium edited by his vegetarian friend Henry Salt, when he speaks of a picture in an illustrated magazine of a murdered (his deliberate verb) bear 'which I wish I could forget'. Even Shaw might have suffered 'discouragement,' in the evolutionary terminology of *Back to Methuselah*, had he had to read, let alone write, such a book as *Victims of Science*.

In 1885, when he resigned his Slade professorship because the University of Oxford had resolved to build a vivisection laboratory, John Ruskin did not foresee a United Kingdom where there were more than five million experiments on animals in a year (1976). No more did Bernard Shaw foresee that the 'routine' practice of vivisection would spread from laboratories to industry and that manufacturers of almost any kind of substance, including cosmetics, sold to the public would, either voluntarily or under coercion from government regulations, apply the L.D.50 test to it. 'L.D.' stands for 'lethal dose' and the '50' for '50 per cent'; and the test consists of force-feeding the substance by stomach tube to a number of animals in order to find out what dosage it takes to kill 50 per cent of them within fourteen days.

THE VEGETARIAN

Neither did Shaw foresee factory (concentration camp) 'farms' which have deprived human carnivores of the last shred of their fantasy that they are noble savage huntsmen matched in fair contest with the wily veal calf or the robust spring chicken.

Although he was (as he bade the secretary of his later years, Blanche Patch, tell one of his correspondents) 'up to his neck in Darwin' by the time he was sixteen, Shaw was converted to vegetarianism not by science but by something very like its antithesis, namely Percy Bysshe Shelley. Shaw was given all his life to quoting, in support of vegetarianism, Shelley's

> Never again may blood of bird or beast
> Stain with its venomous stream a human feast.

The couplet is from Shelley's poem in twelve cantos of Spenserian stanzas *The Revolt of Islam*, to which the poet prefaced the disarming disclaimer: 'I have made no attempt to recommend the motives which I would substitute for those at present governing mankind, by methodical and systematic argument. I would only awaken the feelings'. . .

The feelings Shelley awoke in Shaw were of liberty, equality and fraternity. (The verse Shaw quoted from begins with the words 'My brethren, we are free!') 'It was Shelley,' he recorded in one of his *Sixteen Self Sketches*, 'who first opened my eyes to the savagery of my diet', though 'it was not until 1880 or thereabouts that the establishment of vegetarian restaurants in London made a change practicable for me'.

Shaw's letters and their editor, Dan H. Laurence, fill in that the vegetarian restaurant he frequented in the 1880s and '90s was the Wheatsheaf in Rathbone Place. By 1910 he was recommending a potential convert to try 'Eustace Miles' Restaurant or the St George's Restaurant opposite the Duke of York's theatre'. In 1948 (in a letter which *The American Vegetarian* published in 1953) he was recalling a dictum of his by then dead friend Henry Salt, 'a champion vegetarian,' to the effect that what London and the vegetarian cause really needed was a vegetarian restaurant so expensive that only those who set fashions could afford to eat there.

Shaw acknowledged his debt to Shelley at the first open meeting, in 1886, of the Shelley Society, where, as he recorded in another Self Sketch, he shocked two members into resignation by declaring himself to be 'like Shelley, a Socialist, Atheist and Vegetarian'. (Modern readers should not too contemptuously dismiss the members of the Shelley Society as typically Victorian hypocrites without finding out how many present-day members of the Shaw Society have contrived not to become marxists, anti-vivisectionists and vegetarians like Shaw.)

However, his Shelleyan access of fellow-feeling with animals was confirmed by the 'methodical and systematic argument' of science. It was in the light of the evolutionary kinship of all the animal species that Shaw habitually called human carnivores (of whom, as he pointed out, he had been one for his first twenty-five years) 'cannibals'.

THE UNSENTIMENTALIST

Shaw was as sensitive by ear as Freud by intellect to human ambivalence and had no difficulty in recognizing sentimentality as the public and hypocritical face of an unacknowledged hostility. The whole Freudian theory of 'the ambivalence of emotions' is condensed into the exchange between Shaw's Don Juan in hell and Doña Ana:

Don Juan: [. . .] You may remember that on earth – though of course we never confessed it – the death of anyone we knew, even those we liked best, was always mingled with a certain satisfaction at being finally done with them.

Ana: Monster! Never, never.

Don Juan: (*placidly*) I see you recognize the feeling.

The unsentimentality Shaw shared with his immediate kin ('Our indifference to oneanother's deaths marked us as a remarkably unsentimental family') was something he transferred to his extended kin, the entire animal kingdom. Evidently he did not entertain, either towards fellow animals or towards fellow Shaws, that violent unconscious hostility or envy which can be contradicted only by the professing of vehement concern – a concern that often, of course, infringes the fellow being's right to go his own way and thereby puts into action the hostility it is designed to conceal. Genuine observance of other beings' rights is always liable to be misunderstood – or, worse, understood: as a danger to the general hypocrisy. As he recorded, Shaw was not invited to speak again by an anti-vivisection group for whom he made a speech against cruelty of all kinds from a platform whose other occupants must have been angry only at the scientists' bid to share the upper-class prerogative of being cruel to animals, since they consisted of huntsmen, partridge-killers and women wearing 'hats and cloaks and head-dresses obtained by wholesale massacres, ruthless trappings, callous **extermination** of our fellow creatures'.

It was as an unsentimentalist and unromantic that Shaw, in the 1890s, sat 'on a vestry committee which licenses slaughter houses' (the vestry concerned being the borough council, which then still bore its ancient ecclesiastical name, of St Pancras). Given that the world was not going to turn vegetarian overnight, Shaw accepted that municipally controlled killing was minimally better from the victims' point of view and vastly better from the citizens' than the anarchy of private-enterprise shambles, just as he agreed with one of his correspondents that 'so-called humane killers should at least be humane', even though 'the whole slaughtering business is a horror'.

Henry Salt, 1932

Shaw's own vegetarianism was the fulfilment of the implicit moral contract between a human evolutionist and his fellow animals. It was perhaps slightly easier for Shaw than for most humans to become a vegetarian, and slightly harder for him to remain one, in that he seems not to have taken great pleasure from food of any kind – except, presumably, the large bits of iced cake which Alice Laden, who became his house-keeper in 1943, noticed that he ate between meals and the sugar which she saw him spoon into his mouth from the sugar bowl in the evenings. By the end of his life he confessed that old age had brought him to anorexia – a small-scale symptom, perhaps, of the same psychological condition that led to the death of one of his elder sisters, Lucy, of voluntary starvation.

Having undertaken a moral contract with the animal kingdom, Shaw declined to yield to the sentimental (that is, coldly and materially calculating) view that those who observe it are rewarded by an instant dividend in the form of good health. Indeed, no more than Voltaire was he given to admitting that his health *was* good. Vegetarianism did not cure the headaches he regularly suffered until he was seventy; and in yet more extreme old age he maintained that his diet of cooked pulses and macaroni had filled him with poison that did not abate until he took to raw grated vegetables instead.

Nonetheless, the health and efficiency that were apparent to others and the longevity that, of its nature, became increasingly undeniable were often wielded by his fellow human vegetarians as propaganda. Shaw described the claim that vegetarianism is a panacea for bodily ills as a 'blazing lie', insisted 'I have never ascribed my longevity to my vegetarian diet' and scrupulously drew attention to the good health and longevity of previous, carnivorous Shaws.

However, he was, of course, equally scrupulous and scientific about demolishing the more common lie that humans cannot be healthy without eating corpses; and in 1945 he offered readers of the *Strand Magazine* the socio-economic reminder that 'the British people are now trading on the vitality they have inherited from generations of men and women who did not eat meat for the conclusive reason that they could not afford it'.

Of the yet more sentimental (that is, yet more unscrupulous) claim of vegetarian propagandists that vegetarianism is a spiritual panacea Shaw made even shorter work by his habit of observing that vegetarians (among whom he cited at various times bulls, elephants, Adolf Hitler and Bernard Shaw) are often 'rather more pugnacious and ferocious than carnivora'.

The moral position Shaw maintained for seven decades not only with consistency but with sweetness of temper was that, as a human, you have a right to kill (but not to torture – whence his preference for painless execution of criminals rather than life imprisonment) a fellow being, including a human one, if to do so is essential to the continuation of your own life.

(Below) *Shaw eating cake between meals.* (Opposite) *Alice Laden, Shaw's housekeeper*

In 1898, when the failure of his injured foot to respond to their treatment was attributed by his doctors to his 'vegetarian follies', Shaw recognized their opinion as medical nonsense and risked nothing by his declaration that 'death is better than cannibalism'. He added the direction that his funeral procession should consist of the mammals, birds and fish whose lives he had spared, 'all wearing white scarves in honour of the man who perished rather than eat his fellow creatures'; and he presently published in a magazine a photograph, taken by his nurse, of himself in a wheelchair with his swathed leg propped before him, which he captioned 'the Dying Vegetarian'. But in 1939, convinced (not necessarily correctly) that his life was in danger from 'pernicious anaemia', he let his doctors give him 'a certain number of injections of liver extract'.

(Left) *GBS, newly married and lame, in his invalid chair*

(Opposite) *GBS could not persuade Charlotte to abandon her fur coat*

Ten years after the liver injections Shaw was still being publicly pestered about them, not only by carnivores, in whom he recognized the guilt of wanton killers seeking to justify itself through him, but by vegetarians hoping to convict him of having fallen from the status of propaganda idol to which they had raised him against his express will. They tested his temper and attested his view that vegetarians are often more pugnacious than carnivores, and their insensitivity drove him, in 1943, to tell the *News Chronicle*'s reporter that he had accepted the injections 'to please my wife'.

That excuse, behind which so many men have screened vain or self-interested acts, was probably in Shaw's case the simple truth. In an intimate relationship the less active conscience always places strains on the more active by dividing it between conviction and the duty of tolerance. Although in 1941 Charlotte Shaw made a partial attempt to share her husband's diet she never shared his convictions. She was a carnivore and the owner of two fur coats. In 1898, when Shaw maintained his vegetarianism

in defiance of the doctors, Charlotte Shaw, newly married to him, was largely of the doctors' persuasion; and one of the strains on Shaw's feelings and conscience (to which he evidently capitulated when the crisis was acted out for a second time in 1939) was that he had, as he told Sidney Webb, to oppose to Charlotte Shaw's 'paroxysms of misgiving exactly the same apparently callous obstinacy I oppose to the outside anti-vegetarian world'.

The challenges of agents provocateurs in the outside world Shaw was able to refuse with greater equanimity. When his leather boots were accused of inconsistency with his vegetarianism, he justly replied that it is meat that is economically the primary product, leather only a by-product. This defence, correct though it is, is one that vegetarians seldom have to rely on now. Plastic shoes let us be seen to be self-consistent. Likewise Shaw would be able now to reduce the list of animal species he thought it justifiable for humans to kill since, if you don't, they will either eat you or eat you out of house and home. Of the fleas, mice, squirrels and rabbits he named, only the fleas can justifiably be exterminated now, since oral contraceptives can provide (the obstacles are not real but bureaucratic) a more effective, as well as a humane, method of limiting populations of birds and mammals.

As unerringly as Don Juan recognized it in Doña Ana, Shaw detected the '*mauvaise honte*' of critics affronted by his vegetarianism.

> You read an article purporting to be a review of my latest book, and discover that what the critic is really doing is defending his private life against mine [. . .] The critic tries to go through his usual imposing pen performance; but the blood of the Deptford Victualling Yard chokes him, and the horrible carcass groves of Farringdon Market rise up before him.

Shaw's egalitarianism towards the other animals was, in fact, as disconcerting to received hypocrisies, romanticisms and sentimentalities as his egalitarianism towards the Shaw family, women or his fellow citizens. To his secretary it seemed strange and 'aloof' in Shaw that he would daily 'soak bits of bread in some of the Marmite vegetable soup with which he began his lunch' and, from the french window, scatter it on the lawn at Ayot St Lawrence but never wait to see the birds fly down and eat it. But then to his secretary it probably never seemed strange or anything so unkind as aloof that she sometimes made her luncheon of a roasted bird.

A DEBT PAID

The policy Shaw laid down in 1914, in his Preface to Henry Salt's symposium, for improving the moral relation of man to the other species included 'a plea for widening the range of fellow-feeling'. Since the humanitarian case rests on the value of an individual animal (of this particular guinea pig to his irreplaceable self, not to his or our species), Shaw set about implementing his policy by remarking not only that some species are cuddly in human eyes while others are scaly or creepy but that some individuals within a species are likeable and others not. He instanced two lions of his acquaintance at the Zoo, one of whom was grumpy whereas with the other 'you may play more safely than with most St Bernard dogs'. Such a selective and individualized response, he observed, is what we normally make to our own species, and his plea was that we should widen its range.

In accordance with this policy, not all Shaw's propaganda on behalf of animals is declared as such. *Shaw on Vivisection* might justifiably have been made a longer book by the inclusion of *Androcles and the Lion*, a play whose central dramatic image consists of a frightening animal presented in irresistibly friendly and sympathetic terms. An audience of twentieth-century nominal Christians was beguiled into widening the range of its fellow-feeling by the tale of the primitive Christian (and instinctive animal-sympathizer) Androcles and the Lion who, at their first encounter in the wild, is relieved by Androcles of a disabling thorn in his paw and, at their next encounter, in the Roman arena, displays both gratitude and what Shaw considered to be the supreme evolutionary virtue of self-control by practising vegetarianism for long enough to refuse the offer of Androcles as his next meat tea.

The ancient fable, as Shaw noted, 'figured in natural histories like those of Aelian and was found to please children, in whose story books it has appeared ever since'. No doubt it caught Shaw's attention when he read it in a story book during his own childhood. And what caught his adult imagination was, I think, that to create a drama with the grateful and self-controlled Lion for its hero gave him the opportunity to pay off a debt of conscience he had incurred during his childhood.

The debt was not to a lion but to its domesticated counterpart, a cat. As a controversialist against vivisection, Shaw constantly needed to avoid bringing his arguments into discredit by letting slip the faintest suggestion that he was against science as such. He needed therefore to make it clear that, though he was maintaining that scientific curiosity must be subject to moral law, he was no stranger to scientific curiosity himself and far from opposed to it in itself. In the Preface to *The Doctor's Dilemma* he adduced in evidence the story, which he repeated several times in other excursions against vivisection, of an animal experiment he had himself conducted as a child, when he tested the truth of the folklore dictum that cats always fall on their feet by pushing the family cat out of a window – though fellow-feeling with cats (combined no doubt with scepticism about the validity of folklore dicta) constrained him to make the test from no higher than a first-storey window.

Shaw always had a fellow-feeling with cats

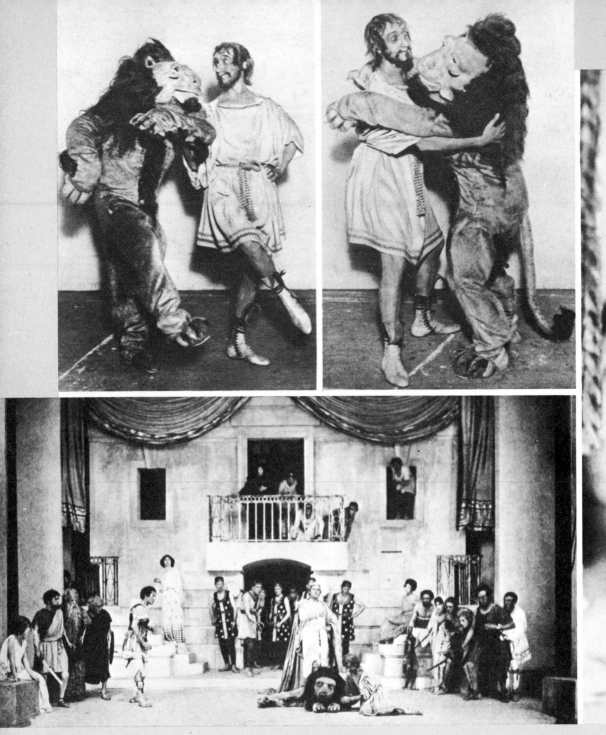

Scenes from Androcles and the Lion *at the St James's Theatre, 1924, with O. P. Heggie as Androcles and Edward Sillward as the Lion*

One of the later occasions on which Shaw recounted this anecdote was in the course of an anti-vivisection controversy in the correspondence columns of the *New Statesman* in 1938, where he adduced it as evidence that he was a 'Man of Science'. After telling the story he commented: 'This was not cruelty on my part: if I had been told that my father could fly I should have pushed him off the top of Nelson's Pillar without a moment's hesitation to see him do it.'

The sudden appearance of Shaw's father, by way of a ferocious analogy, in Shaw's commentary makes me think that Shaw made a habit of remembering his own comparatively minor childhood atrocity against a cat in order to avoid remembering (it was no doubt one of the images, like the picture of the dead bear in the magazine, that Shaw wished he could forget) the much worse atrocity that his father had, during *his* childhood, committed against a cat. As Shaw recorded in 1919, 'He once told me how in his boyhood he had found a stray cat, and brought it home with him and fed it. But next morning he let his dog course it and kill it. He was still conscience stricken by this atrocity, and warned me that no man capable of it deserved or could have any good fortune or happiness afterwards.'

THE SEVENTEENTH SELF SKETCH?
Thus *Androcles and the Lion* pays the debts of conscience the Shaw family owed to the cat family.

In a programme note he composed for the English first night (1 September 1913) of *Androcles*, which I am grateful to Mr J.S. Collis for showing me and to Mr Michael Holroyd for helping me identify, Shaw was at pains, as he was in the following year when he wrote his Preface specifically against killing for 'sport', to emphasize the individuality of animals. The denouement of his play would, he says, 'be incredible of some lions just as the action of Androcles would be incredible of some men. There are lions and lions just as there are men and men.'

The programme note continues, with the same comparison and in much the words that Shaw was to use in the Preface on sport the next year: 'The author of the present version has petted a full-grown lion and has had his advances received with much more cordiality than he could expect from St Bernard dogs.'

As a matter of fact, as Hesketh Pearson recorded, Shaw petted the lion when he visited the Zoo, with the actor who played the Lion, during rehearsals of *Androcles*.

However, although the Lion as produced at the St James's Theatre had a model at the Zoo, the Lion as conceived in the dramatist's heart had, as you might suspect from the ready and repeated choice of a St Bernard when a contrast to him is required, a model nearer home if not, to begin with, more domesticated.

As early as 1890 Shaw had designated himself an untameable (literary) lion. He did so in a letter to Beatrice Potter, who two years later became Beatrice (Mrs Sidney) Webb. He was declining 'to be sent down on approval or return' for inspection by some 'fastidious young lady in search of an eligible Socialist Society to join', and he protested that, however Beatrice Potter might enslave the other Fabians, if she wanted Shaw to go through his 'amusing conversational performances' for her, she 'must come up to town'.

However, eight years after telling Beatrice Potter (Webb) 'this lion is untameable' (as untameable, it should be glozed, as a St Bernard), Shaw was tamed – and by a fastidious woman, in search fairly precisely of an eligible Socialist Society, whom he had met through the Webbs.

What tamed him was what tamed Androcles's Lion: first aid for an injury to his foot.

GBS rehearsing a scene from Androcles and the Lion with Lillah McCarthy and Harley Granville Barker

In April 1898 Shaw developed an abscess on his left instep, the result of lacing his shoe too tightly and then bicycling too far. On 9 May, still vegetarian in despite of the doctors' opinion, he was chloroformed and the abscess opened. The operation disclosed the bone of the foot to be 'carious'. The open wound needed nursing; his unsystematic and overworked style of life needed domesticating. The 'inevitable & predestined agent appointed by Destiny' (as he told the other agent in the matter, Beatrice Webb) was Charlotte Payne-Townshend, who, on 1 June, in the registry office in Henrietta Street, Covent Garden, in the presence of one Fabian witness (Graham Wallas) and one vegetarian-Shelleyan (the 'champion vegetarian' Henry Salt), was married to Shaw 'on one leg' and led him away on crutches to his honeymoon. The Lion who 'holds up his wounded paw and flaps it piteously before' Androcles' is testimony alike to the range of Shaw's fellow-feeling with the beast, and to the versatility of his genius for self sketching.

(Top left) *Beatrice Webb photographed by Shaw;* (top right) *Edward Carpenter;* (below right) *Sidney Webb, c. 1888*

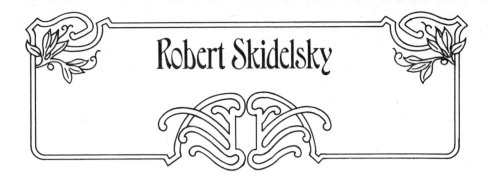

Robert Skidelsky

THE FABIAN ETHIC

Each age invents its own historical heroes. From the past it selects for special admiration those thinkers, artists, public men, who seem psychologically closest to it, to be fighting its own battles. For example, John Stuart Mill has recently found favour as a pioneer of the feminist movement. Edward Carpenter has been revived as a precursor of Gay Liberation. Others fall into disfavour, and must sometimes languish there for decades, even centuries, until a new age once more finds them sympathetic, or relevant.

The original Fabians fall into the second category. I am referring to Beatrice and Sidney Webb and George Bernard Shaw. (Graham Wallas and Sydney Olivier, while important, were less distinctive; H. G. Wells' later involvement in the Society was brief and tempestuous.) My concern here is with their ethic, or attitude to life. I shall try to show how it developed out of Victorian moralism, and determined both their political ideas and life-styles.

The heart of the Fabian ethic was an overwhelming sense of public duty. The Victorians believed that the individual was accountable to God for how he lived his life. The Fabians believed he was accountable to Humanity. In neither case was life to be lived for its own sake – for the enjoyment, or experience, it might intrinsically afford. It must show some result. In 1934, Beatrice Webb wrote to the Bloomsbury novelist, E.M. Forster: 'Why don't you write another great novel giving the essence of the current conflict between those who aim at exquisite relationships within the closed circle of the "elect" and those who aim at hygienic and scientific improvement of the whole race?' Neither the Webbs nor Shaw had time for 'exquisite relationships'. Huge tasks of world construction beckoned; it was these which gave purpose and meaning to human existence. It is easy to see that their admiration for Soviet Russia was no senile aberration. Beatrice Webb saw the Communist Party as a 'puritanical religious order' dedicated to the scientific construction of Utopia. Bernard Shaw saw Soviet Russia as the first Fabian state.

It is precisely this *selfless* ideal which makes the Fabians seem remote from us. Monasticism, even of the secular variety, is out of fashion. The most striking revolution in the West has not been the socialist revolution which the Fabians wanted, but the sexual revolution they feared. This in turn has been part of a wider liberation of self from the Puritan restraints of the nineteenth century. The Fabians wanted to redirect the Puritan instincts from the service of God to the service of Humanity. We have been engaged in abolishing them altogether.

The Fabian ethic was exemplified in life-style. The most striking feature of the lives of the Webbs and Shaw is the great outpouring of impersonal energy. Shaw's John Tanner wanted to be 'used for a purpose recognized by yourself as a mighty one'. Both Shaw and the Webbs trained themselves to become efficient instruments of social progress. They also determined to train their friends. People were objects to be animated (or permeated) with the collectivist spirit; no wonder they tended to fall away exhausted.

By contrast, the great attempt of our time has been to carve out an autonomous place for love, friendship, art. We like to enjoy relationships and experiences, for their own sake, not for the good they will do the world. This doesn't altogether exclude involvement in public affairs. But political categories, as Richard Sennett has remarked, are increasingly translated into psychological categories. 'Caring' for others is considered psychologically admirable; but the great impersonal causes to which Shaw and the Webbs devoted their lives are likely to be interpreted as projections of neurotic fantasies. Even before the First World War, Beatrice Webb was complaining that the young Cambridge Fabians were more interested in sexual questions than in social reconstruction. Freud was to have more impact on the twentieth-century West than Auguste Comte.

The clear Fabian line of division between personal and public concerns took some time to establish itself. The pre-history of the Fabian Society presents a more complex psychological picture. In the early 1880s, Sheila Rowbotham and Jeffrey Weeks have observed, 'the boundaries between [the] moral, aesthetic and political revolt were still fluid'.[1] The Fabian Society had its origins in the Fellowship of the New Life founded in 1882 by the Scottish philosopher, Thomas Davidson, an enthusiastic student of religious communities. His aim was to promote social improvement through individual ethical perfection. Individuals should aim to realize their own highest possibilities; their example would infect others. Among those associated with the Fellowship, Edward Carpenter represents the most sustained attempt to combine socialism with self-culture. His doctrine, example, and legacy, need some consideration.

Carpenter's philosophy rested on two fundamental principles. Man must try to realize his own possibilities; and all social improvement rested on individual improvement. It seemed a neat way of combining personal and public concerns. However, there were two snags. Shaw remarked that the ideal society 'would have to wait an unreasonably long time' if it depended on all its individuals reaching perfection. The other problem was that Carpenter defined self-realization in ethical terms. This ignored the conflict between instinctual drives and ethical imperatives. In time, the programme of self-development would become divorced both from social reconstruction and from the moral underpinnings which Carpenter gave it.

As with all reformers, the date of his birth is important in understanding Carpenter's ideas. He was born in 1844, over a decade ahead of the leading Fabians. His crisis of identity took place before the economic convulsions which produced the socialist revival: he resigned his Cambridge fellowship and curacy in 1874. On the other hand, like the Fabians, he was victim and product of what G.M. Young has called the 'moralizing society' created by Evangelicalism. His own upbringing, and the fact that he had to live, work, and publish in Victorian England combined to give his quest for self-expression its characteristically moralizing tone; it had to be fitted into a scheme of improved living which appealed to the moral susceptibilities of his time. What made Carpenter a rebel was his homosexuality. This was probably denied physical expression till middle age: he was fifty before he 'came out' with George

Merill. So his revolt against conventional morality had to take indirect forms. What he did was to attack the uselessness and dishonesty of upper-class life. In appealing to wealthy despoilers to 'simplify' their lives, he was asking the Victorians to live up to their moral ideals, not just pay them lipservice. This 'simplified life', he hoped, would provide the ethical basis of socialism. The homosexual element was idealized in a vision of a world united by the 'love of comrades', a theme derived from Walt Whitman. In 1883, Carpenter took a seven-acre small holding at Millthorpe in Derbyshire, cultivating it as a market gardener.

What was his vision of self-development? Three interconnected themes, heavily derived from Ruskin, Whitman, and Thoreau, run through his writings: the duty and dignity of manual labour; the drastic reduction of possessions; and the maintenance of vital health.

Manual labour was important for several reasons. It renewed contact between man and Nature. It was the only genuine title to property: the upper classes must become producers, not just consumers, of wealth. It would also reunite the classes in a common experience: like de Tocqueville, Carpenter believed that it was industrial specialization which sundered society by separating life-styles.

Reduction of possessions also had a dual object: to remove the parasitic element in private property, and to free the individual from being a slave to them. Carpenter believed that possessions over and above those that a person created by his own labour (for direct use or exchange) represented, in Marxist terms, surplus value extracted from the unpaid labour of others. More directly, great houses and estates could be maintained only by others' labour: one important aim of simplifying life was to get rid of servants. But the stately mansion was also a prison of the soul – it tied the individual to artificial manners, clothes, respectability. Carpenter painted a grim picture of great houses with 'books rotting by hundreds on the library shelves', 'boudoirs and bedrooms seldom opened, with fusty smelling furniture', 'forgotten dresses lying in the deeps of unexplored wardrobes', 'accumulations of money, of certificates and securities, of jewels and plate, hoarded away in safes and strongboxes. . .'

Vital health was the third element in the simple life. Carpenter was convinced that the upper classes suffered more than others from bad health. Vigorous manual work would partly remedy this; but it also needed a most careful attention to clothes and diet. Carpenter painted a harrowing picture of upper-class attire: 'the pure human heart grown feeble and weary in its isolation and imprisonment, the sexual parts degenerated and ashamed of themselves, the liver diseased, and the lungs straitened down to mere sighs and conventional disconsolate sounds beneath their cerements'. In his writings at least he attached more importance to liberating the feet than the sexual parts. He was the great apostle of sandals, and spent much of his time at Millthorpe making them. For the rest of the body, he recommended suits of hand-spun, unlined wool, with outside pockets. As for food, Carpenter rejected meat as an 'artificial stimulant'. The main meal of the day should consist of a 'central dish' such as a 'vast vegetable pie' round which would circle 'satellite platters' of oatmeal cakes and fresh fruit. Though strict moderation was to be the rule, Carpenter did not exclude the 'occasional orgy' to restore moral tone and prevent a lapse into 'pharisaism'.[2]

In these ways the improved life of the individual could become the basis and the means of the improved life of the race: for the voluntary simplification of the lives of the rich automatically entailed a redistribution of wealth to the poor. However, Carpenter's attempt to base socialism on individual perfection proved unsuccessful. Those interested in pursuing the New Life lost interest in its bearing on social reform; while those who wanted to transform society favoured a more direct approach. This split became clear when a group of New Lifers headed by Edward Pease and Hubert Bland broke off to found the Fabian Society in 1884. The same year, William Morris and some anarchist New Lifers left the Marxist Social Democratic Federation to pursue a more hedonistic ideal in the Socialist League.

The Fellowship's vision of the 'simplified life' continued to exert its attractions. One offshoot was the progressive movement in education: both Reddie, the founder of Abbotsholme (where Lytton Strachey spent some hardy, if miserable, months), and Badley, the founder of Bedales, were strongly influenced by Carpenter. The Arts and Crafts movement owes something to his example; as does the 'garden suburb'. Middle-class intellectuals earnestly simplified their lives by acquiring labourers' cottages in Surrey, where they grew food, made sandals, and communed with Nature: Shaw has left a memorable account of a weekend spent with Henry and Kate Salt at Tilford, near Farnham, during which his woollen clothes shrank every time they had to be dried out after exhausting rambles in the pouring rain.

As the connection between the New Life and institutional change faded, so sexual radicalism became a more prominent feature of the former. The Anarchists in the Socialist League, inspired by the example of Eleanor Marx and Edward Aveling, started to 'live out' their companionate sexual ideals, regardless of the effect on orthodox schemes of social reform. We see here the start of the 'privatization' of radical politics: politics become the direct, not sublimated, expression of psychological drives. Carpenter's own sexual radicalism became more explicit when he set up house with Merill in 1896 and published *Love's Coming of Age* in 1896, and *The Intermediate Sex* in 1908. Lowes Dickinson and E.M. Forster took this aspect of the New Life back with them to Cambridge after visits to Millthorpe; the latter after having had his bottom traumatically pinched by Merill. Carpenter also seems to have influenced D.H. Lawrence through their mutual friends, William and Sally Hopkins and Alice Dax of the Eastwood set near Nottingham; and Havelock Ellis, another New Lifer, and a pioneer of sexual psychology.

The practical Socialist case against the Fellowship's philosophy is obvious. The abolition of poverty could not wait till every man had divested himself voluntarily of his possessions. Moreover, for a socialist movement trying to win a mass following, these middle-class experiments in new styles of living were not only irrelevant but counter-productive. After a visit to the Salts at Tilford, the frock-coated Hyndman wrote to Shaw: 'I do not want the movement to become a depository of old cranks, humanitarians, vegetarians, anti-vivisectionists and anti-vaccinationists, arty-crafties and all the rest of them. We are scientific socialists and have no room for sentimentalists. They confuse the issue.'

More importantly, the ideal of self-culture for its own sake was unacceptable to moralists. Here was the weakness in the Fellowship's position. What was self-improvement for? It was no longer possible to answer 'for the service of God'. The inability of the twentieth century to give a satisfactory answer to this question meant, inevitably, that the ideal of self-development would be transformed into one of self-expression. But nineteenth-century moralists, capable only of sublimated pleasures, needed an ideal of service. And this the Fellowship, with its emphasis on individual perfection, failed to provide.

A question from Sidney Webb clarifies the point at issue. He is criticizing Goethe for being 'horribly self-willed'. 'We have no *right*,' he goes on, 'to live our own lives. What shall it profit a man to save his own soul, if thereby even one jot less good is done to the world.' Goethe was 'a great deserter in the army of humanity'. Webb

FABIAN ESSAYS IN SOCIALISM

1889

·LONDON·
·63, FLEET·STREET·E.C·

Cover design for Fabian
Essays 1889 *by Walter Crane*

concluded that individuals were 'parts of a whole, the well-being of which *may be* inimical to our fullest development'. Certainly the time he and Beatrice gave to socialism left little over for the arts. To Sidney's timid wish to 'carve out a little time together for pictures and poetry and music . . . bye and bye', Beatrice sternly replied, 'it will be difficult'.

The feminist movement of the time, an important element in political socialism, was also opposed to any hint of 'anarchy in sexual relations'. In its view, it was the sexual relationship which tied the woman to the home and motherhood. Thus the feminist ideal was that of the celibate woman: as Beatrice Webb put it: 'it would not have been practicable to unite the life of love with the life of reason.' The feminist campaign concentrated on securing women such things as the right to a career and to better education. When feminists offered themselves in marriage, they often did so in forbidding fashion. 'What does a poet think,' wrote Kate Conway to Bruce Glasier, 'of a woman with ink on her finger and a hole in her stocking? What would he say to two thick ankles? What would he say to a woman who would sooner eat bread and butter and drink milk or buy fruit for dinner than cook it . . .?' It was only with the development of efficient contraception and the lessening of guilt about the body that the feminist movement would be weaned from the sexless ideal.

Nevertheless, the quest for a New Life left its mark on the leading Fabians. Both Shaw and the Webbs renounced the ideal of self-development for its own sake but they embraced certain aspects of new living, such as the simplification of domestic arrangements, and the maintenance of health through the right clothes and diet, as the key to personal efficiency in social reconstruction. Personal fulfilment was to be had in submerging the self in great causes; but for this the New Life could provide an appropriate mental and bodily hygiene.

To understand the Fabian shift from individual perfectionism to social reconstruction, dates are again important. Beatrice Potter was born in 1858, Sidney Webb in 1859, Bernard Shaw in 1856. They discovered their purposes in life at precisely the moment when public events had started to acquire an ominous aspect: as Beatrice Webb noted in her diary in 1884, 'social questions are the vital questions of today: they take the place of religion'. In the last decades of the nineteenth century the feeling was growing that society was in a state of crisis; that big changes in social organization were needed if external decline and domestic convulsions were to be avoided.

Here, then, is the objective reason for the shift in attention. But, equally, involvement in public affairs arises from inner needs. Late-Victorian middle-class reformers were people whose upbringing had given them a great sense of sin. With the loss of religious faith, this sense of personal sin became fused with a sense of social guilt; the service of God was transferred to the service of Humanity. A little later the energies liberated from the service of God would go into the expression of self. But this required a very different upbringing, one in which the child would start to be treated as an end or value in itself, not as a sinful creature to be beaten into righteousness. It was the combination of social crisis and spare moral energy which created the middle-class Victorian reform movement and gave it its particular character. Puritanism turned the social question into a moral question.

Consciousness of social crisis dates from the last quarter of the nineteenth century. Before that most people had thought that *laissez-faire*, plus a modicum of private philanthropy, was making things steadily better and would go on doing so. Then came a cluster of unpleasant, inter-related events: the collapse of the mid-nineteenth-century boom, followed by twenty years of violent economic oscillations; the emergence of new great industrial powers which threatened Britain's economic supremacy and the security of its Empire; and the parallel rise of democracy and industrial militancy, through the two suffrage acts and the start of the 'new unionism'. Much of Shaw's writing is an index of the concerns created by these happenings: the heightened awareness of the competitive struggle, the premonitions of international and domestic anarchy, the lack of faith in the capacity of democratic politicians, the fear that the degraded masses will take horrible revenge on their oppressors. The last was given a new immediacy by the revelation of widespread 'poverty in the midst of plenty'. In the 1880s, Charles Booth started his mammoth survey of poverty in London. It revealed that thirty per cent of the inhabitants of the richest city in the world lived at or beneath the poverty line. This scale of destitution emphasized the irrelevance of private philanthropy, the waste of human resources, the potential threat to the stability of the state.

That economic fluctuations and widespread poverty revealed grave imperfections in social organization is undeniable. The way they were interpreted, however, owes a good deal to the intellectual and moral consciousness of the age. On the one side, Britain's economic problems were fitted into a Darwinian view of life. The contemporary phase in history was widely seen as a struggle between great empires in which success would go to those which were more efficiently organized. Thus Beatrice Webb thought that the Japanese victory in the Russo-Japanese war of 1904–5 would

alter not merely the balance of power, but the balance of ideas – it will tell against Christianity as the one religion, against materialistic individualism, against autocracy, against luxury, in favour of organisation, collective regulation, scientific education, physical and mental training – but on the whole *not* in favour of democracy. They have suddenly raised the standard of international efficiency . . .

(Below) *A London slum in 1889 and* (inset) *the despair that poverty could create*

Here was one very important root of Fabian collectivism; the chief weapon in the Fabian armoury of permeation. The survival of Britain as a world power required the building of a healthy race – healthy in mind, body, and morals. This required both social and eugenic 'drainage', particularly to get rid of poverty.

But it was the moral interpretation of Britain's crisis which best explains the character of the Fabian attack and the nature of the Fabian remedies. Britain's economic failure was blamed on the moral failure of capitalist civilization; particularly its growing tendency to separate wealth from work. The Fabians inherited the moral critique of the New Lifers. The economic failures of the late nineteenth century enabled them to attack the weakest point of the Victorian compromise: the anomaly of great possessions in the moral scheme of life.

The pursuit of self-enrichment had always been hard to reconcile with the moral notions of the Victorians: hence the flight of the bourgeoisie from money-making to imperial and social service. The way the Victorians had combined the two was to justify private riches as a reward for moral virtue (abstinence) and, in Fabian language, as a 'rent' which society paid to outstanding individuals for the hire of their wealth-producing, or other, capacities. But the emergence of a large and expanding class of wealthy *rentiers* living off past accumulations rather than present efforts, as well as a new group of ostentatiously wealthy South African millionaires, broke the moral link between wealth and virtue. It was the moral resentment felt by the first Fabians against this parasitic and luxurious class which led them to question its economic justification. Basically, what the Fabians argued was that private capital no longer justified its 'rent'. Increments of wealth were being collectively produced, but privately appropriated. The existence of a large class of unproductive *rentiers* was a 'tax' on the rest of the community; a tax which explained poverty. The community should reverse the process: it should tax the wealthy out of existence, using the proceeds to establish minimum conditions of life for all. As private production became increasingly unprofitable the municipalities, representing associations of consumers, should take it over. In this way, the lives of the rich would be compulsorily 'simplified' without having to wait for their individual ethical perfection.

In Fabian eyes, the chief offence of capitalism was to create loafers and idlers at each end of the social scale. According to Shaw, the real competition in the modern world was not between Bombay and Manchester but 'the competition of Regent Street with the Rue de Tivoli, of Brighton and the South Coast with the Riviera . . .' In socialist morality, the 'burden of labour' would be a 'debt of honour' which the individual owed society. Capitalism aimed to support a small group of rich in unproductive idleness; socialism would impose 'compulsory industrial and civil service' on the poor as well as the rich.

The dedication to work, the hatred of idleness, lies deep in the Victorian moral outlook. But one cannot fully understand the political expression it took with Beatrice Webb and Bernard Shaw without considering their personal and social circumstances. A certain character-type is inevitably associated with any widely held morality: the same psychological traits are to be found, in some degree, in all the eminent Victorians. Nevertheless, the personal ethics of Beatrice Webb and Bernard Shaw reflect some desperate and unusual features in their own early circumstances.

Both Beatrice and Shaw were neglected children. Beatrice's father was affectionate and easy-going, but had to spread his love round nine daughters, and Beatrice was not his favourite. Her Puritanical mother, on the other hand, positively resented her. This neglect, only partly offset by the usual saintly Victorian nanny, resulted in a

Shaw and the Fabian Baby by *Vicky from* Fabian Quarterly Jubilee Number, *April 1944*

'morbid and at times near-suicidal childhood', punctuated by 'chronic psychosomatic illnesses'.[3] Shaw, too, had a miserable childhood. His father was nicknamed 'the Hermit' by his children; his mother, a stern Puritan, lavished on him, in Michael Holroyd's words, 'the full force of maternal indifference'. He seems to have had no important relationship with his two sisters. Both children thus grew up unloved. The self-hatred that resulted dominated their lives. Theirs was a despair reconciled to life through work and service.

Both families had the virtues of their vices: they starved the affections, but provided, by way of compensation, marvellous food for the intellect and imagination. Beatrice's mind was nourished in the family library, by a circle of family friends which included Herbert Spencer, T.H. Huxley, and J.A. Froude, and by an atmosphere of complete intellectual freedom. Shaw's house was full of music; his mind was peopled by the heroes and heroines of grand opera, most of whose arias he could hum or whistle by the time he was twelve; he spent many hours in Dublin's art galleries, starving, as he put it, on 'imaginary feasts'. * Moreover, the adults in their lives, precisely because they were so remote and forbidding, could provide models for emulation. Beatrice's neglectful mother was a model of the intellectual woman; the philosopher, Herbert Spencer, a close family friend, provided an ideal of unselfish devotion to truth and social betterment. Lucinda Shaw was a complete failure as a mother; but Shaw could worship her on the opera stage, where she performed with an agreeable mezzo-soprano voice. Her singing teacher, George 'Vandeleur' Lee, who moved to the Shaw home to form an apparently harmonious trio, provided with his 'Method' of vocal training, an example of systematic dedication to his craft. In their later indifference to personal relationships and surroundings and their dedication to things of the mind and spirit, both children reflected the balance of their upbringings.

Their social circumstances were, of course, very different. Beatrice came from a well-connected, upper-class, English family; Shaw from an Irish family of 'feudal downstarts', linked by history, kinship, and aspiration with the Protestant Irish gentry, but by actual circumstances with Dublin's petty bourgeois Bohemia. But both found similar difficulties in realizing their exceptional talents in a world which reserved its choicest prizes for wealthy and well-born males. Educational opportunities both for women and for 'aspiring intellectual proletarians' (the phrase is Norman MacKenzie's) were still severely restricted; the best careers were the preserve of those who went to public schools and the still-male ancient universities.

For Beatrice, there beckoned the conventional life of the upper-class woman: to flirt and to marry; to be adored from afar while her husband hunted and shot and dabbled in politics; to be accomplished, but never serious; to produce children, but not look after them; to preside over a household of servants; in short, to be decorative, but useless. All this she rejected with open eyes: 'it will be necessary for women with strong natures to remain celibate,' she noted in her diary. Inevitably, the renunciation involved left a strong sense of bitterness. She came to believe that the 'nice girl' was an 'insidious parasite'; her resentment came to focus on the whole class of 'useless' women and men. What the world offered to someone with Shaw's background was the modest career of the clerk on the proverbial stool. He worked as one for almost five miserable years in a Dublin estate agency. Moving to London in 1876 in his twentieth year he determined to make himself into a writer, at whatever cost. And the costs were heavy. For years he lived off his mother while he wrote five unsuccessful novels. He slowly acquired self-confidence by studying books on etiquette at the British Museum, speaking at debating societies, deliberately cultivating the over-confident, paradoxical style which would force the world to take notice of him.

* C. E. M. Joad has acutely remarked that throughout his life Shaw tended to 'find in music what men who live out more fully and variously to the full scope and range of their senses normally find in nature, in sexual relations, in the athletic pleasures of the body and the sensations of the palate'. (Joad, *Shaw*, 1949, p. 59)

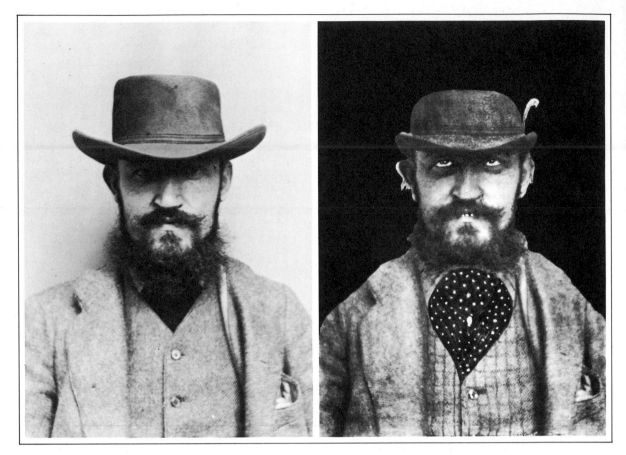

'Nothing is more difficult,' he later wrote, 'than to realise a superiority which the world has always treated as an inferiority.' His early plays were fierce and brilliant attacks on the artificial system of conventional morality which crushes human vitality. He came to see this conventional morality as a product of a parasitic, functionless, class. In this mood, he was attracted by Henry George's doctrine that an idle class of landlords had creamed off collectively-produced wealth for their own enjoyment. With the help of Ricardo, Marx, and Jevons, he and his fellow Fabian musketeers worked out an economic justification for dispossessing the wealthy of their crippling gains. But this was to be done not to put the idle poor in power. As an unrecognized genius with squirarchical pretensions, Shaw felt very strongly that the new state should be run by the best: he felt himself to be an aristocratic revolutionary. Thus the artist became a socialist; the pen would be at the service of the cause; the plays would get the 'bluebooks over the footlights'. Shaw's plays were much more than the sermons he sometimes made them out to be: that is why they survive. But, as with Beatrice Webb, the moral climate as well as the actual conditions of the times conspired with personal circumstances to force genius into the service of humanity.

The life-styles of Beatrice Webb and Bernard Shaw were inseparable from their creeds. Idleness was as much a hell to them as it was a disaster for society. Nevertheless, a distinction must be made between Shaw's and Beatrice's attitudes to work. Shaw worked to realize himself as an artist as much as to change society. Beatrice, who had a low opinion of her abilities, worked entirely in the service of humanity. Sidney

(Left) *The Socialist. From a photograph taken in July 1891* (Right) *The Socialist by Max Beerbohm*

Shaw making a public address at Portsmouth, 1910

Webb provided her with an economic justification for a moral compulsion. *Rentiers* had a duty to render unpaid social labour. 'Unless each individual,' he wrote, 'does work in utility equal to the utility of the commodities he consumes, he is a dead loss to the world.'

They lived up to their principles. Their work schedules were forbidding. For a decade from 1885, Shaw worked eighteen hours a day, seven days a week. He exercised his faculties on socialist pamphleteering, journalism, public speaking, service on the St Pancras Vestry, writing novels and plays, and carrying on a gigantic correspondence. He believed he owed his genius to his will to work. 'Anyone,' he wrote, 'can get my skill for the same price, and a good many people could probably get it cheaper.' Early in their partnership the Webbs, too, devised a punishing work plan to which they more or less kept for the remainder of their active lives.

There were many relapses, particularly by Beatrice, but on the whole they thrived on it. After several weeks of non-stop work, Shaw wrote to Beatrice in 1898: 'By this time I was in an almost superhuman condition – fleshless, bloodless, vaporous, ethereal and stupendous in literary efficiency. . .' Ten years later Beatrice could report that Sidney and she were 'living at the highest pressure of brainwork' on the most 'hygienic basis – up at 6.30, cold bath and quick walk or ride, work from 7.30 to 1 o'clock, bread and cheese lunch, short rest, another walk, then tea and work until 6 or 6.30'. She could hardly sleep from 'brain excitement'.

The main challenge to their programme, as to any monastic deal, was posed by what Beatrice called 'human nature'. Her own sexual renunciation was not easily

achieved. She was a beautiful and passionate woman; in her mid-twenties she had
fallen for Joseph Chamberlain. But she was not prepared to sacrifice her ideals for the
conventional marriage to the Liberal statesman which was probably on offer; and
decided on a sexless life of social investigation. Personal happiness for her became
an 'utterly remote thing'.

It was in this mood that she married Sidney in 1892. The winning of Beatrice was
Sidney's greatest success in Fabian permeation. She did not love him, but he won her
by persistently parading his character defects, which excited her 'mother's pity', and
by stressing the advantages to socialism which would follow from pooling their
talents. Their marriage was undertaken in the Fabian spirit of self-sacrifice. She told
Sidney that she was marrying his 'head only'; the experience convinced her that it was
safe for a 'brain-working woman to marry – if only she can find her Sidney'. Certainly
their union ushered in years of intellectual and administrative fecundity. When, in
the mid-nineteen-hundreds, H.G. Wells, an uncomfortable Fabian at the best of
times, raised the challenge of 'free love' (on the ground that it would extend knowledge of human nature), Beatrice was strongly disapproving. 'That way madness lies,'
she commented, and wondered, in Shavian fashion, whether man would

> only evolve upwards by the subordination of his physical desires. . . . I suggested to Sidney
> for consideration whether our philosophy was not tending to the restriction of all physical
> desires to the maintenance of health in the individual and the race – meaning by health, the
> longest continued and greatest intensity of mental activity – and to the continuance of the
> species at its highest level of quality.

With Shaw the problem of 'human nature' seems to have been solved more easily,
at any rate as he described it. Although Beatrice disapproved of his 'philandering'
with actresses, it was as Michael Holroyd says, little more than an 'ejaculation of
words' on Shaw's part. Virtue, Shaw wrote, consists not in 'abstaining from vice,
but in not desiring it'. Like his Julius Caesar, he came to feel he had no unhealthy
passions to control. He described himself a 'voluptuary rather than an ascetic . . . I
. . . never deny myself a Beethoven symphony . . .' On the other hand, he remained
a virgin till he was twenty-nine. He did not apparently feel any great sense of loss,
remarking briskly 'I am too busy and preoccupied to make opportunities for myself'.
Bertha Newcombe, looking back in 1928 on her affair with Shaw, thought him a
'passionless man'. To Ellen Terry, Shaw wrote 'I am fond of woman . . . but I am
in earnest about quite other things . . . I require whole populations and historical
epochs to engage my interests seriously'. His marriage to Charlotte Payne-Townshend
in 1898 was in the Fabian tradition. She took down his dictation, nursed him, and

(Below) *A study of six
socialists from a drawing by
H. G. Wells*

(Opposite) *GBS and H. G.
Wells*

Burns   Hardie   Shaw   Webb   Hyndman   Me

had plenty of money to service the writing machine. To Beatrice Webb he wrote: 'The thing being cleared thus of all such illusions as love interest, happiness interest, and all the rest of the vulgarity of marriage, I . . . hopped down to the Registrar.'

Friendship for its own sake had little place in the Fabian scheme of life. Nevertheless, the Webbs and Shaw had a different attitude to relationships. For the Webbs, friends were mainly 'instruments' for advancing the cause. They gathered the great to their house, giving them less food and drink than they wanted, and more collectivism than they could stand. Beatrice was far from being insensitive to human character. She felt the 'peculiar charm' of Bertrand Russell; she clearly liked Balfour for his own sake, and was drawn to the elegant living and clever chatter of the Souls. She felt uneasy about manipulating people, though Sidney revelled in it. Yet the half-submerged wish to form human attachments ran up against her renunciation of self for the cause. 'I do not wish to forgo the society of my own class,' she wrote 'and yet to enjoy means wasted energy.' As she approached middle age she conceded that she had become 'too utilitarian to make new friends'.

Shaw, too, had a manipulative view of human beings. But he saw them less as instruments of social plotting than as outlets for his insatiable reforming zeal. In his letters, he poured out an endless stream of advice and exhortation, parodying the manner of an improving schoolmaster. He breezily told the drama critic William Archer to 'take more exercise and earlier hours'. To the actress Florence Farr he confessed an 'extraordinary desire to make the most of you – to make effective and visible *all* your artistic potentialities'. He urged Janet Achurch to take more Shaw and less morphine. To Golding Bright he wrote, 'Make attainment of EFFICIENCY your sole object for the next fifteen years'. The famous Fabian quartet – Webb, Shaw, Olivier and Wallas – had succeeded, Shaw felt, because they were on 'quite ruthless terms with each other'. The Fabian family found their friendships in work, not play. The contrast is with Bloomsbury whose members played with each other, but worked on their own.

What is striking about Shaw's relationships, as revealed by his correspondence, is that they were quite impersonal. His advice was only slightly individuated. It was not based on personal needs, as they might strike a sensitive onlooker, but on general principles which Shaw had worked out for his own case. As he put it to Alice Lockett, his first girlfriend, his exhortation was directed at the nine-tenths of her personality which was exactly like his; the tenth of individual differences was of no importance. It was very much this attitude which informed his relationship with his public. Shaw was a great artist, who deliberately renounced an artistic creed. When Henry James sent him his play, *The Saloon*, based on his story *Owen Wingate*, Shaw told him that 'it is a really damnable sin to draw with such consummate art a household of rubbish. . . . People don't want works of art from you: they want help . . . above all, encouragement'. To this Henry James replied that 'all *direct* "encouragement" . . . is more likely than not to be shallow and misleading, and to make [a man] turn on you with a vengeance for offering him some scheme that takes account of but a tenth of his attributes'. This difference between the two men on the function of art turns directly on their different philosophies of life. For Shaw the world consisted of a Life Force only slightly differentiated into individual human beings. A sermon could directly activate the universal energy in everyone. For James, the world was peopled with individuals, who share common experiences, but who have completely different needs. Shaw's was closer to the traditional religious outlook, James' to the contemporary disintegration of common values. Beatrice's attitude was the same as Shaw's. She could not get on terms with Virginia Woolf: 'Her men and women do not interest me . . . no predominant aims . . . one state of mind follows another without any particular reason.'

True to their principles, the great Fabians treated their bodies as machines to be kept in the highest state of efficiency. Shaw was a lifelong follower of the 'sanitary woollen system' devised by Dr Gustav Jaeger, who denounced the evil effects of cotton and linen. His views on diet were even more stringent than Carpenter's. Man should eat 'good bread and fruit and nothing else'. Beatrice, too, had an obsession about overeating and overdrinking. It would be pleasant to think that it was their 'training' which kept them at work for so long. Productive to the end, Shaw died at ninety-four, soon after falling off a tree he was pruning. Beatrice lived to be eighty-five; Sidney till eighty-eight. Their huge, if unreadable, volumes on Soviet Russia were written when both were in their late seventies. To the last, they remained true to their creeds.

Shaw in his all-wool Jaeger suit, c. 1885

(Opposite top) *Beatrice Webb;* (below) *Sidney Webb*

What I have tried to do is to explain the Fabian response to the crisis of their age in terms of its psychological compulsions. These compulsions produced a moral energy which issued in both a creed and a life-style. It is because our own psychological conditions are so different that we no longer accept either.

The moral revulsion against idleness, so central to the Fabian outlook, has diminished. Steep progressive taxation has decimated the class of idle *rentiers*, thus restoring the connection between wealth and work. In that sense, Fabianism has triumphed. The 'involuntary' idleness which Victorian conventions imposed on upper- and middle-class women is also largely a thing of the past. But more fundamentally, there has been a marked decline in the Puritan work ethic in all classes. An affluent, technically advanced, society both requires less effort from its members and provides many more varieties of pleasure. It thus breaks down the psychological compulsion to work. Probably the hardest workers today are the millionaires: they need to be. It is a joke Shaw would have appreciated.

The decline in the sense of sin, in part the result of the growing ease of life, has also lessened our need for a secular creed. Both Shaw and the Webbs tried to overcome the 'death of God' by establishing new Gods. They failed mainly because we no longer feel the need for them. The purely philosophical criticisms of Shaw's Life Force, his God-substitute, while valid in their own terms, overlook the weakening of the compulsion to seek what T.H. Huxley called 'something, not ourselves, which makes for righteousness'.

The collapse of these drives has destroyed the Fabian attempt to establish an 'ethic' based on self-sacrificing service to an impersonal cause. According to Shaw, the individual should seek his gratification in serving the Life Force; for the Webbs, it was in the service of Humanity. This type of ethic has long been in decay. This is not to say that intellect is now less of a passion for clever people than it was in Shaw's day. But increasingly 'thought' is pursued for its own sake, as one of the many manifestations of the 'monstrous self' which Beatrice tried to batten down, rather than as a duty to the evolutionary process. Also today's outlook is much more hedonistic than it was in Shaw's day. To what extent acceptance of pleasure as a desirable end will lessen the will to achievement is not clear.

It is thus their psychological remoteness which has caused the first Fabians to lose favour. When her full diaries are published Beatrice Webb may yet find her true historical place as a writer and social observer of genius. Shaw's plays will surely live on as plays. But it is their joint *messages* which are, for the moment, stone dead. Whether or not we ever again take Beatrice Webb and Shaw seriously on their own terms depends very much on what happens to our hedonistic civilization. If we can continue to play without disaster, their creeds will remain museum pieces. If life forces a new religion on us, they may yet find themselves among its prophets.

The Fabian window at the Beatrice Webb House, Leith Hill, Surrey. The large figures (left to right) are Edward Pease, Sidney Webb and George Bernard Shaw. The kneeling figures, all Fabians, are (left to right) H. G. Wells, Charles Charrington, Aylmer Maude, G. Sterling Taylor, Lawson Dodd, Mrs Pember Reeves, Mary Hankinson, Miss Mabel Atkinson, Mrs Boyd Dawson and Caroline Townshend, who made the window. The window was commissioned by Shaw in 1910

...RE MOULDIT NEARER TO THE HEARTS DESIRE

PRAY
DEVOUTLY
HAMMER
STOUTLY

PLAYS
PLEASANT
PLAYS
UNPLEASANT
PLAYS FOR
PURITANS
MAN & SUPERMAN
GETTING MARRIED
JOHN BULL'S OTHER ISLE

MINORITY REPORT
ON THE POOR LAW
INDUSTRIAL
DEMOCRACY
HISTORY OF
TRADE UNIONISM
ENGLISH
LOCAL GOVERNMENT
FABIAN TRACTS
AND ESSAYS.

THE CRITIC'S CRITIC

Shaw's three-year stint as theatre critic on the *Saturday Review* has generally been dismissed as yet another instance of his prodigious journalistic facility in pretty well any field from sport to fashion; or, alternatively (in the version enthusiastically preferred by Shaw himself), as no more than preliminary skirmishing in the full-scale theatrical campaign subsequently mounted through his plays. Neither view will bear investigation. In the first place, no one has left a richer or more discerning record of our theatre in the 'nineties than Shaw who, for all his theoretical claims to bigotry and bias ('my criticism has not, I hope, any other fault than the inevitable one of extreme unfairness'[1]) set the greatest possible store in practice by that objectivity which he rightly held to be 'the cardinal faculty of the critic'[2]. In the second place, his role as theatrical revolutionary has been greatly exaggerated. Not that anyone would deny him a prominent place in the progressive critical camp led by William Archer of *The World* and vehemently opposed by the forces of reaction under Clement Scott of the *Daily Telegraph*. Scott and Shaw joined public battle on more than one occasion: the curious point is that, as polemicist, Shaw had rather more in common with the die-hard anti-Ibsenite, pro-censorship and arch-conservative Scott than either might have cared to acknowledge; and that the din surrounding these and other similarly racketty encounters has tended to distract attention from the unexpectedly subtle and dispassionate undertones of Shaw's criticism. Indeed any but the most perfunctory reading of that criticism is bound to suggest that, far from softening up the ground for the Shavian drama, Shaw as Saturday Reviewer was in fact preparing what amounted to a scathing, closely argued and virtually irrefutable case against Shaw as playwright.

ROLLING STONES

Perhaps the commonest, certainly among the most congenial, of Shaw's reactions to the theatre is that mood of 'malevolent exasperation' which must settle sooner or later on any sensitive or serious dramatic critic: 'My labours, it must be remembered, are the labours of Sisyphus: every week I roll my heavy stone to the top of the hill; and every week I find it at the bottom again. . .'[3] What depressed Shaw was not so much the fatigue as the futility of his labours, and still worse their deadly repetition. People who have not tried it often assume that regular attendance at first nights ought to sharpen the critic's responses and refine his judgement. In practice, the opposite is true: indiscriminate playgoing sours the temper, blunts the sensitivity, coarsens the palate and destroys the sense of humour (Shaw, who detected all these symptoms in

Wooden sculpture of GBS

himself, came eventually to suspect that it had damaged his brain as well). No wonder if most critics eventually succumb to what Shaw called 'servile puffery', for the fact is that prolonged exposure to the fifth-rate makes it more, not less, difficult for the professional than for the layman to respond to anything new, delicate or demanding. It takes heroic self-confidence and stamina to withstand a nightly diet of pap, and it is precisely this combination which makes Shaw *par excellence* the theatre critic's theatre critic.

Admittedly, some of the absurdities which drove him to distraction were peculiar to a period of transition. In the 1890s stage lighting at the more popular theatres was often rudimentary, high spots in the drama were still underlined by sweet or stirring music from the orchestra, and stylistic consistency freely sacrificed to spectacular effects like Augustin Daly's thunderstorm in *Two Gentlemen of Verona*, 'immediately after which Valentine enters and delivers his speech sitting down on a bank of moss, as an outlaw in tights naturally would after a terrific shower'. Audiences might be beginning to grow restive at the conventions of melodrama and the well-made play ('Nowadays an actor cannot open a letter or toss off somebody else's glass of poison without having to face a brutal outburst of jeering'[4]), but even the most advanced playwrights had by no means cast them off. José Echegaray's *Mariana* and Hermann Sudermann's *Magda* (*Heimat*), both hailed by Shaw as masterpieces of the modern school, still rely heavily on the old rhetorical usages from the I-had-rather-see-her-dead-at-my-feet type of cliché to the explanatory aside. Villains were still hissed. Water scenes were all the rage, and so were real horses, and real battles with real guns (though Shaw drew the line at the real baby in Wilson Barrett's *The Manxman*).

Nearly a century later the water, the horses, and the orchestra writhing in its pit 'like a heap of trodden worms' have vanished as completely as the jeers of the gallery and the sound of carpenters hammering behind the drop curtain. We have endorsed, more or less shakily, Shaw's views on censorship, civic theatres, municipal subsidy, ensemble playing, flexible staging and the National Theatre itself. But we still have ways of inducing that 'involuntary start of terror among the critics'[5] produced in his day by the announcement of a new historical play in blank verse. Each fresh genera-

Theatre queue at the London Pavilion around the turn of the century

tion of playgoers has to chart its own course between, on the one hand, the sham serious drama designed to collect all the credit without any of the drawbacks of genuine innovation; and, on the other, the bland commercial article turned out by 'playwrights who seek safety and success in the assumption that it is impossible to underrate the taste and intelligence of the British public'. [6] Shaw was a dab hand at detecting both types of fake. Even after all this time one can't but applaud the righteous satisfaction with which he gloats, however prematurely, over a clutch of Christmas closures in 1895: 'nobody need be surprised if I raise an exultant and derisive laugh at the clouds of defeat, disappointment, failure, perhaps ruin, which overhang the theatre at present. Where is your Manxman now, with his hired baby and his real water?' [7]

MIGHT AS WELL PLAY JULIET

It is this sense of personal grievance which gives Shaw's criticism its zest and accuracy. For only someone capable of appreciating the full enormity of what passes in the West End for entertainment can, as he repeatedly asserted, fully assess its high points. Given 'the present commercially precarious and artistically quite miserable condition of our drama', [8] it is scarcely surprising if these peaks nearly always turned out in practice to be feats of acting, celebrated with such loud emphatic vigour that it is easy to forget the precise and detailed observation on which Shaw's enthusiasm rests. The splendid series of articles alternately trumpeting the virtues of Eleonore Duse, and scourging Sarah Bernhardt's vices, provides one obvious example; another is what amounts to a running serial on the glory and decay of the old school exemplified, in Shaw's youth, by the tragedian Barry Sullivan ('there was hardly any part sufficiently heroic for him to be natural in it' [9]). The specialities of contemporary comedians like Charles Wyndham or John Hare are explored with particular relish: take, for instance, this comparison of Hare with Coquelin in the great mother-in-law joke from Sydney Grundy's *Mamma* (adapted from *Les Surprises de divorce*), when the hero discovers that the tremendous labours he has just expended on getting rid of his wife's mother have all been in vain:

(Left) *Elenore Duse;* (centre) *Sarah Bernhardt;* (right) *Barry Sullivan*

Coquelin clowned it, even to the length of bounding into the air and throwing forward his arms and legs as if to frighten off some dangerous animal. But he did not produce the electric effect of Mr Hare's white, tense face and appalled stare, conveying somehow a mad speed of emotion and a frightful suspense of action never to be forgotten by any playgoer with the true dramatic memory.[10]

Shaw in this vein is a match for any critic in the classic tradition from Colley Cibber and Hazlitt to Max Beerbohm or Kenneth Tynan: knowledgeable, incisive, often killingly funny and so vivid one feels as though one had been at the play oneself. He has the essential knack of hitting off a performance in a single stroke as well as a taste for comparative analysis. His demolition jobs are neatness itself, ranging from the merest flick of the wrist for Beerbohm Tree's Falstaff ('No doubt, in the course of a month or two, when he begins to pick up a few of the lines of the part, he will improve on his first effort . . . Mr Tree might as well try to play Juliet') to the avuncular mildness with which he scolds Ellen Terry for her theatrical sweet tooth; commiserates with Johnston Forbes Robertson as Romeo in the duel ('Mr Forbes Robertson . . . fights with unconcealed repugnance: he makes you feel that to do it in that disorderly way, without seconds, without a doctor, shewing temper about it, and actually calling his adversary names, jars unspeakably on him'); or calls Mrs Patrick Campbell to order for getting hopelessly out of her depth in Ibsen's *Little Eyolf*.

There is something decidedly more formidable, and possibly less disinterested, about Shaw's repeated attacks on Henry Irving which culminated in 1896 in a notice of *Richard III* carrying the clear implication that the actor was drunk (as perhaps he had been though Shaw afterwards, somewhat disingenuously, denied that he had suspected it). Shaw made no bones about Irving's genius. What he minded was its being squandered on 'costly Bardicide' at the Lyceum – the heavily-cut Shakespearian texts, the over-elaborate stagings, the inadequate use of Ellen Terry's talents, the frequent perversity of Irving's acting and the mediocrity of nearly everybody else's. Above all he resented Irving's invariable preference for the cheap, the sensational and the second-hand when it came to new plays. Shaw's view was no doubt lopsided, unappreciative, perhaps malicious, certainly politically motivated in the sense that the Lyceum was for him a stronghold of theatrical oppression. But even Irving's most fervent admirers have scarcely left a more memorable tribute than Shaw's to

that strange Lyceum intensity which comes from the perpetual struggle between Sir Henry Irving and Shakespear . . . the craft, the skill double-distilled by constant peril, the subtlety, the dark rays of heat generated by intense friction, the relentless parental tenacity and cunning with which Sir Henry nurses his own pet creations on Shakespearian food like a fox rearing its litter in the den of a lioness . . .

This passage comes in the middle of a review of Forbes Robertson's *Hamlet* which is one of Shaw's finest pieces of sustained analysis. The production, the uncut text, the passionate intelligence of Forbes Robertson as the prince combine with the miraculous force and shapeliness of the play itself to satisfy for once his most exacting demands. Everything comes alive from the meanest bit part ('Mr Martin Harvey is the best Osric I have seen: he plays Osric from Osric's own point of view, which is, that Osric is a gallant and distinguished courtier, and not, as usual, from Hamlet's, which is that Osric is "a waterfly" ') to Mrs Campbell's highly unorthodox Ophelia (a 'wandering, silly, vague Ophelia, who no sooner catches an emotional impulse than it drifts away from her again, emptying her voice of its tone in a way that makes one shiver').

The production was staged to fill a gap at the Lyceum in 1897, and it might be

(Top left) *Mrs Patrick Campbell as Ophelia in November 1897;* (top right) *Forbes Robertson as Hamlet;* (below) *Mrs Patrick Campbell as Juliet and Forbes Robertson as Romeo*

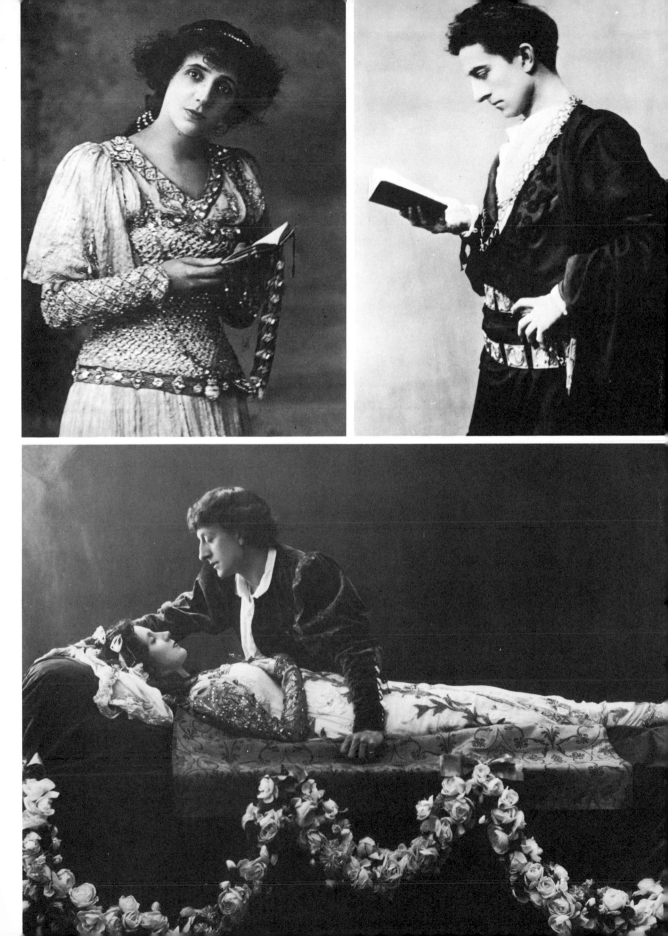

argued that Shaw used it as no more than another stick with which to beat Irving (who had turned down *The Man of Destiny* earlier that year, apparently as a direct result of its author's *Richard III* review). But there is no mistaking the genuine relief and generosity of Shaw's responses. They come from exactly the same source as his irritation with Irving, or for that matter his derisive rejoicing over the collapse of Wilson Barrett's *Manxman*: exultation and derision being, after all, no more than complementary aspects of what Shaw called 'the true critic's passion'.[11]

CALLING A SPADE A SPADE

London in the 1890s held no fiercer exponent of this doctrine than the *Daily Telegraph*'s Clement Scott who, after thirty years in drama criticism, was by now generally acknowledged head of his profession. Impetuous, opinionated and immensely influential, Scott had at least as keen a sense as Shaw of his own mission to the English stage. Fighting was his delight, and fate had twice granted him the chance of taking part in first-class theatre rows: first in the 1860s, when he had championed Tom Robertson, the Bancrofts and their naturalistic school against an outraged older generation; and again in the 'nineties, when he stood firm once more against a younger generation whose chief spokesmen were Messrs Shaw, Archer and A.B. Walkley.

Scott was the original of the critic Cuthbertson in Shaw's *The Philanderer* who spent his time 'witnessing scenes of suffering nobly endured and sacrifice willingly rendered by womanly women and manly men . . .' When Ibsen's *Ghosts* was first performed in England in 1891, it was Scott who had led the outcry against 'this morbid and sickening dissection of corrupt humanity'.[12] For Scott, Irving and the Lyceum represented the summit to which serious theatre might attain. In modern drama he thrilled to 'the clean, human and wholesome school of plays'[13] – tear-jerkers like *The Manxman*, sentimental comedies like A.W. Pinero's *Sweet Lavender* ('only a tale of man's sure trust and woman's gentle confidence'[14]), or the nobler sort of melodrama like H. A. Jones' *The Silver King* ('seldom before had such a sermon been presented against the

(Left) *Clement Scott*
(Right) *A. W. Pinero*

(Opposite) *A fashionplate Pinero strolls past Shaw and says 'Though it is an arguable point whether I be as I was once reputed, and as I still venture to deem myself, the most intellectual, I remain, beyond dispute, the dressiest of contemporary British dramatists.'*

curse of drunkenness and the mad frenzy of youth'[15]). In the frequent controversies over religion or sex which blew up in Ibsen's wake, Scott was heart and soul behind the censor: he had, as he often said, the strongest possible moral objections to calling a spade a spade. Part of the reason for his popularity was no doubt that he embodied to a remarkable degree the aspirations, gullibilities and moral muddle-headedness of contemporary audiences.

It is hard now to fathom the workings of a mind so pure that anything as innocuous as Pinero's problem plays could send it into a flat spin ('He detested pessimism in any form, and the Tanqueray, Ebbsmith and *Gay Lord Quex* families were absolutely shunned by him as any pestilential disease would have been'.[16]) But Pinero's impact had been shattering on all sides. Even Archer – Ibsen's translator, Shaw's mentor, the sternest and most rigorous of critics – had detected an 'astonishing advance in philosophical insight and technical skill'[17] in *The Second Mrs Tanqueray,* and tendered still more fervent congratulations on *The Notorious Mrs Ebbsmith.* Admittedly these were counsels of despair: Archer had suffered for much longer than Shaw from the vapidity and staleness of contemporary drama. Nonetheless the fact remains that Shaw kept his head when all about were losing theirs, refusing steadily to allow Pinero any idea 'beyond that of doing something daring and bringing down the house by running away from the consequences'.[18] It seemed to him 'the purest snobbery of criticism' to rate the specious logic and deft emotional manipulation of the higher drama above unpretentious comedy or farce. The few 'serious' plays by English contemporaries in which he found a rather firmer grasp of reality (Pinero's *Benefit of the Doubt* was one, Jones' *Michael and his Lost Angel* another) still read comparatively well; but even here Shaw remained perfectly clear as to Pinero's intellectual and emotional limitations, or the essential frivolity of the convention which required Jones to kill off his adulterous heroine in Act IV ('Audrie is dying of nothing but the need for making the audience cry' as Shaw tartly pointed out).

Making audiences cry was a speciality of Scott's ally and collaborator, the actor-manager, playwright and tragedian Wilson Barrett of whom Beerbohm said: 'His talk

is not as our talk, and his walk is in time to some strange music made from shawms and sackbuts by a thousand virgin slaves.'[19] It was Scott who supplied the title for Barrett's biggest box-office success, *The Sign of the Cross*, a tale of Christian slave and Roman soldier, true love and mystic martydom along much the same lines as *Ben Hur* and *Quo Vadis?* The 'pretentious puerility, the hideous vulgarity of the whole thing' reminded Archer of a penny dreadful crossed with a Sunday school picture book.[20] But the production put Shaw in high good humour: 'The influence of Ibsen is apparent throughout,' he wrote, specially commending the heroine's 'frightfully voluptuous death', the profusion of whips, racks, chains, dungeons, uplifted crosses,

Wilson Barrett and Maud Jeffries in The Sign of the Cross

shuddering martyrs, and the music ('hymns for the Christians, waltzes for the Romans, . . . and Gounod's Nazareth on the cornet and sackbut between acts'). Sixteen years later he transferred much of Barrett's plot to *Androcles and the Lion*, casting as his heroine Lillah McCarthy who had played the same role in Barrett's *Sign of the Cross* tour.

A weakness for blockbusters was not the only trait Scott shared with Shaw. Both were playwrights (Scott's chief ventures in this line being adaptations of Shaw's bugbear, Sardou); both prided themselves on their pugnacity ('Mr Clement Scott is as incapable as I am of keeping out of a scrimmage,' wrote Shaw[21]); and both were passionately devoted to Scott's proposition that 'there is no more eloquent power for good, no finer or more splendid missionary to teach high thoughts and honourable deeds than the stage when rightly used'.[22] Their difference lay only in their respective definitions of right usage. Shaw called urgently for more Hedda Gablers and Nora Helmers, more Magdas and Marianas. Scott hankered after the 'sweet pure-minded English girl' in *Sweet Lavender* 'to oppose the feverish, peevish, excited, unwholesome, discontented creature called "woman" on the modern stage',[23] and put paid for good to 'the Ibsen reaction, with its unloveliness, its want of faith; its hopeless, despairing creed; its worship of the ugly in art; its grim and repulsive reality. . . .'[24]

Scott's 'Ibsen reaction' was the reverse, indeed a mirror image, of that frank and wholesome optimism which Shaw held to be the keynote of the modern movement (and which corresponded rather more closely to the Shavian drama as it eventually manifested itself than to anything in Ibsen's sombre vision). But the one playwright who had the same unfortunate effect on him as Ibsen on Scott was of course Shakespeare; and Shaw's chief complaint against 'the sententious William' was precisely his pessimism, his lack of public spirit, indifference to the progressive tenets of the 1890s, in short his failure to create Shavian heroes:

> What a crew they are – these Saturday to Monday athletic stockbroker Orlandos, these villains, fools, clowns, drunkards, cowards . . . princes without any sense of public duty, futile pessimists . . . search for statesmanship, or even citizenship, or any sense of the commonwealth, material or spiritual, and you will not find the making of a decent vestryman or curate in the whole horde. As to faith, hope, courage, conviction, or any of the true heroic qualities, you find nothing but death made sensational, despair made stage-sublime, sex made romantic, and barrennness covered up by sentimentality and the mechanical lilt of blank verse.[25]

POOR FOOLISH OLD SWAN

Anyone accustomed to Shaw's cool and humorous approach to his contemporaries will have been struck, again and again, by how sharply the tone deteriorates when he comes to Shakespeare. Time has perhaps lent a certain period charm to his portrait of the Bard as a late-Victorian duffer with a philosophical range barely up to 'the level of a sixth-rate Kingsley',[26] a grasp of practical politics which 'would hardly impress the Thames Conservancy Board'[27], and an infinite capacity for manufacturing 'commonplaces against which a Polytechnic debating club would revolt'[28]. But on the whole the Shakespearian campaign shows Shaw at his most tiresome, rattly and repetitive, close to incoherence in his tirade against *As You Like It* ('canting snivelling, hypocritical unctuousness'), or the notorious review of *Cymbeline* ('vulgar, foolish, offensive, indecent, and exasperating beyond all tolerance') which includes perhaps his most famous piece of childish swank: 'With the single exception of Homer, there is no eminent writer, not even Sir Walter Scott, whom I can despise so entirely as I despise Shakespear when I measure my mind against his'.

·MAN
AND
SUPER
·MAN·
II

ALL THE WORLD'S A STAGE SOCIETY.

ICN FOR A STATUE OF "JOHN BULL'S OTHER PLAYWRIGHT."
AFTER CERTAIN HINTS BY "G.B.S."

John Bull's Other Playwright
(Punch: *3 October 1906*)

Partly no doubt this parody of vanity, petulance and folly was designed in protest against the glib endorsement by more easygoing colleagues of almost any lunacy perpetrated in Shakespeare's name. Contemporary canons of Shakespearian production meant interrupting an often cruelly mutilated text to erect as many as sixteen full-scale scene changes (not forgetting real water, real horses and the very latest thing in portable electric light bulbs for Titania's fairies). Worse still was the national addiction to bardolatry, for Shaw reacted badly to that element of punishment religiously accepted by audiences prepared to bore themselves silly in Shakespeare's name.

But dislike of cultural snobbery will not entirely account for the streak of private venom which seems linked in Shaw to an almost painfully acute sensitivity to Shakespearian rhetoric. It is as though he resented his own susceptibility, or felt that it involved him in some sort of involuntary capitulation: the tantrums thrown at the start of so many of his Shakespearian reviews seem necessary to clear the air, as it were, before he can admit how deeply he has been moved – overpowered is his own word – by the beauties of the play in question. Time after time he breaks off in the middle of administering the most tremendous wigging to marvel at some mighty line or subtle play of feeling. The second half of the vituperative *Cymbeline* review is devoted to paying delicate and quite ungrudging tribute to both Irving and his text. Parts of *As You Like It* made Shaw threaten to vomit but even here he cannot help being momentarily distracted by disinterested professional appreciation: 'And such prose! The first scene alone, with its energy of exposition, each phrase driving its meaning and feeling in up to the head at one brief, sure stroke, is worth ten acts of the ordinary Elizabethan sing-song.'

Inevitably his insights come in spurts and flashes, prompted more often than not by the attempts of supercilious actors or officious managements to correct 'the poor foolish old Swan, than whom they all knew so much better!'[29] It was an unsuccessful ghost in *Hamlet* which produced Shaw's own unforgettable account of why 'the Ghost's part is one of the wonders of the play'. A piece of injudicious cutting in *A Midsummer Night's Dream* – when Daly lopped off alternate lines from the antiphonal duet for star-crossed lovers in Act One – made him bitterly regret 'an effect which sets the whole scene throbbing with their absorption in one another'. Asides like these show that Shaw made no idle boast when he claimed to have been soaked in Shakespeare from an early age. His hints on interpretation, from Imogen to Romeo, and Helena to Hamlet, are invariably illuminating and profoundly attentive to the text. And, if he is good on the changing inflections of mood, the finest variations in tone or execution, he is still better on the separate role played by each part in building an orchestral whole, and on the musical or structural means by which these effects are achieved: 'Even the individualisation . . . owes all its magic to the turn of the line, which lets you into the secret of its utterer's mood and temperament, not by its commonplace meaning, but by some subtle exaltation, or stultification, or slyness, or delicacy, or hesitancy, or what not in the sound of it'.

This comes from a marvellously lucid essay on the musical meaning of *All's Well that Ends Well* which (considering that it was inspired by the efforts of as lamentable a bunch of amateurs as ever trod church hall) must be among the most remarkable pieces of practical criticism ever published in a weekly paper. Its rapturous pleasure in the poetry itself is reinforced by a firm grasp of Shakespeare's emotional truth and density, for Shaw at his best had not only a refined and extraordinarily responsive musical imagination: he had also a fundamental sense of form and – rare in any prac-tising critic – an instinct for the interpenetration of thought with feeling which lies at the heart of Shakespeare's grandest and most sophisticated conceptions. Any number of casual passages – his succinct structural analysis of *Hamlet*, for instance, or the brief defence of blank verse in his *Midsummer Night's Dream* review – make nonsense of Shaw's own tireless insistence that form may be divorced from content. So does his magnificent analysis of the musical tempi and emotional climaxes of *Julius Caesar*. Admittedly, he prefaced the *Caesar* review with another brutal onslaught on Shakespeare's feebleness of mind, just as he later tried to retract, or at least excuse, what had come to seem an over-enthusiastic endorsement of *Hamlet*'s philosophy. Both instances point to the unmistakeable uneasiness which runs right through Shaw's attempts to come to grips with Shakespeare.

The fact is that Shaw knew very well, at the deepest and most fastidious level of his consciousness, that art cannot be essentially didactic. This knowledge is the root of his innate love and sympathy with Shakespeare; it underlies his feeling for Ibsen (the reviews of *Rosmersholm* and *Peer Gynt* make it very clear that, however much he admired Ibsen's revolutionary teachings, what moved him most was something altogether harder to define); and it is flatly incompatible with the comparatively much cruder set of attitudes which inform his bullying attacks on Shakespeare, and were subsequently embedded in all but the earliest and least pretentious of his own plays.

MORE THAN HUMAN NATURE CAN BEAR

It was not for nothing that Shaw's earliest impulse to write plays came from his very first sight of Henry Irving in sentimental comedy: 'I instinctively felt that a new drama inhered in this man, though I had then no conscious notion that I was destined to write it. . . .'[30] The passage, written in 1929 nearly forty years after Shaw's first play had been performed, goes on to discuss the need for creating a new stage world, lifting the theatre out of its rut and heading it 'towards unexplored regions of drama', without pointing out that in the event Shaw had proved no more capable of these feats than Irving.

It is a commonplace that there could scarcely have been dramatic regions already more thoroughly explored than those in which Shaw chose to pitch his tent. His entire career as a dramatist shows no advance, in point of innovation, on his original scheme of taking nineteenth-century stereotypes and turning them on their heads. His cast lists, from *Widowers' Houses* to *Back to Methuselah*, stick more or less to the stock lines of 'business' traditionally laid down for ingenue and villain, low comedian and heavy father, Utility or Walking Gentleman (Shaw called explicitly for three of these in casting *Candida* alone). Martin Meisel, in his fascinating and exhaustive survey of Shaw's borrowings, lists no less than five 'womanly women' – Julia in *The Philanderer*, Blanche Sartorius in *Widowers' Houses*, Ann Whitefield in *Man and Superman*, Hesione Hushabye in *Heartbreak House* and Orinthia in *The Apple Cart* – all directly descended from 'the dark, passionate, female Heavy of Melodrama'.[31] As to plots, Shaw helped himself no less liberally to all the standard formulae of popular success: in Meisel's book *Mrs Warren's Profession*, for instance, is a variation on *The Second Mrs Tanqueray* and *Candida* on Sardou's *Divorçons*, just as *Androcles and the Lion* rearranges the slave-and-martyr theme from *The Sign of the Cross*.

Shaw, of course, had no illusions as to the provenance of his 'hackneyed claptraps'[32]: when actors threw up their parts in bewilderment and audiences reeled at his audacity, one of his favourite ploys was to point with an air of injured innocence to the irreproachable conventionality of his construction and technique. Thus *Widowers' Houses*, 'far from being a play of so new a sort that its very title to the name of drama is questionable'[33] was a run-of-the-mill 'blue-book' play, and *The Man of Destiny* no more than a 'commercial traveller's sample'[34] designed to demonstrate its author's mastery of stage tricks. He protested that *The Devil's Disciple* was a catalogue of virtually every cliché known to melodrama, and drew up his own list ('the reading of the will, the oppressed orphan finding a protector, the arrest, the heroic sacrifice, the court martial, the scaffold, the reprieve at the last moment'[35]) to prove it. When productions of his plays caused public commotion, Shaw put it down to modern thought, modestly disclaiming responsibility for an originality which was 'not any invention of my own, but simply the novelty of the advanced thought of my day. As such, it will assuredly lose its gloss with the lapse of time, and leave *The Devil's Disciple* exposed as the threadbare popular melodrama it technically is.'[36] This ability to superimpose apparent novelty on an essentially trite conception was perhaps the most useful of all the lessons Shaw learnt from the playwrights he criticized. For what he is here describing is, after all, precisely the confidence trick which, as a critic, he had so mercilessly exposed in Pinero when that luckless impostor 'invented

Scenes from The Devil's Disciple *first presented at the Savoy Theatre in 1907*

a new sort of play by taking the ordinary article and giving it an air of novel, profound and original thought'.[37]

Shaw as Saturday Reviewer had described often enough the process whereby his contemporaries assembled their despised 'problem' plays from a construction kit of ready-made character and incident. The rare exceptions – principally the 'real live works' of H.A. Jones – were praised for their creative imagination, original observation, above all for their organic rather than mechanical construction: in short, for a method the opposite of that which, by Shaw's own account, produced the Shavian drama. The two contradictory approaches are nicely illustrated by a passage in his review of *Michael and his Lost Angel*, discussing the climax in which Jones' adulterous clergyman publicly confesses his sin from his own altar steps (a proceeding which caused such scandal in 1896 that the management withdrew the play after a ten-night run). In his notice, Shaw had no sooner praised the rare emotional honesty of this scene than the critic in him was, so to speak, supplanted by the dramatist, blandly offering to supply a brand new Shavian hero on the grounds that Jones' Michael, though 'perfectly true to nature', was no friend to up-to-date thought ('Here you have the disqualification of *Michael and his Lost Angel* for full tragic honours. It is a play without a hero. Let me rewrite the last three acts, and you shall have your Reverend Michael embracing the answer of his own soul, thundering it from the steps of his altar, and marching out . . . with colours flying and head erect and unashamed. . . .') This high-handed moralistic approach suggests that Shaw and the great Victorian public were not so far apart as either supposed. However different their ostensible objections to the scene in question, both shied violently away from what had threatened to develop into a disquieting truthfulness on stage.

In a sense one might say that Shaw as theatre critic was serving an apprenticeship which bore frightful fruit in his plays. For up-to-date thought is the most perishable of commodities. Notions that scandalized the 'nineties have long since lost their power to shock, turning imperceptibly into comfortable commonplaces well suited to the stale and trivial atmosphere from which the Shavian drama sprang, and owing what interest they still retain to that provoking tone which at once titillates and reassures an audience in almost equal measure. Shaw himself, unlike Peer Gynt, foresaw a future when 'my gold will have turned into withered leaves'.[38] He lived to see his plays a box-office success; since his death they have become, on an international scale, a safe commercial draw; and, as overtones of parody fade from characters whose ideas no longer impose the smallest mental strain, it is increasingly hard to discount in Shaw the complacency, the condescension, the effect of synthetic significance grafted onto stock dramatic situations which he himself understood so well in Pinero:

> In this way he conquered the public by the exquisite flattery of giving them plays that they really liked, whilst persuading them that such appreciation was only possible from persons of great culture and intellectual acuteness. The vogue of *The Second Mrs Tanqueray* . . . combined the delights of an evening at a play which would not have puzzled Madame Celeste with a sense of being immensely in the modern movement.[39]

The basic objection to this kind of play is that it implies, on the part of the playwright, a want of respect for his own characters' integrity coupled with a smug indifference to his audience's independent powers of thought and judgment. 'To be publicly and obviously played down to is more than human nature can bear,' as Shaw said[40]; and admirers of the critic who set his face uncompromisingly against the scoring of cheap points must bear, if only for that reason, a heavy grudge against the playwright who betrayed him.

THE PLAYS

The Shaw revival in Britain began on 15 March 1965 with Ronald Eyre's production of *Widowers' Houses* at the Theatre Royal, Stratford East. Not that Shaw had ever vanished down the star-trap. Discounting the 2281 nights of *My Fair Lady*, the West End public had lately seen three of Frank Hauser's elegant Oxford transfers; the English Stage Company played Shaw alongside John Osborne and *Saint Joan* followed *Hamlet* in the opening season of the National Theatre. None of which had the slightest effect on Shaw's reputation. Shavians and anti-Shavians alike emerged from these shows with unaltered minds. The familiar features of the Ayot St Lawrence sage grinned down from the stage as rigidly as a totem pole, exhibited to ritual observers who turned up to have their prejudices and enthusiasms reinforced.

The production of *Widowers' Houses* was an event of an entirely different kind. Shaw's first play had never found a place in the standard repertory, and most of the Stratford audience must have been seeing it for the first time. Instead of witnessing the return of a venerable relic on the cultural merry-go-round, they were brought face to face with an unknown young author, and in circumstances as unsmart as those of the play's 1892 Independent Theatre premiere. It helped that Shaw's study of slum landlordism arrived in the wake of the Rachman case, but the work itself was quite enough to demolish a whole swathe of Shavian preconceptions and reveal an alarmingly human face under the grinning mask.

Before meeting the world-famous author, Harpo Marx asked if he had started off as Bernie Schwartz. If Harpo had seen *Widowers' Houses*, he would have greeted Mr Schwartz by name and handed him an exploding cigar. Mostly written in the mid-eighties, the play pre-dates the invention of GBS, the playwright's most celebrated character; and point by point it repels all the commonplaces of Shavian criticism. For a start, it is an angry comedy by a practical Socialist concerned with specific reformist issues. Shaw at this time still had political ambitions, and announced that he had written the play 'to induce people to vote on the Progressive side at the next County Council election in London'. Beyond that, it is also the work of a man whose Socialism is rooted in a sense of personal grievance. It really is an Unpleasant Play. However the slum profiteers defend themselves from scene to scene, they finally merge into a repulsive image of the class enemy, in which the audience are invited to recognize their own reflection. And however fair-minded the distribution of arguments, the play is fuelled by a rage far stronger than the interplay of ideas. The snarl of the underdog echoes under the dialogue: witness the parvenu snipping at Cokane, the gentleman parasite, the catroon exhibitions of snobbery, the manipulation of events to show the corrupting power of money.

GBS at Hammersmith Terrace, 1891

Shaw famously defined poverty as a disease of the poor. In *Widowers' Houses* it still figures as a crime of the rich, who stir the Fabian virtuoso to the pre-political gut response of the psalmist: 'Woe, for they chant to the sound of harps and anoint themselves, but are not grieved for the afflication of the people.' Shaw is allegedly incapable of portraying human suffering. What about the suffering of Blanche's terrorized maid and the wretched Lickcheese when he loses his job? Sex likewise is supposed to be a Shavian blind spot. That would have been news to spectators recoiling from the sadistically erotic Blanche, a bourgeois cousin of Strindberg's Miss Julie. No one would have predicted from this sulphurous piece that Shaw would conquer as a comic writer, still less that he would be strictured for his unfeeling flippancy. And where, in its terse unsparing length, are there grounds for the view that he had every stylistic gift except brevity?

With artists who live to a great age it is usual that the closer they approach our own time, the further they recede from us. And of no artist is this more true than of Shaw, notwithstanding his sagacious remarks on the atom bomb and his last-minute enrolment in the British Interplanetary Society. Any idea of what Shaw had been was erased by what he had become. The public who had ostracized him as a traitor for his views on the 1914–18 war, now revered him as a national monument, licensed to say anything because they were no longer listening. Those who were still listening observed Shaw, the champion of the underdog, change into the Shaw of *Geneva*, cracking jokes against capitalist Jews in Hitler's Germany. And where other veteran artists at least had the tact to disappear into their work, Shaw, the chirpy nonagenarian, was always around, explaining, correcting, touching up his own legend, and determined to stay in the game. 'Another fiasco like that of *Buoyant Billions* would damage me seriously,' he wrote in 1950, at the unwelcome news that Esmé Percy was planning a full-scale West End production of *Farfetched Fables*. As he said himself, GBS was a wonderful old boy. Everyone said so. It was a good excuse for ignoring what he had been as a man. And perhaps still was, under the carnival mask. 'I am writing,' he told Clare Winsten in 1950, 'a play in which there is an old man who has a house-keeper who is so houseproud that she gradually eliminates everything that is personal in the house until he feels a perfect stranger there.' It is not the subject you would expect from the vainglorious old world-changer, gorged on international attention and ironically aloof from the common human bonds.

I have never been able to see much sense in Shaw's obsession with Shakespeare as his number one professional adversary, but there is at least one negative point of comparison. We know nothing about Shakespeare's life. We know too much about Shaw's. But when it comes to relating their work to its psychic roots – as one can, say, with Dostoevsky or Strindberg – both men are equally mysterious. Comment on Shakespeare is inhibited by his supreme rank among the literary immortals. Comment on Shaw is inhibited by the suspicion that whatever you say about him, he has probably said it much better himself – and then contradicted it. The received idea of Shaw is that he dragged everything into the open; that he knew his own mind and spoke it at the top of his voice so that even the stupidest listeners would get the point. In the words of the burglar in *Too True to be Good*, 'I can explain anything to anybody, and I love doing it.' But all the explanations left the 1965 public unprepared for the experience of his first play, which revealed the forgotten darker side of Shaw and restored our contact with him as a modern writer. Since then, it has been the privilege of a new generation of playgoers to get to know him from the beginning. *Widowers' Houses* was promptly followed by revivals of the other *Plays Unpleasant* and two of the middle-period comedies: the Edinburgh Festival and Birmingham weighed in with

Sketch for the backdrop for Back to Methusalah: *Paul Shelving*

ROBERT LORAINE

MAN & SUPERMAN
BY G. BERNARD SHAW.

two amazing late works, and the Shavian boom was under way, reaching an appropriate climax in 1969 with the National Theatre's full version of the *Methuselah* cycle. The torrent then settled into a steady stream, and by the mid-seventies all the major plays had returned to the London stage with the unaccountable exceptions of *Androcles and the Lion* and the Don Juan in Hell scene from *Man and Superman*. This time round, the author has not been on hand to supervise productions, organize advance publicity, and criticize the critics' heads off: so at least we have had the chance to attend to Shaw without distracting cartwheels from GBS.

Early in his career, Shaw proclaimed himself an old-fashioned playwright, and modern scholarship has seized gratefully on this admission and computed his debts to Scribe, Brieux, romantic comedy, the problem play, extravaganza and other contents of the Victorian property basket. No one, so far as I know, has followed up his equal acknowledgement to opera and to Mozart as his supreme dramatic teachers; though modern directors like Clifford Williams have paid close attention to the musical expression marks with which Shaw decorated his prompt copies. Obviously the example of the past was of immense importance to him, and nobody is in any danger of missing it.

What repeatedly takes you by surprise are the occasions when he anticipates the styles of the future. The weird nursery rhyme ritual between Shotover and his daughters in the first act of *Heartbreak House* leads straight into the world of T.S. Eliot's riddling guardians in *The Cocktail Party*. 'How much did the clock strike, Phyllis?' enquires the Lady in *The Fatal Gazogene*. 'Sixteen, my lady,' replies the menial, and we are off into Ionesco territory, complete with a character eating the ceiling. There are Beckett images, like the Preacher in the howling wilderness in *Too True to be Good*, and the 'silenced' priest Keegan conversing with a grasshopper. Shaw is probably the last influence any of these writers would recognize, and all I am suggesting is that his genius pushed him into areas of feeling generally considered to be outside his range. In particular, his extension of Victorian burlesque yielded an effect indistinguishable from surrealism. Consider Shaw's stage pictures rather than his dialogue: a Magritte-like terrain dotted with bourgeois manikins, unperturbed by the dynamite in the gravel pit, visitors from the sky, bombardment by passing airships, giant microbes, and the sight of the local mayoress going off into a Delphic trance. It is customary to explain away all such effects, down to the lady in *Buoyant Billions* who stills alligators with a saxophone, as a throwback to extravaganza; but you could equally well cite them as early stirrings of the theatre of the absurd.

Turn up the dialogue, of course, and reason resumes control: events and images fall into place as a supporting pretext for the dance of ideas. 'Intellectual passion drives out sensuality,' said Leonardo, putting it better than Shaw ever did; perhaps because, in Shaw, the exercise of the intellect periodically lapses into smart duels of opinion, agile sophistries, and those curious key passages – like Dick Dudgeon's or Lavinia's declarations of faith – where the play's argument reaches its climax only to expire into hot air. (The only such climax that really comes off is Dubedat's dying speech in *The Doctor's Dilemma*, which Shaw lifted from a story by Wagner.) 'That Bernadette Shaw?' giggles the drag queen in Peter Nichols' *Privates on Parade*: 'What a chatterbox!' The manikins keep at it hammer and tongs, never at a loss for something to say, bobbing along with buoyancy, casting no shadow behind them. But under the words something can be heard echoing with the desolate resonance that E.M. Forster heard from the Marabar caves.

The poster for Man and Superman, *Criterion Theatre, 1911*

As a director of actors, Shaw found one outlet for his frustrated musicianship: defining shifts in mood as precise modulations (he claimed D-flat major, a very comfortable scale for the amateur pianist, as the 'Shavian key'), insisting on the paramount importance of contrast in timbre and tempo, and conceiving each role in terms of a singer's range. But in advising others on how to direct his plays, he also said, 'the first rule . . . is that there must never be a moment of silence from the rise of the curtain to its fall.' What a baffling statement for a musician to make! What kind of music can exist without rests? Happily, the directors of the past fifteen years have ignored this rule. We have, after all, been going through the golden age of the theatrical pause. Shavian actors have been given a chance to breathe, and productions like John Schlesinger's *Heartbreak House* (National Theatre, 1975) or Clifford Williams' *Too True To Be Good* (Aldwych, 1975), occupied a zone of ominous suprapersonal comedy not all that remote from Beckett. Let me defend that modish comparison. The grand theme of both Shaw and Beckett is man's insignificance within the universe: and in both, the characters try to hold the cosmic silence at bay with a compulsive flood of words. With Beckett, of course, the words keep breaking down, as the characters glumly recognize themselves as one of the Almighty's little jokes. Shaw's people make no such confession, and keep things going until the curtain falls. But with both writers the underlying emotion is identical: abject terror of the universal void, and the emptiness within themselves.

Shaw had a word for that emotion. He called it cowardice: typically, a confident old-fashioned moral judgment. You can fight stupidity, he said, but you cannot fight cowardice. And observing that all men, himself included, were cowards without a religion, he equipped himself with one and became, as he said, a man with some business in the world. The Shavian trick was to overcome the sense of human futility by surrendering to the powers that render human life futile. In this way, he exchanged his role as a helpless victim for that of spearhead of the universal Will. From his magpie pickings from Carlyle, Schopenhauer, Bunyan, Marx, and Lamarck, he built his own nest of Creative Evolution, in which he could survey the world without despair and go about his work in confidence that it mattered. Hence the sheer volume and energy of his creative output: hence also his unfeeling response to social evils after 1918, his enthusiasm for dictatorships of both Left and Right, his support for extermination programmes of the unfit, his incurable optimism.

Nothing in that list sets him further apart from mid-century experience than the last item. It was the sight of the old world-betterer (the subtitle of his last full-length play) still preaching his crazy home-made gospel in the aftermath of Auschwitz and Hiroshima that condemned Shaw to his immediate posthumous reputation as the last of the Victorian idealists: the very tribe on which, as a young man, he had declared war. Now that we have renewed contact with the young Shaw and retraced his route to the Ayot sanctuary, we can discount that view as the product of an even more blinkered pessimism. If one thing is clear about the roots of Shavian 'metabiology' it is that it sprang from an intimate acquaintance with despair. He had plenty of cause for despair in his youth, and however jocular his early journalism, it is full of black images of defeat – solitary drinkers staring into their glasses, worn-out slaves of the theatrical tread-mill, not to mention the searing descriptions of death and degradation he extracted from the performances of Calvé and Yvette Guilbert. 'The world,' he wrote in *Man and Superman*, 'will not bear thinking of to those who know what it is.' And in that play, the one passage that sticks in everybody's memory is the Devil's speech on the arts of death. As for Shaw's own black Irish background, there is no need to turn up the letters: Larry Doyle says it all in *John Bull's Other Island*:

> Oh, the dreaming! the dreaming! . . . An Irishman's imagination never lets him alone,
> never convinces him, never satisfies him; but it makes him that he can't face reality nor

A 1932 production of Too Good to be True *at the New Theatre with Leonara Corbett as the patient, Ernest Thesiger as Monsieur, Donald Wolfit as the doctor, Ellen Pollach as the nurse and Cedric Hardwicke as the burglar*

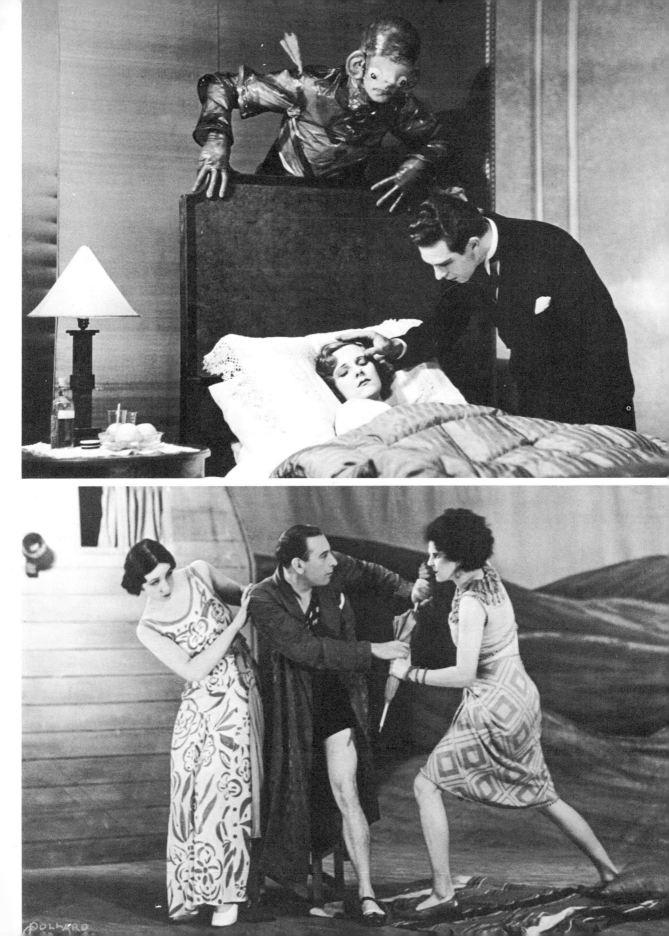

deal with it nor conquer it: he can only sneer at them that do. . . . At last you get that you can bear nothing real at all: you'd rather starve than cook a meal; you'd rather go shabby and dirty than set your mind to take care of your clothes and wash yourself; you nag and squabble at home because your wife isn't an angel, and she despises you because you're not a hero; and you hate the whole lot round you because they're only poor useless devils like yourself.

If Shaw settled for an optimistic creed, it was because he knew the alternative too well. For him, the question was not whether Creative Evolution was objectively 'true', but that life was unendurable without it. Perhaps he made a tactical error in passing off his faith as a science, and leaving it open to demolition by Wells and the scientific establishment: though it is interesting that Arthur Koestler, in a like state of despair, has lately turned back to Lamarckian functional adaptation and revived

Shaw's photograph of Rodin at work on The Thinker

the Shavian hope that giraffes grow long necks to reach the top leaves. But whatever the biological grounds for the theory, there is no doubt that it worked personally for Shaw. Consider his changing physique. In youth, the face of an undernourished curate: in maturity, a head which Rodin sculpted as 'une vrai tête de Christ.' Consider his staying power. 'When we are young,' Chekhov said, 'we all chirp rapturously like sparrows on a heap of muck, but at the age of forty we are already old and start thinking of death.' Back comes Shaw's answer: 'We are all beginners at forty.'

What I wish to dispute is the persisting idea of Shaw as a Victorian survivor. Intellectually he came of age in Victoria's England, but the faith with which he armed himself to face the twentieth century arose neither from Victorian materialist self-satisfaction nor Victorian religious doubt. Partly an antidote to Bunyanesque 'discouragement', it is more akin to the system-building of the eighteenth-century *philosophes*, and the posture of men like Swift and Dr Johnson who clung so tenaciously to reason and the hope of salvation precisely because they went in daily fear of madness and chaos.

It is his determination to find some grounds for hope that sets Shaw apart from the mainstream of twentieth-century European writing, which obsessively annotates the decline of the West. Unwaveringly attached to the issues of his own time, Shaw has therefore been excluded from the ranks of modern authors. To reassert his membership, you have only to quote Orwell's modernist slogan: 'When you are on a sinking ship, your thoughts will be about sinking ships.' There it is: the dominant image of *Heartbreak House*, Shaw's only difference from his fellow castaways being that he still placed some trust in navigation.

No doubt any philosophy student could make mincemeat of Creative Evolution as a logically constructed system. But it would be a waste of time. In philosophy as in playwriting, Shaw did not believe in construction: he believed in growth. Visitors to his temple may find it leaky, but for him it held water as an organic extension of his own experience. Let me drop this apologetic line. Shaw was not some minor poet struggling along with the help of a personal survival kit: he was the greatest world teacher ever to have arisen from these islands, the means by which countless adolescents have woken up and learned to think for themselves, the knight-errant intellectual who used his sword for common humanity; and, like Bunyan's Pilgrim, he drew his strength from his religion.

As a practical creed, Creative Evolution had another advantage. It was not a closed system. And as Shaw came to it by degrees through his knowledge of the world, he escaped the usual penalties of conversion. He had the exhilaration of being used for a mighty purpose without paying the price of intellectual enslavement. 'I am free from the indecision which is called an open mind,' he said; but he went on to concede that, if he met good enough arguments, his mind could be changed – unlike those of his contemporaries who had barricaded themselves behind Marxist or Roman Catholic imperatives. His sense of mission was as strong as theirs, and if you choose to regard his life as a tragedy, it is that he utterly failed in his main purpose. 'For me,' he said, 'the play is not the thing . . . "For art's sake" alone I would not face the toil of writing a single sentence.' He wrote to change the world, but for any direct influence he exerted he might as well never have written at all. As Maurice Valency says of his courageous speech in defence of Roger Casement: 'The speech was much admired and Casement was hanged.' But in this case, it seems that Creative Evolution divined better than Shaw what he was most fit for, and armed him with a creed that allowed the artist in him to survive.

The most revealing comparison is with Tolstoy – another mighty would-be world-changer, creator of a personal religion, vegetarian, and notable anti-Shakespearian. In Tolstoy, the philosopher sacrificed the artist, with lamentable effect on his own work and his judgment of the works of other men. Shaw likewise embraced the role of artist-philosopher and dissociated himself from the company of those who, like Shakespeare and Dickens, 'are concerned with the diversities of the world instead of with its unities'. But in all his quarrels with Shakespeare, down to the final round of fisticuffs in *Shakes versus Shav*, there is no trace of the closed-system bigotry of, say, Tolstoy's essay on *King Lear*. And throughout his life he gave generous acknowledgment to writers like Chekhov, Lawrence, and Joyce from whom the philosopher in him must have violently recoiled. As for his own work, you have only to remember the notorious disparity between the plays and their prefaces to see how completely Shaw the artist escaped the clutch of his philosophic *alter ego*.

To return to the beginning, it was the anarchic disruption of the original plans for *Widowers' Houses* that led Shaw's collaborator, William Archer, to conclude that his Irish protégé had better stick to pamphleteering and leave the stage alone. The familiar story is that Shaw, writing the dialogue for a plot supplied by Archer, ran out of events half way through and went on to devise a third act wildly out of keeping with Archer's cherished prescriptions for well-made plays. The less publicized side of the story is that of their original agreement. As planned, *Widowers' Houses* (based on an Augier comedy) was to have imported French social criticism onto the English stage. Besides his championship of Ibsen, Shaw at that time was a keen advocate of Eugène Brieux, and he declared his own position in terms that apply exactly to agitational plays like Brieux's *Damaged Goods*. 'If people are rotting and starving in all directions, and nobody else has the heart or brains to make a disturbance about it, the great writers must.' He wrote an enthusiastic preface to an English edition of Brieux (claiming him as the greatest French writer since Molière) whose way of making a disturbance may be gauged from the Doctor's final speech in *Damaged Goods* (concerning marital syphilis):

> This poor girl is typical. The whole problem is summed up in her: she is at once the product and the cause. We set the ball rolling, others keep it up, and it runs back to bruise our own shins. I have nothing more to say. But if you give a thought or two to what you have just seen when you are sitting in the Chamber [of Deputies], we shall not have wasted our time.

Programme for Widowers' Houses *at the Royalty Theatre, 1891*

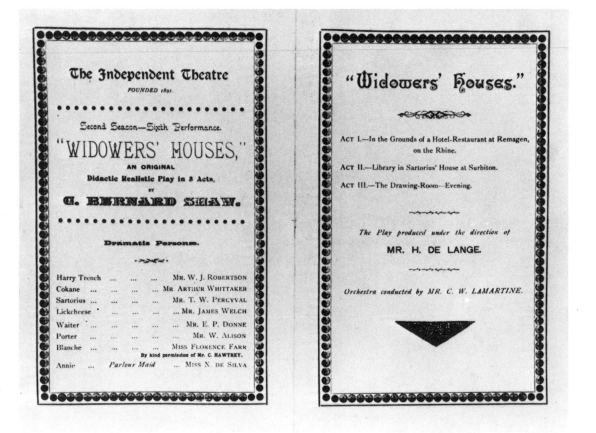

Just the approach you would expect from Shaw, the St Pancras vestryman, urging people to 'vote on the Progressive side at the next County Council election'. Except that no such passage occurs in any work by Shaw. Instead, the public theme intrudes *Widowers' Houses* by stealth: breaking into the light comedy atmosphere like a malignant tumour so as to poison the characters' privileged little world of love affairs and social climbing, and then spreading out to infect the audience as well. The degree of rage and human complexity which Shaw brought to this exercise far exceeds the requirements of any agitational work. He began as he went on, by overshooting the target. He set out to write a 'blue book' play, destined for oblivion as soon as its message had been digested. Such oblivion has befallen writers like Brieux who practised exactly what they preached. But Shaw's *Plays Unpleasant* have long outlived their originating social impulse, and have furnished a model for the puritan playwrights of later generations. David Hare's *Knuckle*, to pick an example from the 1970s, involves spectators in the armaments trade just as Shaw involved them in the slum property market.

I have returned to *Widowers' Houses* partly because it shows how irrepressibly Shaw's imagination broke free even when handcuffed into a Scribean plot dictated by someone else. It is also a peculiarly accessible play for modern English audiences. The theatrical upheaval of the late 1950s was a direct continuation of the pre-1914 new drama crusade, and Shaw would have been as much at home in the Royal Court Theatre of George Devine and John Osborne as he was in the Court of Granville-Barker and Gilbert Murray. *Widowers' Houses*, though it only resurfaced in the mid-sixties, would have fitted perfectly into the opening 1956 'breakthrough' season as the work of an angry outsider, tearing into the smug assumptions of middle-class English playgoers. Never mind; there were other people around at the time to write that kind of play. Where are they now? Spinning round in narrow, self-preoccupied circles, sniping peevishly at a world they receive mainly through newspapers and television, they do not rouse much faith in the artistic potential of angry outsiders who make the transition to middle-class affluence. One index of Shaw's resilience is that he embarked on the greatest phase of his career after making the transition which, to lesser artists, has so often been a sentence of death. His contemporaries were not to know what lay in store. Soon after Shaw capitulated to his Irish millionairess in 1898, he was the subject of a Beerbohm cartoon entitled 'Popular Notion of Bernard Shaw since Marriage'. It represented the erstwhile champion of the oppressed as a fat plutocrat, and Charlotte had to be restrained from buying it 'with the object of concealing or destroying it'. Characteristically, it was Shaw who communicated this domestic detail to the artist; and he celebrated his arrival among the rich with the composition of his most revolutionary work, *Man and Superman*. He is not, in short, to be judged by the diminished expectations of our time.

I am not trying to argue that money was unimportant to Shaw; rather that it was of supreme importance in his artistic development. In private life, of course, he advertised himself as a skinflint, and some of the cases he supported suffered once he was in a position to give them material assistance. Rebuffing an appeal from Israel Gollancz in connection with his cherished National Theatre project, he wrote: 'It is quite impossible for me to take part in asking people privately to give thirty thousand pounds to the S.M.N.T. They would immediately ask me why I did not give it myself.' As a poor man, Shaw enjoyed the ideological advantages of poverty: as an orator, journalist and playwright he could adopt a clear-cut revolutionary position in confidence of having nothing to lose. Marriage to Charlotte, no matter how scrupulously he respected her money, cut the revolutionary ground from under his feet.

But whatever the turmoils of social conscience this may have aroused in Shaw, they were resolved in the composition of *Man and Superman*.

Mendoza: I am a brigand: I live by robbing the rich.
Tanner: I am a gentleman: I live by robbing the poor. Shake hands.

Quite apart from its open references to *Don Giovanni*, this play is the supreme instance of Shaw's dramatic debt to Mozart. Emotionally, one curiosity of *Man and Superman* is that although the Don Juan legend is turned inside out to present the hero as a blameless victim, the piece as a whole retains an obsession with shame, betrayal, false relationships, hypocrisy and moral torment. Tavy and Ramsden are the most obviously stricken, as two ethical impostors repeatedly laid low by the Shavian cudgel. Tanner, though not a target for so blunt an instrument, is in the falsest position of all. The gentleman revolutionist: not even the most sanctimonious Victorian mill-owner could match that for conscience-saving mendacity. Imagine how the Shaw of *Widowers' Houses* would have handled such a crew. But in *Man and Superman*, personal suffering and personal rancour are transposed into a major key where Shaw and Mozart meet in the zone of Olympian comedy. If that sounds like uplift, I make no apology. Uplift is the only available word for the sense of exhilaration these two artists convey. For both of them, creative self-respect begins with the assumption that it is possible to tell the whole truth without resort to moralizing or personal confession. Presenting work to the public means appearing fully dressed to face the world. It means finding a just point of balance between the mess of common humanity and the geometry of artistic design. Mozart's and Shaw's characters alike have air and space around them: they occupy a world where the most wounding things can be said without anybody walking off in a huff, and where every inhabitant, however trapped or vilified by dramatic circumstances, is equally at liberty to make sublime music. There exists also a submerged affinity between them in the melancholy that runs through their work like a dark river under a serene classical landscape. Mozart's way of clouding even the sunniest dance tune with a poisonous harmonic inflection finds its counterpart in the periodic glimpses of Shavian desolation: lines that come booming up from the Marabar caves, like Shotover's 'Give me deeper darkness. Money is not made in the light.'

For Shaw, as for any classical artist, raw human emotion was so much untreated sewage. Even as a reviewer, he found it proper to let his enthusiasms (if not his hates) subside before committing them to print. So far as *Man and Superman* is concerned, no wild speculation is needed to divine its emotional sources. The piece clearly arises from a mortified conscience and the sense of irrevocable compromise. The very form of the play supplies evidence for this. Its intellectual sinew is mostly confined to the dedicatory letter and the appendix, where Shaw lays his cards on the table as an artist and as a revolutionary, and even the *Revolutionist's Handbook*, with its deadly slogan 'Every man over forty is a scoundrel', is hived off as the gospel of John Tanner, 'Member of the Idle Rich Class'. Within the play itself, the character of Tanner does not coincide with that of his stern legendary prototype in the third act, for the obvious reason that Don Juan has cast off the lumber of personal relationships and social responsibilities, whereas poor Tanner is still thrashing about in a net of scheming women, numskull parents, and servants he cannot quite bring himself to do without. He may see himself transcending them all and graduating to the Shavian elysium as a 'master of reality', but what probably lies in store for him is abject surrender: in another twenty years he will be another Roebuck Ramsden.

Man and Superman *at the Criterion Theatre, 1911*

The dramatic trick is the same one that Ibsen played in *Hedda Gabler*. The character

(Right) *Lillah McCarthy*

Lillah McCarthy and Granville Barker (top left), Edmund Gwenn (top right), Lillah McCarthy (below left) and Granville Barker and Edmund Gwenn (below right) in Man and Superman *at the Royal Court Theatre, 1905*

who apparently dominates everyone through superior intelligence and force of personality turns out to be the weakest figure on the stage. The individual intellect is no match for the bovine multitude: it is no good being a superman if you are surrounded by sub-men. Unless, that is, the superman also happens to be an artist. Tanner, luckily for the play, is not an artist: instead, he is in the hands of an artist who converts his defeat into a form of triumph by ironizing it from start to finish.

Shaw's style is often likened to that of a schoolmaster, which is an inexact comparison if it implies sarcasm. Sarcasm represents an unfair abuse of power by the strong over the weak. Shaw's characteristic instrument is irony: the traditional weapon of the weak against the strong. At its simplest, it takes the form of single-scene encounters between an ironist and an impostor; that most ancient of all comic relationships, recurring in the innumerable anti-climaxes where Shaw takes the wind out of somebody's sails. In *Man and Superman* it is co-extensive with the entire play, with Tanner combining the roles of ironist and impostor. From scene to scene he may tie Ramsden and Tavy up in knots; but in the end it is they, the immovable mass of solid middle-class opinion, who call his bluff. They, not he, are the masters of reality. All Tanner can do is break lance after lance on their armour-plated hides. 'Go on talking,' purrs Ann at the end, to a chorus of 'universal laughter' as the cage snaps shut behind him.

A deep sense of political impotence, personal compromise and social isolation underlies the story of Jack Tanner. Shaw's achievement was to pick up the pieces and shape them into a comedy whose sovereign quality needs no recommendation from me (though it is worth noting how soon solid middle-class opinion swung round in its favour. For instance, when Ben Iden Payne left the pre-1914 Manchester Gaiety Theatre to run his own touring company, '*Man and Superman* so far exceeded the other plays in popularity that we decided to have two companies, one performing only that play'.) Shaw subtitled the work 'A Comedy and a Philosophy'; not, significantly, a 'philosophic comedy'. The two elements are separated. The romantic comedy is sandwiched between the dedicatory letter, in which he delivers his artistic creed, and the *Handbook*, which contains some of the blackest pages he ever wrote. To put it mildly, the relationship between these components is oblique: but one can sum it up as a devastating exhibition of the futility of the teaching process written by a man whose life's mission was to teach.

Teaching is the central passion in all Shaw's major plays: whenever they record a victory, it is the victory of Pygmalion – the release of a free, autonomous creature from the petrified forest of unexamined values and social conditioning. Tanner is the unique exception in this company: the teacher who is incapable of learning (even Higgins gets a lesson or two from Eliza). And in this respect, his story has a cruelly exact bearing on the subsequent career of his creator, the prophet-philosopher delivering his message to the world in full knowledge that nobody is listening: 'My gift has possession of me: I must preach and preach and preach no matter how late the hour and how short the day, no matter whether I have nothing to say.'

The speaker is Aubrey in *Too True to be Good*. Again, not an artist. And again, the force of his statement hits the audience because it comes from a character ironized by dramatic context, and not *ex cathedra* from the author. It is this teasing relationship between Shaw and his principal characters that constitutes the central Shavian riddle. He drew his intellectual self-respect and his reason for continuing to write from the conviction that he had something definite to say: but as soon as he moved from editorializing into dialogue, precisely what he is saying becomes a matter for dispute. Tramline intellectual dogmatism gives way to something altogether more elusive.

Shaw allied himself with writers who presented a co-ordinated view of the universe: 'artist-philosophers are the only sort of artists I take quite seriously.' Set that statement alongside his equally revealing claim that Mozart possessed 'the unscrupulous moral versatility of a born dramatist'. When Shaw the dramatist gets into the saddle, it is his moral versatility that holds the show on the road, not his philosophic integrity. With the exception of Ibsen, none of the writers in his list of avatars (Bunyan, Shelley, Schopenhauer, Wagner, Tolstoy, etc.) is primarily a dramatist. Which raises the further question of why such a man, who also proclaimed himself an implacable opponent of democracy, should have chosen to garble his message to mankind by presenting it in the supremely democratic form of the stage play.

The pert answer to that is that Shaw was no philosopher anyway. And it is true that where a Schopenhauer or a Tolstoy drives his argument through to break new moral grounds, with Shaw the action often goes round in a circle, taking a keen look at the latest sexual manners and revolutionary fashions, and winding up more or less where it started: endorsing marriage, patriotism, and even allowing some virtue in the medical profession. Not for nothing did he go on those world cruises with Charlotte. 'I,' he confessed, 'have had no heroic adventures': even Tanner got captured by bandits.

GBS at Reid's, Madeira in 1927, taking dancing lessons from Mr and Mrs Max Rinder – 'The only man who taught me anything'

The answer will not do, because Shaw evidently had no choice in the matter. From his point of view, Creative Evolution had called him to do its work with the best means that lay to hand: which in his case meant the exercise of an incomparable theatrical imagination. The critical luxury of splitting the art apart from the dogma was not one he could allow himself. For him, the medium really was the message. The Life Force supplied him at once with his theme and his source of creative energy; and we may accept the word of so vain a man when he describes his own part in the process of composition as merely that of 'an amanuensis or an organ-blower'. In an often-quoted letter of 1934, Shaw confided to Leonora Ervine that 'my bolt is shot'. This sounds like an open confession of impotence, authorizing posterity to ignore *The Millionairess*, *Geneva*, and the other products of his last years. However, the letter goes on to make a crucial proviso: his bolt is shot, Shaw says, 'as far as any definite target is concerned . . . I shoot into the air more and more extravagantly without any premeditation whatever.' This, of course, is in flat contradiction to everything he had to say on the subject from youth to middle age, when power of expression was entirely dependent on having a definite target. 'Effectiveness of assertion is the Alpha and Omega of style. He who has nothing to assert has no style and can have none.' He prefixes that assertion with a patronizing dismissal of the stylistic parlour games played by writers in their dotage; but when he himself reached old age and had nothing left to assert, he found himself still possessed by his gift. The Life Force did not so easily relax its grip. The play, after all, was the thing.

Shaw first entered the theatre as a blatant careerist. As he acknowledged to Archer, he was at once a critical old hand and an artistic novice, and he set about the task of self-promotion with a journalist's understanding of how reputations are made: getting his foot into the most accessible door and writing for the market. Today, it would be a matter of graduating to the West End and the big subsidized companies via television and the fringe. In Shaw's time, it meant declaring war on commercial drama from the platform of the Independent Theatre, while keeping a sharp eye on the Haymarket and Irving's Lyceum.

The manoeuvre was not unsuccessful. Shaw made his mark with the minority audience (in spite of the ban on *Mrs Warren's Profession*), and went on to wind his tentacles round the carriage trade in the *Plays Pleasant*. Like *Plays Unpleasant*, they were aptly named. In the words of the aperient advertisement which Edward Thomas bestowed on the poems of Ella Wheeler Wilcox, they 'would move an elephant and not harm a child'. They retain a firm place in the popular repertory and the vitality still to take you by surprise: but there is no overlooking the element of sheer ingratiation – in marked contrast to the usual Shavian astringency – with which they strive to please. Pinero never disinfected Ibsen for the squeamish London public with the ruthless hygiene of *Candida*. No part of Shaw's output does less to support his boasted 'flair for human nature'. Situations like the Marchbanks–Candida–Morell triangle, and the Valentine-Gloria relationship in *You Never Can Tell*, come about only by man-handling the characters into pleasant attitudes. And coming from a writer so preoccupied with the marks of consanguinity, the families in these plays seem to be made up of changelings. The blustering vulgarian Burgess is wholly incredible as Candida's father (they never get a scene together), and Mr Crampton hardly less so as the sire of Gloria and the terrible twins. What remains, of course, is the fashionable feminist debate articulated through brazenly traditional stage types and a plot guaranteed as clean as a whistle.

It has been argued that this is part of the huge Shavian joke; and that parodying the behaviour of the Victorian middle-classes and parodying their favourite forms of stage

The audience of You Never Can Tell *as seen from the front*

Shavians at the Savoy

(1) In the Stalls (Half a Guinea)

(2) In the Circle (Seven and Sixpence)

(3) In the Pit (Half a Crown)

(5) One of our future Monuments?

(4) In the Gallery (A Bob)

entertainment was all the same thing to him. But the argument evaporates in performance. Shaw's characters were more self-aware, more active, better able to defend
themselves with their mouths than those to which his public were accustomed; he
also excelled in the specifically Victorian game of mock-heroic burlesque. But the
success of his plots as a conventional success. Whatever their other qualities, *The
Devil's Disciple* is a robust, nuts-and-bolts melodrama, *Mrs Warren's Profession* a tightly
organized problem play complete with *scène à faire*, and so on.

If Shaw was no innovator in the matter of plot, I suspect this was because he was
not interested in it. He was interested in growth areas. Characters could grow. Ideas
could grow. But stories were a dead end. 'The writing of practicable stage plays does
not present an infinite scope to human talent; and the playwrights who magnify its
difficulties are humbugs. . . . It is . . . the outlook on life that changes, not the craft
of the playwright.' In the early plays, particularly in the *Plays Pleasant*, he set up as a
craftsman. He mounted the cart, blew the trumpet and showed the world he could
do it: gradually extending his range from small theatres to grander addresses. The act
paid off, but at a cost. These are not the plays you would expect from a man who saw
the difference between organic development and construction as a difference between
life and death. They are, on the contrary, models of conscientious construction, often
bursting with rebelliously vital material, but always subduing it to the discipline of
an imposed form.

How long Shaw could have kept this up is anybody's guess. It was his artistic
instinct to work within the limits of the possible, and self-violation seemed the
unavoidable price of capturing the public. However, Mother Nature's fist then struck
him down with the worst illness of his life: Charlotte waved her golden wand over the
scene, *The Devil's Disciple* made a fortune in America, and Shaw's bondage to the
well-made play was at an end. He celebrated this release by making a bonfire of the
box set and its wooden inhabitants in *Caesar and Cleopatra*: when the Library of
Alexandria goes up in the second act, the collected works of Scribe, Dumas and Pinero
went up with it. Or, if that metaphor seems a bit ruthless, Shaw took freehold possession of the Victorian theatrical mansion; and instead of living in as a discontented
servant, he came and went as he pleased as its master, leaving the windows open for
his guests.

Coming into sudden wealth is an experience shared by several of Shaw's characters,
both before and after he underwent it himself; one can draw an easy ironic contrast
between the corrupting influence of money on Lickcheese in *Widowers' Houses* and its
liberating effect on Doolittle *père*. But whether the transformation is negative or
positive, it invariably transmits a sense of exile: uprooting Lickcheese and Doolittle
alike from their own class without giving them a home anywhere else. So far as Shaw
is concerned, the sense of exile is endemic from the start. Colin Wilson built his
'Outsider' theory around the case of the uppity Irish nobody who transcended British
society as a substitute for getting into it. However, as a young man Shaw put prodigious energy into seeking out men, movements and ideas with which he might find a
common cause. It was a case of a lone wolf in search of a pack, and it led only into
the transitory alliances of debating societies and flirtatious Fabian weekends. In the
aftermath of his marriage, Shaw progressively abandoned the pursuit of ideological
allies, along with pursuit of the carriage-trade audience, and surrendered uncondi-
tionally to his gift. Perhaps not even he would have equated money with the Life
Force: but it is a matter of simple chronology that after marriage his writing became
increasingly improvisational, and that this method of composition yielded his
greatest work.

The cant opinion on Shaw the playwright used to be that he was a 'bad master': and it is true that no one would study him as a craftsman, as one might study Chekhov or even Pinero. Plot aside, there are other technical blind spots, including his defective sense of theatrical time (for instance, the instantaneous deluge of eggs in the first scene of *Saint Joan*) and his unsuccessful attempts to twist mythological patterns to his own advantage (such as the unsatisfactory ending of *Pygmalion*, where Cinderella is done out of her Prince).

The side of Shaw I always dread is the gentleman pugilist. Pakenham Beatty, Shaw's chief sparring partner during his brief career in the ring, used to send him letters addressed to 'Gully Belcher Shaw Esq.' and Gully lived on to swagger through his plays as the 'drunken, stagey, brassbowelled barnstormers' who convey so insistent an impression of false hair on the chest. I hold Gully likewise responsible for thinking up names like Holy Joe and Foul-mouthed Frank, and for devising those strings of gutless oaths and insults ('blithering baboon', 'despicable pantaloon', etc.) which disfigure Shavian diction like a pub chorus breaking up the Ninth Symphony. Gully accompanies the fastidious, physically unadventurous Shaw like a paid heavy, advertising his patron's robust masculinity and common touch with low-life caricatures like Drinkwater and Snobby Brice, where we observe Shaw labouring over the elements of Cockney with the same academic zeal he put into his juvenile harmony exercises from Logier's *Thoroughbass*. There are no phonetic pedantries when Shaw, most musically, returns to the dialect of his homeland in *John Bull's Other Island* and *O'Flaherty V.C.*

It is, therefore, a moment of great relief to me when Shaw finally ditches Gully and comes clean in *Pygmalion*. The Shavian red herring, linking Higgins with the philologist Henry Sweet, has fooled nobody (least of all those acquainted with the laborious Sweet) into missing the uncommonly direct and critical self-portraiture of the role, which suggests one explanation of why Shaw, normally courteous to his actors, treated Beerbohm Tree with abominable rudeness during rehearsals for the 1914 production. Higgins, when he first appears, is not even introduced by name: he is that universally mistrusted outsider, the 'Note Taker'; and although he can place any accent from Selsey to Hoxton and Lisson Grove, the scholarly slummer has no idea of what is going on inside his subjects' heads. That, indeed, is the mainspring of the comedy's development. Eliza is a double example of the improvisation process. For, just as Shaw claimed to have no foreknowledge of how his characters would work out, so Higgins is farcically unprepared for his protégée's transformation. It is a scene of Nietzschean irony: the reward of the successful teacher is to be brutally rejected by the pupil. The Shavian twist is that this means solitude for both of them. The price of becoming a free, independent creature, of growing into a 'tower of strength' like the new, improved Miss Doolittle, is the renunciation of common human affection. Hence Shaw's recurring difficulty in reconciling his dramas of intellectual awakening with the kind of plot that implies wedding bells. *Pygmalion*, for this reason, combines one of his finest climaxes with one of his most frustrating endings; the frustration being heightened by the fact that Higgins and Eliza wind up as two of a kind and that a line like 'I have my own spark of divine fire', ridiculous when Higgins says it, could also be spoken in deadly earnest by Eliza.

As a self-portrait, Higgins offers the clearest single instance of Shaw's genius for projecting sad personal insights into the domain of supra-personal comedy: and, as such, it forms the strongest counter-argument to those who object to the absence of pain in his work. Something supremely positive has been extracted from a negative experience. There is nothing sad or painful about Higgins, and how much more alive

he thereby becomes to the world at large. The same goes for his bachelor self-sufficiency and for Shavian solitude in general. It is our habit now to look on solitude as a tragic condition of human life. With Shaw it is a source of exhilaration and the foundation of his defiant optimism.

So much was as clear to his public of fifty years ago as it is now; and it neglects the ambiguity of his best work in which, as I have tried to argue, all the brilliantly devastating qualities for which the word 'Shavian' was coined are undercut by a persisting melancholy. On some occasions (as he was the first to acknowledge privately) this prevented him from finishing a work properly: *John Bull*, for instance, and even *Mrs Warren*, trail off into lingeringly unresolved discord. In his time, this would have been set down as yet another item in the endless list of Shavian contradictions to swell the 'fool's cry of paradox'. Nowadays we prefer the word 'ambiguity', and list it as a virtue; which is less foolish if one takes it to mean that plays are wiser than their authors, and that great writers follow the method of the Hopi goddess who taught her people to weave, always incorporating a flaw in the design through which the spirit could escape. Precisely because they are not closed structures saying what Shaw said they were saying, we now find *The Doctor's Dilemma* contributing to the debate on the medical termination of life and *Major Barbara* being cited in explanation of the Baader-Meinhof gang. As he put it, 'Every jest is an earnest in the womb of time.'

The worst thing one can say of *Back to Methuselah*, the apex of Shaw's career as an artist-philosopher, is that it does form a closed circle. For once there is perfect agreement between the play and its preface. It seems that Shaw undertook the work as an evangelical duty, knowing what he had to say in advance and succumbing to no creative distractions along the route. As a result, his most ambitious adventure into the unknown is lacking in mystery. The play has not borne new fruit with the passage of time, and its composition was evidently a barren experience for Shaw himself, who read one draft to Barker and announced that he was thoroughly bored with it: 'It has never seemed quite so tedious before.'

With this work, of course, we reach the threshold of Shaw's old age and his transformation from a fighting artist into a cultural institution. Whether or not you accept that this process began to take effect from the time of his marriage, something certainly happened to change him from a passionate participant in the human comedy to an amused spectator at mankind's follies. What connection is there between the forty-year-old Shaw who wrote, 'You must transact business, wirepull politics, discuss religion, give and receive hate, love and friendship, with all sorts of people, before you can acquire the sense of humanity', and the Shaw of fifty-nine who declared, 'If the human race wishes me to respect it, it must behave very differently'? Into his early middle age, the fiery, red-bearded demolition merchant was insistently likened to Mephistopheles: the very embodiment of Goethe's 'spirit that denies'. Thereafter we meet a different personage, still gifted with the same prodigious mental energy, but now withdrawn into a magic circle seemingly invulnerable to normal human sympathies and afflictions, and uncannily retaining his full intellectual power beyond the normal human span – at what dreadful secret price? If we seek a companion archetype for this lonely latter phase, the only candidate is Faust, who duly crops up in the person of Captain Shotover, who 'sold himself to the devil in Zanzibar'.

Shotover and Keegan, in *John Bull*, are the clearest examples of the desolate void underlying Shaw's brisk, puritan work ethic. Shotover hovers on the brink of comedy: Keegan is not comic at all. They have several features in common. They are both physically restless, becoming very uncomfortable if pinned down for polite

Herbert Tree as Higgins in Pygmalion at Her Majesty's Theatre, 1914

conversation. They are both impotent, Shotover by virtue of his age, Keegan through being 'silenced' by his Church. Like Shotover in Zanzibar, Keegan has struck some mysteriously fateful bargain with a 'black man'. Each, in terms of his own calling, views the world with unrelieved despair. Shotover, the ex-sailor, sees it as a masterless ship heading for the rocks. Keegan, the ex-priest, sees it as a literal hell. To the extent that these two characters occupy the moral centre of the plays in which they appear, they are speaking for Shaw. And although I would not care to press the Faustian analogy any further than that, one is left speculating about whatever transaction it was that set Shaw so curiously apart from the human race. Was there a black man somewhere in his own past?

The likeliest approach to this question is through a subject beloved by anti-Shavians and which I have so far ignored: Shaw's sexual disgust. 'Love has pitched his mansion in the place of excrement' as Yeats puts it in 'Crazy Jane Talks With The Bishop'. Shaw had a rooted objection to this bit of natural economy, and he came down firmly on the bishop's side: better live in a heavenly mansion than a foul sty. Sexual stirrings, he said, always prompted him 'as a gentleman to apologize for my disgraceful behaviour'. At the same time, perhaps egged on by Gully, he was quite keen to broadcast his prowess as a he-man and itemize his bachelor affairs. Not counting the ludicrous post-marital entanglement with Mrs Patrick Campbell, he was into his forties before he concluded his virgin pact with Charlotte: roughly the same age as Andy Warhol when he announced his retirement from the game.

If we look to the plays for help in resolving this contradiction, we find any amount of oblique eroticism, but no reciprocal relationships. There are characters who invade marriages as travelling companions, *à la* Judge Brack. There are the 'Virgin Mother', charmers who seduce their menfolk into the paths of virtue; and professional enchantresses like Orinthia and Mrs George who zoom off into the higher syntax at the threat of physical contact. Lovers are unmasked as teacher and pupil, parent and child. Sex is carefully displaced into a learning aid. But it is not altogether under Shaw's control, and is apt to crop up in the oddest places, especially when there is no danger of consummation: as in the third part of *Methuselah* where the President gets a television flash of the Minister of Health in her knickers. Throughout the plays of Shaw, somebody is hammering on the bedroom door, and nobody gets through it. The subject was evidently one of lasting fear and fascination for him, and from his one direct portrait of lust in action in *Widowers' Houses* it appears that his interest focused on aggressively dominant women whom he proceeded to unsex or disarm in his plays.

Relying on the testimony of acquaintances like St John Ervine, who spoke of Shaw's 'mortal terror' of women in his later years, one can draw a reductive equation between life and art and interpret the regiment of overwhelming stage females as a menagerie of caged beasts, performing tricks for a master who would dread to meet them in the wild. For people unsympathetic to Shaw, that is the end of the matter. But I would suggest that more is involved than the banalities of the bedroom, and the real issue is that of Shaw's sexual identity. Eric Bentley, Shaw's most penetrating critic, notes a recurring sexual division in the plays. Shaw 'tended to identify both himself and free vitality with the Eternal Feminine and to identify the enemy with the society-ridden male.' The society in question is British society, for which Shaw had great respect as a blundering, thick-witted force which nevertheless got something done in the world; unlike the sensitive, intelligent futility of his native land. He dramatizes the national relationship with classical finality in *John Bull*, and what emerges is the picture of an unhappy marriage between the brutally efficient British husband and the long-suffering Irish mate.

Mrs Patrick Campbell

The young Shaw, tongue-tied in company, given to blushing embarrassment, was very much an Irish virgin, and the great personal drama of his early life was to renounce the victim's role and join the winning side, clipping on a big red beard and proving himself twice as tough as any British adversary. Feminism was one of his first causes and, fashion aside, you can see why. It applied to his own case. Like Annie Besant and Beatrice Webb, he knew that his only hope of getting into the exclusive gentlemen's club was to smash the door in and beat the resident drones at their own game. Shaw openly assumed the role of an adoptive Englishman. It casts some curious light on the Shavian enigma – the psychological blind spots, the sense of solitude behind the mask, the incessant performance element, as well as his sexual evasiveness – if you also consider him as an adoptive male. If we seek an archetype for this heroic masquerade, it is there in the person of Saint Joan.

WOMEN AND THE BODY POLITIC

'I say, Archer, my God, what women!' R. L. Stevenson exclaimed to William Archer after reading Shaw's 'shilling shocker' *Cashel Byron's Profession*. From Mrs Warren, Major Barbara and St Joan, to Lina Szczepanowska the Polish acrobat-pilot of *Misalliance*, Lysistrata the Powermistress-General from *The Apple Cart* and the affluent domineering Epifania Fitzfassenden of *The Millionairess*, the formidable phalanx of new women – unwomenly women – boss women – that was to advance from Shaw's plays wonderfully justifies Stevenson's exclamation.

'I am a first class ladies tailor,' Shaw admitted to Mrs Patrick Campbell. But some women saw his creations as an embarrassing army of dummies. For them, the best of Shaw in this respect was his insistence on the virtue of independence. Vivie Warren in *Mrs Warren's Profession* achieves this, as Shaw himself did, by substituting work for people; Lesbia Grantham in *Getting Married* defines her independence by reason of her freedom from the necessity of marriage ('If I am to be a mother, I really cannot have a man bothering me to be a wife at the same time'); Eliza Doolittle establishes her independence through education in *Pygmalion*. But Cleopatra, at the end of *Caesar and Cleopatra*, is still immature. By preferring the romantic prospect of Anthony to the distant example of Shaw's superman Caesar, she shows that she has not yet grown from a child into a woman – and maybe never will. In which case, she is better left to Shakespeare.

But there is another breed of women, of whom Candida and Ann Whitefield are fair examples, that may appear positively anti-feminist. The box-office success of *Candida* depended on a sentimental misunderstanding of the play that had been invited by Shaw's failure to make his purpose clear. He was to claim that it won the hearts of women by turning Ibsen's *A Doll's House* upside down and revealing the doll in the house to be the man. To the feminist mind, the danger of this was that it provided a sympathetic case for doing nothing and gave intellectual respectability to Mrs Humphry Ward, the most influential of those women opposing suffrage. For if, despite appearances, women organized most matters as they wanted, why weaken their power with emancipation? Shaw's failure lay in glossing over the odiousness of Candida and concealing the revulsion from domestic ideals that is the true 'secret in the poet's heart' and the awareness of which provides his moment of growing up. Shaw described *Candida* as a 'mystery play', and it remained mysterious to the thousands of Candidamaniacs happily filling the theatres. The theme of the play was set down some thirty years later when Shaw was making notes for *The Intelligent Woman's Guide to Socialism and Capitalism*:

George Bernard Shaw

A slave state is always ruled by those who can get round the masters. The slavery of women means the tyranny of women. No fascinating woman ever wants to emancipate her sex; her object is to gather power into the hands of Man because she knows she can govern him.

A cunning and attractive woman disguises her strength as womanly timidity, her unscrupulousness as womanly innocence, her impunities as womanly defencelessness: simple men are duped by them.

Ann Whitefield in *Man and Superman* is another cunning and attractive woman driven by the creaking institutions of an out-of-date society to behave like 'a cad': 'A woman seeking a husband is the most unscrupulous of all the beasts of prey.' But it was not this unscrupulousness, nor the inversion of Tennyson's 'Man is the hunter; woman is his game' that infuriated some women: it was Shaw's apparent assumption that the social purpose of women was the breeding of children.

Man and Superman was Shaw's first attempt, in reaction from Darwin's *Origin of Species*, to dramatize his creed of Creative Evolution. In the philosophical system he put together, women are not treated as objects of men's desire, but as imperfect contrivances employed by the Life Force in its trial-and-error experiments for improving the future. This had resulted in the Duel of Sex, an inevitable phase in mankind's development that Shaw hoped would soon end 'in frank confession and good-humoured laughter'. As a man-huntress and slave of Nature, Ann Whitefield was Everywoman: but she was not all women. Elsewhere he insisted that 'motherhood is not every woman's vocation'. Woman had two classes of champion to contend with: those who wished to see immediate and obligatory freedom fastened on all of them; and those who denied them every freedom they didn't already have and resented what they did have. From *Mrs Warren's Profession* onwards, Shaw campaigned in the theatre for the economic independence of women which would give them individual choice as to the direction they wished to go. They would do best for society, he believed, what they did best for themselves. In attempting to unite individual talent with collectivist principles, he demonstrated the unwearying inclusiveness of his philosophy.

It was difficult to avoid the amiability of his impersonal embrace. Everything he seemed to say, was what it was – and another thing. Women were the same as men: but different. But of the two, he calculated, women were fractionally less idiotic than men. 'The only decent government is government by a body of men and women,' he said in 1906; 'but if only one sex must govern, then I should say, let it be women – put the men out! Such an enormous amount of work done is of the nature of national housekeeping, that obviously women should have a hand in it.' Shaw favoured women over men in much the same spirit as he advertised Roman Catholics being a trifle superior to Protestants. Both preferences were the product of a Protestant gentleman who delighted in perverse exhibitions of fairness.

Certain consequences followed from the fact only women became pregnant. Had Shaw had the making of the world in the first place, and not merely the re-making of it, things might have been ordered more sensibly. However the rules had been laid down and the worst thing you could do was to complain of them. Every grievance was an asset in the womb of time. The advantage to women came in the form of greater natural wisdom about sex. They could hardly help themselves. Shaw maintained that the instinct of women acted as a sophisticated compass in steering our course for the future. His disenchantment with the human experiment expanded during and after the First World War. In *Heartbreak House* – 'my *Lear*' he called it – he shows us what he supposed to be a 'Bloomsburgian' culture where the feminine instinct has been

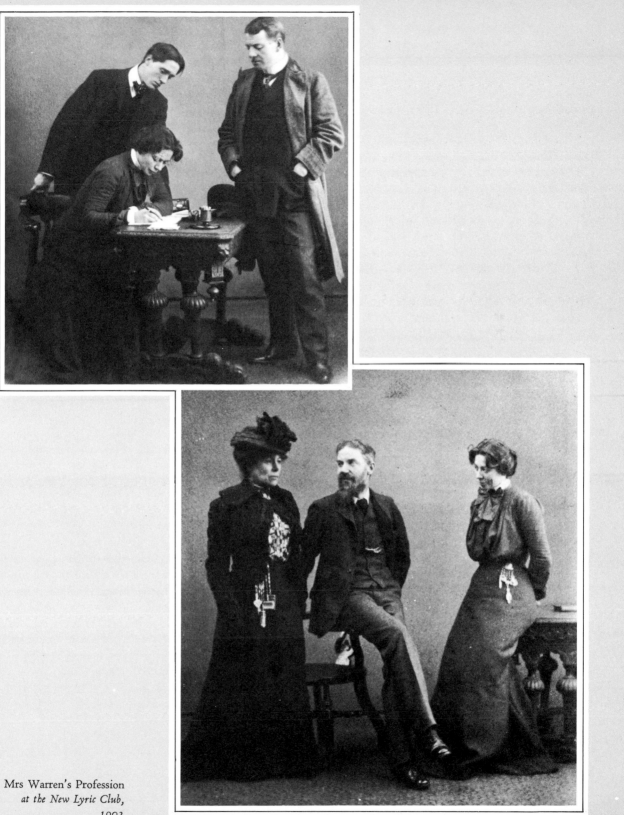

Mrs Warren's Profession
at the New Lyric Club,
1902

*Frank Harris: a photograph
sent to Hesketh Pearson in
1927*

trivialized in such a way that it no longer gives us our true bearings, and we drift towards the rocks. We had defaulted in our contract with the Life Force and would probably be superseded by another partner.

Shaw's pessimism, which is full of vitality, lies concealed beneath the waves of brilliant Shavianism that ebb and flow with his alternating despair and expectation. Life for Shaw meant continually renewed hope; and hope was a matter of willpower. But increasingly as he grew older hope became more distant and fantastical. *St Joan* tells us that this world is not ready yet to receive its saints. So the Fabian patience must be extended beyond all human experience. Shaw's blueprint for Utopia is *Back to Methuselah*, and it was this Metabiological Pentateuch that increased for some of his audience their earlier uneasiness at his attitude to women.

The standard argument against the women in Shaw's plays – that they *weren't* women – had been put, most appropriately, by Frank Harris. These creatures, Harris explained, 'are distinctly unpleasant, practically unsexed women. Their bodies are as dry as their minds, and even when they run after their men . . . the pursuit has about as much sex appeal as a timetable.' Harris suspected that such women had been born of a union between Ibsen and Shaw in their well-publicized elopement from Victorian sentiment. Shaw, who had the re-writing of Harris's biography after Harris died, passed this passage for publication or perhaps mischievously drafted it in the Harris style himself. He was fond of placing on the pages of other writers the theory that he had dreamed up his women characters in reaction to the romantic logic of the stage. In the ghostwritten introduction he provided for a lecture in 1911 by H. M. Walbrook on 'The Women in Bernard Shaw's Plays', Shaw allows it to be discovered that

> there are no women in Bernard Shaw's plays. Dont think that I mean that they are untrue to life. I mean exactly the contrary. For I will tell you another secret. There are no women in the real world. Believe me, ladies and gentlemen, woman, of whom we hear so much, is a stage invention, and . . . a very tiresome one. There is no such thing as a woman; and Bernard Shaw's greatness consists in his having discovered that fact, whilst all the others were turning out heroines that were getting womanlier and womanlier and womanlier until they had lost all semblance of humanity, and bored everybody to distraction . . . the reason the women in his plays were so uncommonly good is that he always assumes that a woman is just like a man.

In the interests of political equality, Shaw's insistence that 'a man is a woman without petticoats' was refreshing; as a single shot against the vulgar idealization of women, his assumption that 'a woman is a person exactly like myself' was at least as telling as he intended. Throughout his plays he emphasizes what men and women share. 'I am a woman,' says the man in *Village Wooing* to the girl; 'and you are a man, with a slight difference that doesn't matter except on special occasions.' Or, to put it another way, GBS was as much a woman as Lady Astor was a man. His world was full of beings who, if not actually androgynous, have only the *minds* of women and who eventually find their natural home in *Back to Methuselah*. The Ancients of that world are cerebral arch-sensualists in whom, during the course of evolution, the ecstasy of intellect has replaced sexual passion. For Shaw, the most fastidious of men, one advantage of this would be that the reproductive function was fulfilled in a less unpresentable manner. While denying that he was a misogynist, he could not but regret that Nature 'in a fit of economy, has combined a merely excretory function with a creatively ejaculatory one in the same bodily part . . .' The syringing of women by men was an indignity that had 'compensations which, *when experienced*, overwhelm all the objections to it,' he told St John Ervine. '. . . I am myself only too susceptible to them; Yet I always feel obliged, as a gentleman to apologise for my disgraceful behaviour; and I would be shot rather than be guilty of it in public.' Shaw's revulsion to the idea of sexual intercourse affected the tone of his writing. It was this synthetic tone against which some women revolted even when they were attracted to the moral elegance of his argument.

Shaw's dialectical genius is at its most powerful in some of his non-dramatic works. His *Intelligent Woman's Guide* might be said to have been written to mitigate the harm done to the country and to women by forcing on them the single solution of the Vote. The origin of this book was a request from his sister-in-law for 'a few of your ideas of Socialism' for 'the Study Circle to which I belong'. The two hundred thousand words that were let loose make up Shaw's political testament. The book shows an understanding of the practice of patriarchy far ahead of its time. Shaw ignores the 'femaleness' of women, but treats them as the outsiders and have-nots of a male culture, and analyses in a most practical way the limits imposed on them by that culture. He does not propose socialism as a cure-all, but attempts to trace specific 'evils' to inequality of income. The tone is neither militant nor patronizing: it is Shaw at his most natural.

This first full-dress political treatise to be addressed specifically to women was the climax to a volume of work enabling Shaw to claim that he had challenged John Stuart Mill's supremacy as a woman's author. It had started with Ibsen. Ibsen had changed the mind of Europe and in *The Quintessence of Ibsenism* Shaw played variations on a neo-Ibsenite philosophy of which he was the solitary exponent. The result was in part a sophisticated feminist document which was proclaimed (by the author) to have broken up homes and made suffragettes of the most unlikely readers. The early chapters, culminating in 'The Womanly Woman', are a beautifully planned demolition of the nineteenth-century woman-on-a-pedestal.

> Now of all the idealist abominations that make society pestiferous, I doubt if there be any so mean as that of forcing self-sacrifice on a woman under pretence that she likes it; and, if she ventures to contradict the pretence, declaring her no true woman . . .
>
> . . . The domestic career is no more natural to all women than the military career is natural to all men; and although in a population emergency it might become necessary for every ablebodied woman to risk her life in childbed just as it might become necessary in a military emergency for every man to risk his life in the battlefield, yet even then it would by no means follow that the child-bearing would endow the mother with domestic aptitudes and capacities as it would endow her with milk. It is of course quite true that the majority of women are kind to children and prefer their own to other people's. But exactly the same thing is true of the majority of men, who nevertheless do not consider that their proper sphere is the nursery . . . If we have come to think that the nursery and the kitchen are the natural sphere of a woman, we have done so exactly as English children come to think that a cage is the natural sphere of a parrot: because they have never seen one anywhere else . . .
>
> The sum of the matter is that unless Woman repudiates her womanliness, her duty to her husband, to her children, to society, to the law, and to everyone but herself, she cannot emancipate herself.

The ingenious exercise of protecting women against their protectors appealed to Shaw. If you accepted the reactionary idealism that separated women from men by insisting on the selfless purity of women, then, he argued, were you not guaranteeing the impurity of all business and politics from which, with such ruthless sentimentality, you were excluding them? He believed that society changed only when women wanted it to – though the reconnaissance work towards such change was often made by men. Men tended to be idealists; women were more practical: a combination of idealism and practicality made for reality. To substitute this reality for the artificial segregation of society was the aim of Shaw's political work.

'On the woman's suffrage question, I have never had any particular doubts,' Shaw once remarked. There were Conservative, Labour and Liberal parties in Britain: but, unfortunately for women, the country had no Shaw party. 'If it had,' he declared in 1907, 'that party would be uncompromisingly on the side of giving suffrage to women.'

He did his best to transform the Fabian Society into a Shaw party. Despite some oscillations, his political record, though not easy to appreciate and often assailed for its waywardness, was so infuriatingly consistent that all his literary skill was needed to confuse it. Fabian Tract No 2, a manifesto drafted by Shaw in 1884, lists as one of the opinions that Fabians desired to spread (and the consequences of which they wanted to discuss) 'that Men no longer need special political privileges to protect them against women: and that the sexes should henceforth enjoy equal political rights.'

But in Victorian and Edwardian politics women were dynamite – especially for a Society that included such serious-minded womanizers as Hubert Bland and H. G. Wells. Shaw's first priority was keeping the Fabians united. In this he was not greatly dissimilar to the party politicians he scorned. Preventing people who were substantially in agreement on most subjects from violent assaults on one another required an enormous expenditure of Shavian paradoxes. But Shaw believed that the call of respectability was a far more powerful force for change in Britain than any appeal to revolution, and that the anarchy of 'free love' could set British Socialism back a hundred years. In such matters Shaw's conversion to Marxism had been no conversion at all: he merely sought to convert British Marxists into international bourgeois Shavians.

So, for the sake of the larger cause, political emancipation slipped down the Fabian scale of priorities and it was not until 1907, when the anarchist Charlotte Wilson rejoined the Society, that the Fabians were converted ('at pistol point', Margaret Cole has written) to 'the establishment of equal citizenship between men and women'. In his 'Draft of Propositions on which to found a revised Basis', Shaw enunciated his political beliefs:

> The Fabian Society seeks to establish equality as the universal relation between citizens without distinction of sex, color, occupation, age, talent, character, heredity or what not. . . . The Fabian Society not only aims at complete political equality as between the sexes, but at their economic independence. It advocates the explicit recognition by legally secured rights or payments of the value of the domestic work of women to their immediate domestic partners and to the State as housekeepers, child bearers, nurses and matrons.

There were few more ridiculous figures, Shaw maintained, than the male suffraget. Though his opinions appear to have been as radical as those of most Edwardian feminists, he did not advertise his political work on their behalf with his usual Shavian panache. One of the reasons for this was his belief that women could achieve their ends at least as effectively without the magnanimous interference of men, and that the experience of conducting their campaign themselves, with all its frustrations and indignities, would serve as an intensive course in political education.

Though he had been an early suffragist, advocating when in 1889 he was invited to consider standing as a Liberal candidate 'suffrage for women in exactly the same terms as men', he was sometimes assailed in later years by ardent feminists who accused him of having contributed nothing. 'Do you suppose that the walls of Jericho, which stand against Mrs Pankhurst's devotion and suffering will fall at the wave of my pen or a   *Mrs Emily Pankhurst*

clever platform speech?' he asked Maud Arncliffe Sennett. 'Such credulity makes me despair of the movement.' It was even possible in 1914 for the composer Dame Ethel Smyth to inquire why he did not interest himself in the suffrage question. 'I can only put a similar question to you,' he replied.

Why is it that you have never thought of devoting yourself to musical composition? It is a light employment though the actual pen and ink work of scoring is tedious. You will find the transposing instruments rather puzzling at first; . . . if you suggest anything that is worth doing that I can do and that I have not already done five or six times over, by all means let me know what it is. How little effect I am likely to produce is shewn by the fact that even you, who are specially interested in the question, do not even know whether I am in favor of the vote or not.

Shaw believed himself to be 'as sound a Feminist as Mary Wollstonecraft'. At heart a suffragist he was on friendly terms with Mrs Fawcett, but also remained a good ally to Mrs Pankhurst until their opposing attitudes to the war drove them apart. After seeing *Man and Superman*, Mrs Pankhurst had declared that Ann Whitefield 'strengthened her purpose and fortified her courage'. It was her courage that

particularly impressed Shaw. In a letter to *The Times* (19 June 1913) he protested strongly against her treatment under the vindictive Cat and Mouse Act and combined this protest with an attack on what he described as the Prime Minister's rabbit theory:

> In the debate on the Dickinson Bill Mr Asquith for the first time opposed the franchise for women explicitly on the ground that woman is not the female of the human species, but a distinct and inferior species, naturally disqualified from voting as a rabbit is disqualified from voting. This is a very common opinion. . . . Many men would vote for anything rather than be suspected of the rabbit theory. It makes it difficult to vote for the Liberal Party and then look the women of one's household in the face.

Shaw's articles and letters were often taken from *The Times* and *New Statesman* and reported in *Votes for Women*, and other feminist papers such as *Suffragette*. He was a brilliant propagandist and especially good at embarrassing the government. On 12 November 1915, for example, *Votes for Women* carried his suggestion of how the country could pay its debt to Edith Cavell.

The size of the demonstration for women's rights in Hyde Park, 21 June 1908, and two feminist newspapers, show the growing strength of the movement

We cannot vapour about chivalry, because if she had come back alive to demand the political rights granted to the meanest of men, and had broken a shop-window to compel attention to her claim, she would have been mobbed, insulted, and subjected to gross physical violence, with the full approval of many of the writers who are now canonising her. What we can do is very simple. We can enfranchise her sex in recognition of her proof of its valour. . . . If this proposal is received in dead silence, I shall know that Edith Cavell's sacrifice has been rejected by her country.

Shaw came out particularly strongly against imprisonment and forcible feeding. In one of his letters to *The Times* (31 October 1906) he framed his opposition to the imprisonment of Mrs Cobden-Sanderson as a civilized Shavian petition to the Home Secretary:

Two women – two petticoated, long-stockinged, corseted females have hurled themselves on the British Houses of Parliament. Desperate measures are necessary . . .

. . . To the immortal glory of our Metropolitan Police they did not blench. They carried the lady out. . . . They held on to her like grim death until they had her safe under bolt and bar, until they had stripped her to see that she had no weapons concealed, until a temperate diet of bread and cocoa should have abated her perilous forces . . .

. . . As a taxpayer, I object to having to pay for her bread and cocoa when her husband is not only ready, but apparently even anxious to provide a more generous diet at home. After all, if Mr Cobden-Sanderson is not afraid, surely the rest of us may pluck up a little. . . . If Mrs Cobden-Sanderson must remain a prisoner whilst the Home Secretary is too paralysed with terror to make that stroke of the pen for which every sensible person in the three kingdoms is looking to him, why on earth cannot she be imprisoned in her own house? We should still look ridiculous, but at least the lady would not be a martyr. I suppose nobody in the world really wishes to see one of the nicest women in England suffering from the coarsest indignity and the most injurious form of ill-treatment that the law could inflict on a pickpocket. It gives us an air of having lost our tempers and made fools of ourselves, and of being incapable of acting generously. . . .

Will not the Home Secretary rescue us from a ridiculous, an intolerable, and incidentally a revoltingly spiteful and unmanly situation?

At a meeting in the Kingsway Hall in March 1913, Shaw set out his objections to forcible feeding. Taking special care not to patronize women, he told his audience that he was not a Suffraget speaker. 'I want to point out that our protest against forcible feeding is not only a protest against the forcible feeding of women . . . women were exceedingly well able to take care of themselves . . . Therefore don't understand me as appealing for special consideration for women.' He objected to this 'torture' on legal as well as moral grounds.

I contend that this forcible feeding is illegal. I contend that if you are tried in a public court and sentenced to imprisonment you are sentenced to imprisonment, and not to torture, except in so far as imprisonment may be torture. . . . I contend that if the Government wants to break people's teeth with chisels, and force food into the lungs and run the risk of killing them, to inflict what is unquestionably torture on them, their business is to bring in a bill legalising these operations. There is no reason why they should hold back. They have no shame in doing it without the law. Why should they be ashamed of doing it with the law?

Shaw ended his speech by bringing to the government's notice what he believed was the conscience of the country.

These denials of fundamental rights are really a violation of the soul and are an attack on that sacred part of life which is common to all of us, the thing of which you speak when you talk of the Life Everlasting. I say this not in a mystical sense, but the most obvious common-

A poster showing exactly what forcible feeding meant

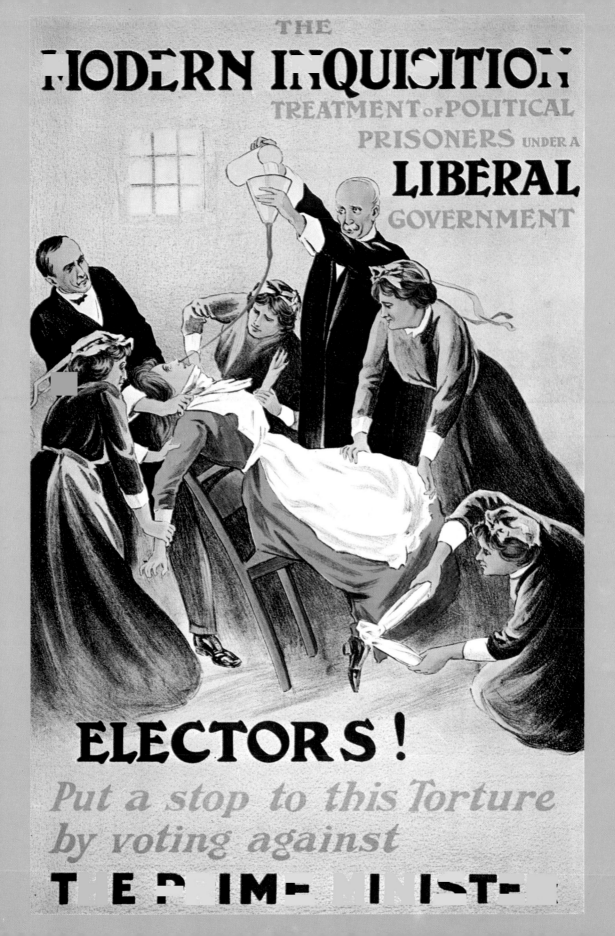

sense, that the denial of any fundamental rights to the person of woman is practically the denial of the Life Everlasting.

Of his many speeches and writings on this subject, the most gloriously Shavian was his response to Herbert Gladstone who had volunteered that forcible feeding was not painful. Shaw took up the challenge and, in *The Times* on 23 November 1909, invited him to dinner.

> It may be that Mr Gladstone is right on this point. I will therefore undertake to procure the co-operation of the Fabian Society in providing for Mr Gladstone a banquet which Sardanapalus would have regarded as an exceptional treat. The rarest wines and delicacies shall be provided absolutely regardless of expense. The only condition we shall make is that Mr Herbert Gladstone shall partake through the nose; and that a cinomatograph machine be at work all the time registering for the public satisfaction the waterings of his mouth, the smackings of his lips, and other unmistakable symptoms of luxurious delight with which he will finally convince us all of the truth of his repeated assurances to us that the forcibly fed Suffragette is enjoying an indulgence rather than suffering martyrdom.

In the eyes of both suffragists and suffragettes, Shaw was unreliable on the one end about which they all seemed to agree: votes for women. Though Mrs Fawcett in June 1910 quoted a telling extract from *Press Cuttings*, most feminists felt that this, his single dramatic treatment of the suffrage movement which he subtitled 'A Topical Sketch Compiled From the Editorial and Correspondence Columns of the Daily Papers During the Women's War of 1909', was well placed in a volume entitled *Translations and Tomfooleries*. It was his flippancy and waywardness that most campaigners dreaded. He paid women the compliment of assuming that they had a sense of humour, and that they could value laughter as a political weapon. In one interview with Maud Churton Braby in 1906, he had claimed that suffrage was nothing to him and that he had no opinion of it since, being a man, he'd already got it. It was the style of such non-interference that could damage the Cause. But then, on being pressed by his interviewer, the well-behaved Fabian exploded: 'Of course, if I were a woman, I'd simply refuse to speak to any man or do anything for men until I'd got the vote. I'd make my husband's life a burden, and everybody miserable generally. Women should have a revolution – they should shoot, kill, maim, destroy – until they are given the vote.'

In fact Shaw cared very little for giving women the vote except as a means of getting them onto public bodies. Unless that happened, the enfranchisement of women would not change society: we would merely be served up with more of the same until 'no sane person will cross the street to vote, though everybody will run down the street to avoid being elected'. At the end of the most disgraceful debate he had ever heard, which took place in the House of Lords, women who had sat on the London vestries were disqualified from sitting on the Borough Councils – which were the vestries under a new name. 'The argument which prevailed,' Shaw wrote, 'was that the Borough Council would contain an alderman and a woman could not possibly be an alder*man*. This joke pleased the House immensely. It stimulated the peers to an exceptional display of facetiousness . . . and women vanished from the London municipalities for some years.' Shaw made an effort to remedy this mischief by writing to *The Times*, 'but *The Times* blushed and threw my letter into the waste paper basket . . .'

There was, in Shaw's view, no other way of making men behave properly and avoiding the schoolboy bad manners of the House of Lords than by appointing women to all public bodies. As an example of the indecency flourishing in exclusively masculine institutions Shaw instanced the Health Committee of which he was a member and which burst into a bray of laughter over a case that depended on a woman being pregnant. If there were no other arguments for giving women the vote, Shaw concluded, he would favour it on the grounds that it would be a step towards making them members of such committees. His support of Israel Zangwill's move to admit women to the Dramatists Club, and his strong criticism of the lack of women on the managing committee of the Academy of Dramatic Art (where female students outnumbered the males) were examples of those actions he pursued on matters where he was personally involved, but which never reached the newspapers and remained unknown to most feminists.

But give him publicity and no one could be certain he would not injure the heroic tone of the movement. Revolutionaries are seldom cursed with humour. He exasperated a few women and offended more men when, in the course of his duties as a St Pancras Vestryman, he agitated for free public lavatories for women and went on to produce for *The Englishwoman* (March 1909) 'The Unmentionable Case for Women's Suffrage'. To some political sensibilities this was grossly unappealing and the story of this battle does not appear even as a footnote in histories of the women's movement. Shaw went so far as to arrange for a dummy lavatory to be placed in Camden Town where it was passionately assailed as an obstruction to traffic, the tradesmen of the district careering into it in such quantities as to make it clear that these were no accidents but the charges of anti-feminist cavalry. The battered structure, shudderingly identified in council as 'this abomination', became a monument to victory when the municipal franchise was extended to women. A woman's free public lavatory was then opened in Leicester Square, and Shaw vainly tried to persuade a lady to enter it. But no lady of his generation might be seen insinuating herself into such a place, and no gentleman could be conscious that such a need existed. To ascribe to the unfashionable theory that women digested their food with the usual consequences, as men did, was a blasphemy that no respectable person would tolerate.

After the Pankhursts had swept Feminism out of the Liberal Parliamentary rut and made Votes for Women into a slogan for saboteurs, Shaw occasionally found himself in hot water. As a collectivist, he did not centre his arguments on the rights of individuals, but treated women as valuable units of governments that had not yet been fitted into the political machinery. But some leaders of the Women's Rights Movement feared that his clever analogies, qualifications, jokes and the philosophy of his politics would confuse a simple theme and enable opponents of enfranchisement to delay reform. First get your votes, they said, then use them to get what you want. The most likely way of converting words into political facts was to reduce them to a slogan and, reinforced by acts of militancy, repeat them loud and often. Disliking such over-simplicity, Shaw warned that a victory gained by such methods could be pyrrhic. You had only to see, he argued, how little use the vote had been to men to understand that anyone expecting Votes for Women to achieve a millennium would be disappointed. Much the same argument as was used by Mrs Humphry Ward against the enfranchizement of women could be employed for taking away the vote from men.

He reduced his own opinion, not to a slogan, but a Shavian paradox that convinced no one – though it may appear to have more truth in it now. Votes for Women would keep women out of Parliament, he said, because too few women would vote for another woman. Looking back from the end of the 1920s, he wrote in *The Intelligent Woman's Guide*:

Only the other day the admission of women to the electorate, for which women fought and died, was expected to raise politics to a nobler plane and purify public life. But at the election which followed, the women voted for hanging the Kaiser; rallied hysterically round the worst male candidates; threw out all the women candidates of tried ability, integrity, and devotion; and elected just one titled lady of great wealth and singular demagogic fascination, who, though she justified their choice subsequently, was then a beginner. In short, the notion that the female voter is more politically intelligent or gentler than the male voter proved as great a delusion as the earlier delusions that the business man was any wiser politically than the country gentleman, or the manual worker than the middle class man.

Shaw's remedy, as he explained to Lady Rhondda, was the Coupled Vote. Since we inhabit a world of men and women in approximately equal numbers, he proposed that the smallest unit of government should not be the individual but a pair. All that was needed was a law declaring single votes to be invalid: all valid votes must go to a man-and-woman. Only on this bicycle-made-for-two, ensuring that all elected bodies were bisexual, could we peddle our way to a state of real democracy instead of the cult to which we paid such unconvincing lip-service. Quarter-of-a-century later Britain had a House of Commons containing over six hundred men and a couple of dozen women; a war cabinet of eight men and no women; and an outer-ministry of eighty-

The twelve women MP's in 1931. (Back row, left to right) Lady Astor, Mrs Helen Shaw, Mrs R. H. Tate, Mrs Thelma Cazalet-Keir, Mrs W. J. Ward, Mrs Ida Copeland, Miss F. Hursbrugh; (front row, left to right) Mrs N. Runge, Lady Iveagh, The Duchess of Atholl, Mrs Irene Ward, The Hon. Mary Pickford

one men and two women. The true battle for the emancipation of women had still not been won by the time Shaw died in 1950.

For most of his adult life, Shaw's Dulcinea had been Equality of Income. He was accused of inconsistency for not loving her sister Equal Pay. But he identified Equal Pay as a manoeuvre designed by the masculine Trade Unions to keep women out of industry – the calculation being that if employers had to pay a woman as much as a man they would invariably choose the man. The third sister, Equality of Opportunity, he treated as a political harlot whose soft words meant nothing. Everyone, he liked to point out, had had the opportunity of writing the plays of G. Bernard Shaw – and not one of them had done so. What was the point of telling a beggar that he had the 'opportunity' of becoming Astronomer Royal? It was simply thoughtless and cruel. Since there could be no equality of ability, no physical equality or equality of parents, the only real equality must be financial. Equality of Income – the same basic wage for the butcher, Prime Minister and chorus girl – was a biological necessity since it would lead to equality of class, to inter-marriageability and, by enabling us to act on our instinctive sexual preferences that had been frozen for centuries into rigid class stratifications, to our full cooperation with the Life Force. 'Miss Murby . . . is firmly persuaded that my views on the production of the Superman involve the forcible coercion by the State of selected women to breed with the selected men,' Shaw told Florence Farr; 'and she, being a good-looking & clever person, very likely to be selected under such a scheme, fears the worst.' But Shaw believed that equality of income would encourage individuality of choice and that we must rely for our future on the freeing of our instincts from the coil of social inhibitions, rather than on any eccentric notions of the master race. There was no need for differentiation of race or class. We were all one with another and should eventually breed all but our individual differences into oblivion.

Since our system of marriage and family life had been responsible for producing people no better than ourselves, major reforms were urgently needed. Shaw advocated revisions to our marriage laws to bring them out of indecency and into line with human nature. He addressed himself to the administration not the heartbeat of love, to legislation rather than Bohemian private enterprise, advising people 'on no account to compromise themselves without the security of an authentic wedding ring'. Otherwise, he insisted, we would go on tolerating that unwholesome morality of marriage where families were supposed to stew in love till they expired, and where children were slowly suffocated by sentimentality. There was no magic in marriage, he warned: perpetual wedlock was a punishment that helped to bring our law into disrepute. As a first condition for the maintenance of marriage, Shaw proposed divorce obtainable, as it were, from the chemist: that is, at the request of either party and with no reasons given. By the time he came to write *Too True to be Good* (1931) he felt that it might be simpler to limit the marriage contract to one year with optional vows of renewal every twelve months. But he was not doctrinaire. Though personally he looked forward to a time when it would be thought shockingly bad form for a daughter to be able to recognize her own mother in the street, he allowed that husbands and wives must be entitled to produce children if they wished. In a reasonable moral climate, however, he could scarcely think that many would do so. In his Preface to *In Good King Charles's Golden Days*, written in 1939 and subtitled 'A True History that never Happened', he explained that Charles II

took his marriage very seriously, and his sex adventures as calls of nature on an entirely different footing. In this he was in the line of evolution, which leads to an increasing separation of the unique and intensely personal and permanent marriage relation from the carnal intercourse [which] . . . being a response to the biological decree that the world must be peopled, may arise irresistibly between persons who could not live together endurably for a week but can produce excellent children.

If it is true, as Hugh Kingsmill maintained, that 'no man can put more virtue into his words than he practices in his life', then the sincerity of Shaw's words must be tested in the context of his life. 'We were not a sentimental family,' he once remarked. His ideas on marriage and the family were the product of complicated methods by which he distilled optimism from his loveless years in Ireland. In Dublin society during the mid-nineteenth century his parents had had little choice but to marry each other for love of money. The Life Force had cooperated well, producing one genius from the match, but the marriage created much unhappiness and left the son bereft of all passions except two: the passion for laughter and reform. His marriage to Charlotte Payne-Townshend was one of his many essays in reformation. He and Charlotte seemed to hold in common one opinion above all others: their determination not to marry. Once more the Life Force interceded and Shaw, under the impression he was dying, offered Charlotte widowhood. So they were married and, having found a house they both disliked, settled comfortably into it for

The exterior of Shaw's Corner as seen from the bottom of the garden

almost forty years. It was an unorthodox marriage. Every Shaw scholar knows how, after an hour's lecture on the intricacies of Shavian economics, Fabianism or alphabetical reform, his scholarship will be tested with questions as to whether Shaw slept with his wife. If he did not, this was at Charlotte's request. Sex was never a central part of their relationship, and Shaw appears to have accepted – a little too readily perhaps – the *marriage blanc* that Charlotte offered. He met the accusation of behaving with unvirile correctitude by hearing the call of nature in the voice of Mrs Patrick Campbell, his Nell Gwynn – even though, handicapped by his Fabian gradualism, he failed to permeate. 'I throw my desperate hands to heaven and ask why one cannot make one beloved woman happy without sacrificing another. We are all slaves of what is best within us and worst without us.'

Money had given Charlotte independence, and it was the strength of her independence (mitigated by waves of jealousy) that Shaw relied on. She continued to eat

GBS and Charlotte in 1905

meat, drink whisky and to involve herself as densely as Shaw's mother had done in the mists of mysticism. Shaw did not lust after her money, having in his middle forties just begun to make money himself. Before their marriage, Rodelle Weintraub has written, 'a contract detailing the distribution of their incomes was drawn up. After the marriage, he refused to file a joint income tax return, although British law required married couples to do so, for he felt it was humiliating for wives who had their own incomes to be treated as appendages of their husbands.' While acknowledging that the principle of taxing family income was sound enough, he sought an amendment (nicknamed the Bernard Shaw Relief Act) to the Income Tax Act to enable husband and wife to make separate returns. 'I have absolutely no means of ascertaining my wife's income except by asking her for the information,' he wrote to the clerk to the Special Commissioners of Income Tax in 1910.

> Her property is a separate property. She keeps a separate banking account at a separate bank. Her solicitor is not my solicitor. I can make a guess at her means from her style of living, exactly as the Surveyor of Income Tax does when he makes a shot at an assessment in the absence of exact information; but beyond that I have no more knowledge of her income than I have of yours. I have therefore asked her to give me a statement. She refuses, on principle. As far as I know, I have no legal means of compelling her to make any such disclosure; and if I had, it does not follow that I am bound to incur law costs to obtain information which is required not by myself but by the State. Clearly, however, it is within the power of the Commissioners to compel my wife to make a full disclosure of her income for the purposes of taxation; but equally clearly they must not communicate that disclosure to me or to any other person. It seems to me under these circumstances that all I can do for you is to tell you who my wife is and leave it to you to ascertain her income and make me pay the tax on it. Even this you cannot do without a violation of secrecy as it will be possible for me by a simple calculation to ascertain my wife's income from your demand.

After a meeting at which Shaw pointed out that they were both 'up against two obstacles – first, an oversight in the Income Tax Acts; and, second, the suffragist movement', the government accepted separate filings, billing Shaw for any shortages.

Shaw's sincerity, which lay in attempting to replace the vices of his family life in Ireland with the virtues of married life in England, cannot be doubted. But was sincerity enough? He would have been the first to point out that Galileo's contemporaries sincerely believed that the sun went round the earth. Shaw's feminism was Hegelian. He stated as fact what he desired to achieve as an end – that men and women were almost identical. He dreamed of combining their minds to form a higher synthesis of political animal. His paradoxes were the instant flash of this synthesis which, he believed, was being postponed by our old-fashioned segregation of the sexes and by unnecessary class barriers. He used Woman the Huntress as a stereotype to combat the Victorian stereotype of the Sexless Angel. But the women he promoted from angels to human beings and married to men in a political union, found that Shavian independence meant a solitude relieved only by the narcotic of work. Shaw's synthesis, with its precious bodily fluid dried up, becomes synthetic. When asked by Louis Wilkinson in 1909 what he considered to be the chief obstacle to the emancipation of women, he gave one word: 'Lust'. It is an answer that, even though he may have meant the lust of women as much as of men, can help to explain his immaculate public record. The man who consistently supported the claim of women to the franchise and who campaigned in his writing and in his life for a new attitude to women, could also affirm that it was 'not the small things that women miss in me, but the big things'.

Margot Peters

'AS LONELY AS GOD'

The trouble with Bernard Shaw is that we always believe what he says. Whether the topic is war, wool, or women, his assertions strike with the force of commandments. The witty paradoxes, the surprise reversals, the absolutist prose style, the brilliant distinction-annihilating exaggerations – all intimidate the would-be critic. We are particularly intimidated when Shaw talks about Shaw.

And so the contradictions in Shaw's nature tend to be ignored, although they are many. He idolized Mozart – and Wagner. He considered himself a realist, yet fell into the wildest romanticisms. He proclaimed total indifference to family ties, yet minutely familiarized himself with his family tree. He was modest and arrogant. He gossiped vigorously, and could be the kindest of friends. He preached selective breeding as eugenic duty to the human race, but fathered no children. He wrote a great deal about sex while dexterously avoiding the actuality. The list is random, fragmentary; yet suggestive that the master of paradox was himself highly paradoxical.[1]

Shaw's attitude towards women, both in life and in art, is not the least of his paradoxes. His first love affair and the novel he wrote in 1883 during its stormiest period reveal conflicts about women that were to characterize his conduct and his writing the rest of his life.

Shaw met Alice Lockett in February 1882 while recuperating from a light attack of scarlet fever at the home of his uncle at Leyton – and fell violently in love. Although an inconveniently swift recuperation sent him back to London, he managed to get temporary employment at Leyton, returned, stayed a week, and pursued Alice. It came to moonlight walks and heavy flirtation. By 17 April Shaw could report to Elinor Huddart, a steady correspondent: 'Alice thinks I am in love with her.'[2] She had every reason to believe it. 'Recklessly I dare again/On this page with ink to rain,' scribbled Shaw in his shorthand notebook:

Alice, Alice
Alice, Alice, Alice
Alice!
Alice!
Alice!
Alice!
Alice!
Alice!
Alice!

George Bernard Shaw

Alice Lockett

Alice!
Alice!
Alice!
Alice!
Alice!
Alice!
Darling Alice!!![3]

The twenty-six-year-old Shaw approached this romance with mixed emotions. His masculine culture defined women precisely for him. Woman was the Ideal Other, the sexless angel in floating skirts, the pure and passive object of chivalrous patronage. Conversely she was the siren, the fatal appeal to the 'lower centres'.

But private forces were at work in Shaw's life that contradicted these familiar stereotypes of women. There had been the day, for example, when Shaw discovered that his father drank. With the loss of faith in his father came Shaw's distrust of the masculine, orthodox, middle-class culture that had betrayed him: Shaw the iconoclast was born. Such filial sympathies as remained were turned to his mother. Her role in the family only convinced him further that middle-class appearances were not to be trusted: Lucinda Shaw was the cool, hard, aggressive, rational partner in the unfortunate marriage, not her husband. Rejecting his father, Shaw tended to identify with his mother, an identification made possible by her 'masculinity', which at the same time encouraged Shaw to develop traditionally feminine characteristics – physical modesty, narcissism, vanity, flirtatiousness, charm, talkativeness – and reject the war-sport-women mentality of the male locker room.

But Shaw's mother did not return this sympathy. 'She did not hate anybody, nor love anybody,'[4] said Shaw, and she managed to wound and alienate him even while he was forced to admire her. Her coldness left him insecure where women were concerned, and also in awe of their powers; and so the image of woman as regenerating angel still held sway. He approached Alice Lockett, it may fairly be said, in a state of high confusion.

The affair, conducted chiefly over tea and at the piano after Alice's singing lessons from Mrs Shaw, teetered violently between bursts of affection and repudiation. Shaw blamed their difficulties on the split personality of Alice. Miss Lockett was prim, prudish, and proper – always tossing her head and defending her dignity and pretending to be sophisticated, but essentially a weak and cowardly person, terrified of her better impulses. Alice was those better impulses: Alice was strong, generous, frank and free.

But Shaw's perceptive analysis stemmed largely from a recognition of his own deep contradictions. 'Have I not also a dual self,' he admitted to Alice, '– an enemy within my gates – an egotistical George Shaw upon whose neck I have to keep a grinding foot – a first cousin of Miss Lockett?'[5] This other self could be diabolically destructive. Yet Shaw did not apparently realize what an impossible situation his contradictions alone created. He could tell Alice, for example, that when she was kind and frankly affectionate 'a set of leading strings' fell from her and hung themselves upon him 'in the form of golden chains'; yet in the same letter warn her that his heart is a machine: 'Believe nothing that I say – and I have a wicked tongue, a deadly pen, and a cold heart. . . .'[6] Understandably angry at this doubletalk, Alice retaliated: 'All people are not machines: some are capable of genuine feelings . . . you are one of the weakest men I have ever met; and in spite of your cleverness I cannot help despising you.'[7] The contradiction of Shaw's demand that Alice be free and affectionate while he proclaimed heartless invulnerability would prove unresolvable.

If Shaw's romantic affairs were at this time turbulent, on the philosophical level he was experiencing a revolution that would shape his social creed for the rest of his life. Before he casually walked into Henry George's lecture on Land Nationalization and Single Tax in September 1882, he had been (as he later explained) a 'born Communist': that is, an immensely gifted individual frustrated and seditious in a social order he cannot understand. George supplied the key that unlocked the mystery: economics. Immediately the scales fell from Shaw's eyes. He saw that 'Property is theft: respectability founded on poverty is blasphemy: marriage founded on property is prostitution: it is easier for a camel to go through the eye of a needle than for a rich man to enter the kingdom of heaven.'[8] He went from the lecture to Marx: he put down *Das Kapital* a socialist: a man with a creed and a cause. He expounded both in his fifth novel.

An Unsocial Socialist levelled a three-pronged attack at Shaw's new social enemies: individualism, private property, and romanticism – or more broadly, at the system which breeds all three: Capitalism. Shaw's hero is Sidney Trefusis, the son of a wealthy self-made capitalist like Dickens' Bounderby, married to Henrietta Jansenius, a conventional middle-class young woman who has the bad grace to protest when her husband, suddenly converted to socialism, disappears one day without a word. She eventually discovers him masquerading as a country bumpkin in corduroys; explanations follow, but Harriet is unreconciled: it is her misfortune that she cannot see, as Trefusis does, that the end of human love is not the private marital love-nest but dedication to the public good. 'I only understand that you hate me,' says Henrietta, 'and want to go away from me.' 'That would be easy to understand,' her husband tells her. 'But the strangeness is that I *love* you and want to go away from you.' Then, taking her in his arms where they are lying on the bank of a canal, Trefusis explains to his wife the capitalist profit system, his mission to liberate his father's labourers, and his preference for his corduroys and two-room cottage to 'our pretty little house and your pretty little ways'.[9]

The scene aptly illustrated Shaw's current personal struggle between romance and his newly conceived social mission: the conflict of Trefusis and Henrietta is very much the conflict of Bernard Shaw and Alice Lockett. Henrietta dies of a chill and a broken heart, not having learned to love the masses more than her husband. It is not too fanciful to suggest that Shaw was trying to bury his own romantic self with her: the birthdate on her tombstone is his own: 26 July 1856.

Sex, as Shaw saw, was still bound to intrude upon human lives; but he had formulated its place both in *Cashel Byron's Profession* and *An Unsocial Socialist*, and would reassert that formulation for the rest of his life: the primary end of sex was not pleasure but procreation. Although the concept seems puritanical and Victorian, Victorian it was not. Couples were not to breed like rabbits, but creatively for the higher evolution of the human race. Mating therefore is a social duty for superior men and women, and Sidney Trefusis is a social socialist in his decision to remarry after Henrietta's death. 'A bachelor is a man who shirks responsibilities and duties,' proclaims Trefusis; 'I seek them, and consider it my duty, with my monstrous superfluity of means, not to let the individualists outbreed me.'[10]

Psychically, however, Shaw experienced conflicts over love and sexual attraction which philosophically he seemed to have resolved. The renunciation of Alice Lockett was not easy. 'If I had your heart, I know I should break it,' he writes her on 19 November 1883, 'and yet I wish I had it.'[11] It is the struggle of the Puritan: reason and feeling, mind and body, conscience and impulse are violently split. Shaw came to realize this psychic chasm within himself. 'Women tend to regard love as a fusion of

body, spirit and mind,' he told Stephen Winsten. 'It has never been so with me.'
What he did not add was that emotionally (not intellectually) he viewed 'body' as
wrong. Thus, of course, it was also incredibly fascinating, while its very fascination
made it the more loathsome and dangerous.

Nowhere is this conflict better illustrated than in Shaw's relationship with Jenny
Patterson, a well-to-do widow at least fifteen years older than Shaw who entered his
life on the heels of Alice Lockett and initiated him sexually on the eve of his twenty-
ninth birthday.[12] Shaw the puritan pretended that she was totally the aggressor in
the affair: that she plied him with unwanted caresses, that he submitted only to
gratify her, and that he only sought her out when, infrequently, he had nothing better
to do. Shaw's diary and the letters that survive from Jenny Patterson to Shaw, however, reveal that while he was at once attracted and repulsed by the sexual liaison, the
attraction was strong. 'Went to JP' is a constant diary entry. He could tell her, 'Be
faithful to me or I will kill you by mere intensity of hate', and she evidently spoke the
truth when she wrote to him, 'You will not believe me I know but it is absolutely
true that often my body has been an unwilling minister to you. In many of your
letters have you not threatened me with your desertion if I did not love you passionately.'[13] It was not the 'love' she loved, she told him, but her lover. Shaw denied this,
but the case of the woman being accused of carnality when she is only submitting to a
man's desire is too familiar. 'In our sexual natures we are torn by an irresistible
attraction and an overwhelming repugnance and disgust,' wrote Shaw in 1915,
describing very well the liaison with Jenny Patterson that lasted eight years.

Fired with self-confidence by Jenny's wholehearted submission and attracted to
women, yet at the same time extremely self-sufficient and scornful of romantic
attachment, Shaw became during these eight years a compulsive philanderer. With
neither body, mind nor spirit engaged simultaneously, he indulged in what he repu-
diated intellectually: romance: the titillation of sexual emotion without its gratification. He teased, charmed, provoked, and flattered like a coquette, drawing back at a
hint of seriousness. Of course, the despicably false relationships between men and
women that Shaw would spend his life attacking made his conduct appear worse than
it was; for women – even the intelligent women that Shaw preferred – were condi-
tioned to take any kind of male attention in deadly earnest.

Shaw's lack of seriousness made him gravitate in these years towards relationships
in which he could play a safely ambiguous third. Eleanor Marx and Edward Aveling,
May Morris and Henry Sparling, Annie Besant and John Robertson, Edith Nesbit
Bland and Hubert Bland, Kate and Henry Salt, Janet Achurch and Charles Charrington – in all these households Shaw paid court more or less seriously to the woman
and was taken more or less seriously in return. The triangle duplicated a domestic
pattern that perhaps provided the emotionally deprived Shaw with what he craved:
he could play the eternal child (as he had never been), coddled by the woman-mother,
accepted yet half-feared by the male-father. Perhaps too the triangle satisfied his
androgynous nature. Certainly it reassuringly duplicated a familiar situation:
Vandeleur Lee, Lucinda Shaw's music mentor, had joined the Shaw household in
Dublin to make an apparently platonic *ménage à trois*. Of course, the situation must be
handled delicately: wives could grow suddenly intense and husbands jealous: but
Shaw balanced carefully on that tightrope, sowing his gallantries thickly with the
names of other females, maintaining a frank camaraderie with the male partner, and
playing the buffoon.

Besides the safety of the triangle, there was safety in the types of women Shaw
preferred: Eleanor Marx Aveling, common-law wife of the philandering Edward

Mrs Jenny Patterson (top left),
Eleanor Marx (top right),
Annie Besant (centre left),
May Morris (centre right),
Edith Nesbit (below left) *and*
Florence Farr (below right)

Aveling; Annie Besant, estranged from her husband and children and a notorious radical; Kate Salt, a lesbian; Edith Bland, a talented writer who was forced to countenance her husband's mistress and illegitimate children under her own roof; Florence Farr, the 'new woman' who kept, according to Shaw, 'a sort of Leporello list of a dozen adventures'; Bertha Newcombe, the Chelsea artist; Janet Achurch, a 'wild and glorious' actress but also a drug addict; Ellen Terry, twice married when she and Shaw began to correspond in 1892, probably Henry Irving's mistress, and mother of two children by her lover Edwin Godwin. The radical Shaw approved these women on principle, the essentially aloof Shaw felt at ease (as he told Frank Harris, he preferred women who knew what they were doing), the wary Shaw felt safeguarded from conventional female demands; yet the puritan Shaw who put social duty before personal freedom must have had strong reservations.

In turn Shaw's sexual reticence made him particularly attractive to types of women who shy away from aggressive masculinity and conversely he found these women congenial. Paradoxically, however, Shaw's reticence aroused aggressiveness in women who might well retreat from ordinary male advances. As a consequence, he developed a seemingly genuine conviction that the female was the driving sexual force in the universe and the male her nearly passive victim. The conviction found early expression in *Don Giovanni Explains,* a short story Shaw wrote as an apologia in 1887 after two years of compulsive trifling with women. Shaw's Don is no libertine, but only a sensitive and chivalrous gentleman who would much prefer to worship *la belle femme* at an ideal and safe distance, if only she would let him.

Shaw's passive Don Giovanni bears superficial resemblance to the Shaw whom Jenny Patterson seduced, Edith Bland hunted down, and Annie Besant tried to bind with a home-made marriage contract. Yet passivity is not really the word to describe Shaw's behaviour. He constantly visited Jenny Patterson. He dashed off dozens of provocative letters to women. He boasted of his entanglements to William Archer, to Sidney Webb, and to all his female victims. He faithfully recorded in his diary his day-to-day progress with women, as well as the scores of his sexual encounters with Jenny. It is more constructive to return to the concept of Shaw the puritan. His repulsion-attraction to sex and the divorce of it from the spirit and mind that he held paramount explain why his conduct is generous and high-minded when his intellect is engaged, and frequently petty or even despicable when sex is in question: matters of sex or romance did not demand better conduct from him. Thus in a letter to Annie Besant he can call Jenny Patterson – who called *him* 'my dear love' – 'no better than a woman of the streets'.[14] For the same reason he generously lauded Annie Besant's benevolence and courage in later years; yet when asked whether she had ever attracted him physically, he said brutally: 'She had absolutely no sex appeal.' So, too, he could look back and say: 'Women have never played an important part in my life. I could always discard them more readily than my friends. . . .'[15]

Alice Lockett had engaged his heart, Jenny Patterson his body, Annie Besant his mind. It remained for Florence Farr Emery to fleetingly engage all three for the first time in his life and the last. She was twenty-eight, educated, separated after four years of marriage to actor Edward Emery, an actress herself, a member of the Yeats–Paget–Todhunter circle of Bedford Park, and a rebel who had 'given home and family as much trial as seemed necessary' and put both behind her.[16] She had the frank warmth that Alice Lockett lacked, the sexual attractiveness missing in May Morris and Kate Salt, the beauty that Annie Besant had lost, a cool unpossessiveness that Jenny Patterson did not know the meaning of.

They had their 'first really intimate conversation' in her rooms at Dalling Road on 15 November 1890. Six months later he could call her 'my other self – no, not my other self, but my very self'. The most enchanting of his surviving love letters is written to her:

> This is to certify that you are my best and dearest love, the regenerator of my heart, the holiest joy of my soul, my treasure, my salvation, my rest, my reward, my darling youngest child, my secret glimpse of heaven, my angel of the Annunciation, not yet herself awake, but rousing me from a long sleep with the beat of her unconscious wings, and shining upon me with her beautiful eyes that are still blind.

Never so intoxicated that he lost his instinct for self-protection, however, Shaw could not resist anti-climax. 'Also to observe incidentally,' he added, 'that Wednesday is the nearest evening that shews blank in my diary.'[17]

Even in the throes of love, Shaw the reformer could not long be idle. It was a role he cultivated in his private relations with women since it dignified romance with purpose. Shaw's first mission was to persuade Florence to stage Ibsen's *Rosmersholm* instead of his *Lady From the Sea*. From then on Shaw began to judge Florence according to the degree she rose to his standards. It was a compulsion both egocentric and disinterested since, as he knew, his standards were high. 'I wish to see you an accomplished actress,' he tells her. 'I will not face the judgment bar at the end of my life with you if I am unable to meet the question, "Why did you suffer her to do her work badly?" '[18]

In this he would be disappointed, for Florence lacked the true artist's religious drive towards perfection. Shaw himself was responsible for his art down to the last comma; he could not admire anyone who felt less. By 1892 he was scolding her sharply: 'In the first scene you are insufferable. You wave your arms about like a fairy in a transformation scene. . . . If you decide at any time to do nothing, shut your mouth, and compose yourself, and *do* nothing. . . .'[19] It is her crime that she neither understands his greatness nor strives to rise to it.

> Cubits high and fathoms deep am I the noblest creature you have yet met in this wood of monkeys where I found you straying. . . . For many years had I wandered alone, sufficient to myself: I will, at a word, wander on again alone. But what will you do – return to the monkeys? It is not possible: self-sufficient must you also become or else find no less a man than I to be your mate.[20]

Florence did, however, return to the monkeys. He cannot help anyone, he tells her, except by taking help from them; and she has no more help to give him. Once he had called Florence his holiest joy; now he tells her she has neither faith, honour, heart, holiness nor religion: 'to be with you is to be in hell.' She had failed him in the deepest sense: by considering art an aesthetic and emotional escape from life instead of, as he did, a brightly polished weapon for reforming it. Like Christian he must trudge on his hard but sanctified way to the Celestial City alone.

Shaw thus repeated his relationship with Alice Lockett more intensely with Florence Farr, and would repeat it essentially in all his more intimate relations with women. Janet Achurch exploded into Shaw's life when she walked on the stage of the Novelty Theatre in June 1889 as Nora Helmer. By the time Janet and her actor husband Charles Charrington left for Australia a month later, Shaw had seen *A Doll's House* five times; romanced the actress at a celebratory cast dinner; sent her *Cashel Byron's Profession*, *An Unsocial Socialist*, and at least three letters; alienated William Archer's wife by rhapsodizing Janet; begun a play 'based on the Archer-Achurch incident'; called on the Charringtons; and turned up at the station to see them off on their tour: had, in short, been 'suddenly magnetized, irradiated, transported, fired, rejuvenated, bewitched by a wild and glorious young woman'.[21]

During the Charringtons' disastrous three years abroad Janet became addicted to morphia, presumably after doctors administered it heavily when she nearly died in childbirth. She had already been addicted to drink. When Shaw saw her play Nora again in London in 1892, she was fighting her way through the performance 'by brute force and stimulants'. It would have been natural now for Shaw to withdraw abruptly from the association; on the contrary, he found in her new inspiration. Her case was painfully familiar: 'I saw the process in my father,' he told her, 'and have never felt anything since.'[22] The way was open for Shaw the reformer to save Janet's soul. He will create an idealized character for her which she will not only play triumphantly on stage but emulate in real life. He could not help anyone except by taking help from them: he now took help from Janet; the result, of course, was *Candida*. And for a time Shaw's mission seemed to be succeeding: Janet, he told her, 'begins to draw on rich stores of life, becomes beautiful, becomes real, becomes almost saintly, looks at me with eyes that have no glamour of morphia in them, and with an affection that is not hysterical . . .'[23] And yet he is still uneasy: temporary salvation is not enough: the question is, how to make Janet religious so that she may recreate herself.

Candida did not save Janet Achurch's soul, however, either as a vehicle for the too emotional actress, or as a model of womanly behaviour. For the character of Candida does not change, as Shaw believed Janet must: she is at the end of the play what she was at the beginning, the mother-sister-nurse-wife of her boy husband Morell: an inspiration to men, not herself inspired. Candida learns nothing. It is Marchbanks the poet who concludes that love, security, and sexual fulfilment are ignoble ends compared to the lust after the inviolability of the soul. Shaw the poet closed the door on Janet with the secret he had meant to tell her locked in his heart.

Shaw had long been a candidate for sainthood. Revulsion had always lurked under the surface of his attraction to sex. If we are to believe his own testimony, the play intended to save Janet instead saved Shaw, lifting him far above the need for sensual pleasure and into the realm of dramatic genius, for 'ability does not become genius until it has risen to the point at which its keenest states of perception touch on ecstasy, on healthy, self-possessed ecstasy, untainted by mere epileptic or drunken incontinence, or sexual incontinence'.[24] And, as he had hoped for Janet, the transformation seemed to be permanent. 'Do you know anyone who will buy for twopence a body for which I have no longer any use?' he writes to her on 29 January 1896, more than a year after beginning *Candida*. 'I have made tolerable love with it in my time; but now I have found nobler instruments – the imagination of a poet, the heart of a child, all discovered through the necessity – the not-to-be-denied inmost necessity – of making my way to an innocent love for Janet. . . . In the old days saints and abbesses used to say "Wait until we die: we shall meet in heaven". Stupid of them, when it is so simple to become an angel on earth.'[25] Apparently Shaw never indulged in sex again. And *Candida* proved to be a significant artistic as well as personal watershed. Henceforth he put both sexual realism and socialist propaganda behind him, and turned to dramatizing sex intellectually as the Will of the Life Force and to portraying idealist heroes whose kingdoms are not of this world. He was uneasy about both defections, wondering whether *Candida* 'was not the beginning of weakness and mollycoddledom', and looking back on *Mrs Warren's Profession* with envy: 'Oh, when I wrote that I *had* some nerve.'

Shaw wrestled many years for Janet's soul. He thought it worth saving: he called her at one point the only great tragic actress that England possessed; he cared for her

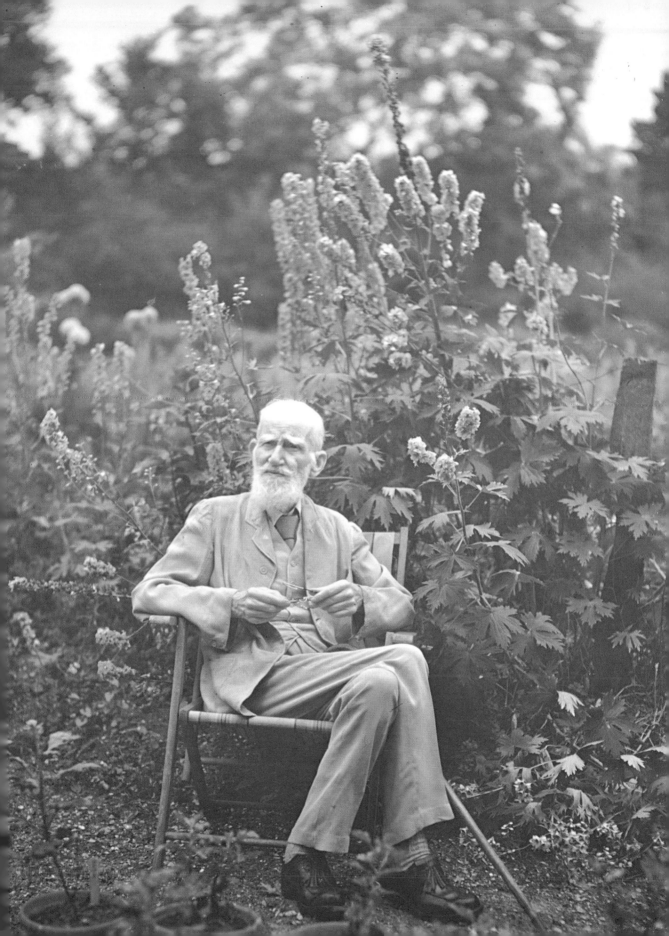

Photo by DOVER ST STUDIOS

HIS MAJESTY'S THEATRE
HERBERT TREE
PYGMALION

SAVOY THEATRE

THE
DEVIL'S
DISCIPLE
By
BERNARD
SHAW

more deeply than he cared for Florence Farr. But disillusionment was inevitable, and as a greater artist than Florence, Janet's fall from grace was more disastrous. Disillusionment with her as a human being was also inevitable, even if Shaw had not now found the new ideal in Ellen Terry and the real in Charlotte Payne Townshend. He takes leave of Janet in much the same language as he had taken leave of Florence Farr: his is the high road to heaven, hers the low road to hell: 'The step up to the plains of heaven was made on your bosom, I know; and it was a higher step than those I had previously taken on other bosoms. But he who mounts does not take the stairs with him. . . .'[26]

If Janet had failed to rise to the plains of heaven (Candida is the Virgin Mother and nothing else, Shaw proclaimed), another woman surely could not fail him. In Ellen Terry he wooed the vision he beheld across the Lyceum footlights: a woman of grace and powerful beauty, but above all an articulate artist, as committed to her work as he to his. She was the Candida he had tried to inspire in Janet and, as he promised her, 'one does not get tired of adoring the Virgin Mother'. Particularly would Shaw not get tired if their passion remained verbal: 'I had rather you remembered one thing I said for three days,' he admitted, 'than *liked* me (only) for 300,000,000,000,000,000 years.' Of course, he teased her with the possibility of a physical passion. But he hung back as did Ellen (taking his cue): a meeting would be a kind of sacrilege: he would be sure to spoil it with 'those philandering follies' that made him 'so ridiculous, so troublesome, so vulgar with women'.[27] And Ellen Terry too provided him with a mission. Although the foremost actress of her time, she had reached a plight familiar to Shaw. She, too, as she told him, could only help others by taking help from them; and in both her artistic and personal relations with Henry Irving, the actor could no longer help her. Shaw offered that help, touting the rejuvenating powers of the New Drama and particularly of Shaw who would create for her a role that fitted like a glove. He cajoled, teased, and harangued her from 1892 until 1906 when Ellen finally consented to appear as Lady Cicely in the play Shaw had written for her in 1899.

Their disembodied relationship, as well as his own conversion to disembodiment, had inspired him to create for Ellen the part of a powerful woman who overwhelms men with moral superiority rather than sex appeal: Lady Cicely is Shaw's virgin as Candida had been his mother. 'In every other play I have ever written – even in Candida,' he told her,'– I have prostituted the actress more or less by making the interest in her partly a sexual interest: only the *man* in the Devil's Disciple draws clear of it. In Lady Cicely I have done without this, and gained a greater fascination by it.'[28] Shaw sent *Captain Brassbound's Conversion* to Ellen and waited for her applause. But he had misjudged her severely: she did not admire his charming spinster; she would far rather play his Cleopatra or Mrs Warren. 'Of course you never *really* meant Lady Cicely for me – but to be published along with other Plays,' she rebuked him. For Shaw it was still another case of a woman falling short of expectation. Knowing Janet Achurch, he had portrayed Candida in meaningful emotional relationships with men. Not knowing Ellen Terry, he seemed to envision her only as a kind of aristocratic Emily Post, reforming the manners and morals of males who cross her path by extending her hand and politely saying 'How d'ye do?' He had listened too closely to the new saintly Shaw who whispered that sexuality was something to be overcome. The result was a lady when Ellen Terry apparently wanted a woman.

Charlotte Payne Townshend, the 'green-eyed millionairess' who married Shaw on 1 June 1898, offered the kind of relationship, therefore, for which Shaw at the height

Posters and cards for You Never Can Tell, Pygmalion, *and* The Devil's Disciple

A programme for a 1906 production of Captain Brassbound's Conversion signed by the cast

of his renunciation was psychically fit. Like Shaw, she had endured 'a perfectly hellish childhood and youth' with an unhappy and destructive mother who had dominated the household. Like Shaw she had learned from her ill-matched parents that marriage 'is not natural – but unnatural and disastrous'. She had extended her horror of marriage to the conception and rearing of children (as the fastidious Shaw might well have, had he been female): 'The idea was physically repulsive to me in the highest degree,' she confided to T. E. Lawrence.[29] Shaw, of course, had long ago formulated the maxim attributed to Jack Tanner: 'the essential function of marriage is the continuance of the race, the accidental function of marriage is the gratification of the amoristic sentiment of mankind.' Shaw now entered a marriage that would function neither essentially nor accidentally; yet he must have found it temperamentally congenial, for it provided in effect for the nurturing of a Superman while not threatening his sainthood. Shaw had indeed found his Virgin Mother, a woman with great strength of character who put him first, as his own mother never had, and who, with her plain Irish face and full figure, looked not unlike Lucinda Shaw. If he missed sexual consummation, he was not going to admit it yet. Marriage, he argued in *The Revolutionist's Handbook and Pocket Companion*, has essentially nothing to do with conjugation: conjugation is essential to nothing but the propagation of the race. Domesticity is the only function essential to marriage.

Had Shaw been a consistent man, he might now have been satisfied with the mind and spirit that Charlotte offered him. But the Puritan rejects sex partly because it fascinates him. 'Someday a pair of dark eyes, a fierce temperament and a woman will obtain you body and soul,' Elinor Huddart had warned.[30] Jenny Patterson's dark eyes and fierce temperament had won Shaw's body and enough of his imagination to inspire Blanche Sartorius and Julia Craven, the latter part requiring, said Shaw in a significant if unintentional tribute to his mistress, 'an actress of great passion and beauty'. Casting about for the perfect Julia for his unlucky *Philanderer*, he had been able to think of no one more right than the dark-eyed, temperamental, passionately beautiful Mrs Patrick Campbell.

Ironically, Beatrice Stella Campbell had cast her spell over Shaw in the kind of play

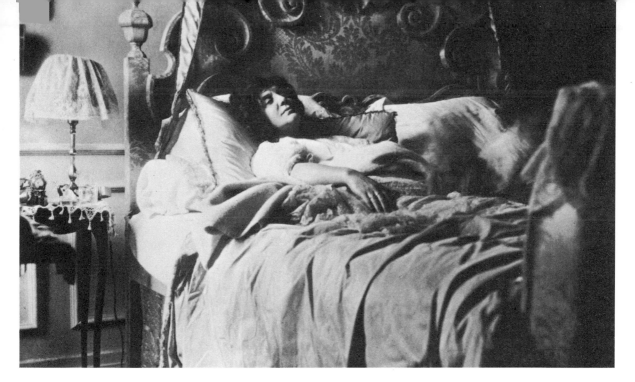

Mrs Patrick Campbell in her bed, photographed by Shaw

he most abhorred and which he dedicated himself to discrediting both as a critic and dramatist: pseudo-Ibsen plays which were 'nothing but the ordinary sensuous ritual of the stage become as frankly pornographic as good manners allowed'.[31] Here was a new mission for Shaw. He would liberate Mrs Campbell from insidious dramas like *The Second Mrs Tanqueray*. Not only would Shaw's heroines be women without a past, they would be women without a future – at least a future with the hero who was to renounce them after reforming them to his satisfaction. The result, of course, was Shaw's most successful play, *Pygmalion*. But Mrs Campbell enthused as little over Eliza Doolittle as had Janet Achurch over Candida or Ellen Terry over Lady Cicely; anti-romance had little appeal, and Shaw had succeeded better in portraying himself as the elusive Higgins.

Having created anti-romantic plays for Stella Campbell, Shaw then fell romantically in love with her at the age of fifty-six. Of course he protected himself with barriers he had been adept at erecting even in Alice Lockett's time. 'Many thanks for Friday and for a Saturday of delightful dreams,' he writes on 30 June 1912, a few weeks after completing *Pygmalion*. 'I did not believe that I had that left in me. I am all right now, down on earth again with all my cymbals and side drums and blaring vulgarities in full blast; but it would be meanly cowardly to pretend that you are not a very wonderful lady, or that the spell did not work most enchantingly on me for fully 12 hours.'[32]

But Shaw was not to escape with twelve hours. The affair followed a now-established pattern. First the simultaneous invitation and warning: then the rapture with his own creation: the ecstatic, orgasmic outpouring of words that replaced the physical: 'Oh, before you go, my Stella, I clasp you to my heart "with such a strained purity".'[33] And, as in the case of Janet Achurch, there came at last the realization that Stella Campbell was after all a human being: a trivial operation inspired the revelation that she was 'a real fellow creature in real pain'.[34]

It seems to have been this discovery that prompted Shaw to arrange a meeting with Stella at the Guildford Hotel at Sandwich, for unlike Janet Achurch, Stella did not have a husband, and apparently Shaw now desired sexual consummation. He went to

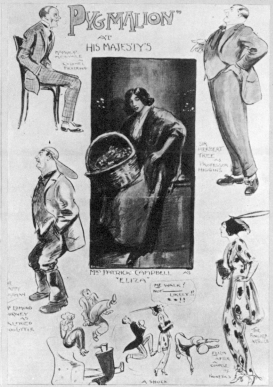

Act III   Pygmalion   47

ottoman, *so pleased to get rid of the visitors that he becomes almost civil.* ~~Freddy comes back from the balcony appears at window~~

CLARA. Oh yes! we have three at-homes to go to still. ~~Good-bye, Professor Higgins.~~

HIGGINS [~~shaking hands with her across the ottoman~~] Good-bye. Be sure you try on that small talk at the three at-homes. Dont be nervous about it. Pitch it in strong.

CLARA [*all smiles*] I will. Good-bye, Mrs Higgins. Good-bye, Colonel Pickering. [*Turning again to Higgins, who is accompanying her to the door*] Such nonsense, all this early Victorian prudery!

HIGGINS. Such damned nonsense!

CLARA. Such bloody nonsense!

MRS EYNSFORD HILL [*convulsively*] Clara!

CLARA. Ha! ha! [*She goes out radiant, conscious of being thoroughly up to date*].

FREDDY [*to Higgins*] Well, I ask you— [*He gives it up, and comes to Mrs Higgins, followed by Higgins, who comes to Mrs Hill*] Good-bye.

MRS HIGGINS [*shaking hands*] Good-bye. Would you like to meet Miss Doolittle again?

FREDDY. Yes, I should, most awfully.

MRS HIGGINS. Well, you know my days.

FREDDY. Yes. Thanks awfully. Good-bye. [*He goes out*].

MRS EYNSFORD HILL. Good-bye, Mr Higgins.

HIGGINS. Good-bye. Good-bye.

MRS EYNSFORD HILL [*to Pickering*] It's no use. I shall never be able to bring myself to use that word.

PICKERING. Dont. It's not compulsory, you know. Youll get on quite well without it.

MRS EYNSFORD HILL. Only, Clara is so down on me if I am not positively reeking with the latest slang. Good-bye.

PICKERING. Good-bye [*They shake hands*].

MRS EYNSFORD HILL [*to Mrs Higgins*] You mustnt mind Clara. We're so poor! and she gets so few parties, poor child! She doesnt quite know. [*Mrs Higgins, seeing that her eyes*

Sandwich on 9 August 1913: he was cruelly hurt there. The story emerges obliquely from the flurry of bitter letters that followed the disaster. Weary of words, Stella evidently wished an immediate, and to her, normal resolution of the year-old romance. Shaw, the artist, wanted seven holy days of aesthetically mounting bliss. After two days Stella fled, bewildered and angered at Shaw's dalliance, having flung in his face meanwhile the news that she intended to marry George Cornwallis West. Shaw took the defection hard, venting all his wrath upon the now fallen angel:'Bah! You have no nerve: you have no brain: you are the caricature of an eighteenth century male sentimentalist, a Hedda Gabler titivated with odds and ends from Burne Jones's ragbag; you know nothing.'[35] He might have flung the same words at Alice Lockett: again the vision had failed: again he had discovered that the woman he enthroned as the Mother of Angels was after all a conventionally romantic woman.

The degree of Shaw's infatuation with Stella Campbell may be gauged by the pain he caused Charlotte, a woman he respected. Her diary, as laconic as Shaw's own, records only for 1913 'G.B.S. told me about Mrs. P.C.' Her travel diary for the same year is perhaps more revealing: among the list of place names appears the jarring word 'Pygmalion'.[36] The affair caused deep estrangement. While Charlotte was 'ill and alone' in London during the first week of 1914, for example, Shaw is still writing to Stella: 'New Years Eve. O night of all nights in the year – of my most immemorial year! Do you remember last New Years Eve? . . . I remember it: it tears me all to pieces: I believe we were both well then, and have been ill ever since.' That winter Charlotte went very little to Ayot St Lawrence. On 8 April 1914 she sailed for America, evidently unable to face the final rehearsals and opening night of *Pygmalion* on the eleventh, not knowing that Stella Campbell had become Mrs Cornwallis West on the sixth.

Stella Campbell finished Shaw's excursions into grand romance, although having constant need to 'refresh his heart' by admiring women, he never gave up flirtation. At the age of sixty-five, however, he was beguiled into repeating the whole process once more with Mary Arthur Tompkins, a young married American who aspired to acting. He rebaptized her Molly Tompkins, scolded her articulation, her heavy make-up, her temper, her handwriting, her domestic chaos, her laziness; yet soon she was Mollissima. He romanced her on the Stresa road; claimed, when she found herself pregnant, to be the spiritual father of the child; provoked her emotions while at the same time warning her not to take him seriously – while Charlotte was left to watch the proceedings through powerful binoculars. Yet her intemperate romanticism could only disillusion him at last: 'you thought that when you had secured your Ogygia and lured me to its shores you could Calypso to my Odysseus and make a hog of me. Aren't you glad you didn't succeed?'[37] As he had told an audience in 1927, 'I am a man of the most extraordinary hardness of heart';[38] and this hardness – the aloofness of age – was now evident. When, after Charlotte's death, Molly Tompkins wrote from New York proposing that she come to Ayot St Lawrence to look after him, Shaw sent back a terrified refusal. This time Molly Tompkins' reply was refreshingly anti-romantic: 'What a way to misconstrue my letter. Come and live with you indeed! Do you think I would give up the serenity of my independence to live with anybody on earth – and be responsible to them for my time and thoughts – even you? Hell no!'[39]

Shaw's behaviour with the many women who attracted him was thus from beginning to end consistently inconsistent. His failure ever to have a 'normal' relationship with a woman (or, depending on one's viewpoint, his success) seems to have been created by an inability to integrate mind, spirit and body. He could not love Jenny

(Top left) *Mrs Patrick Campbell as Eliza in* Pygmalion *before and after her transformation by Professor Higgins.* (Top right) *Sketches of scenes from* Pygmalion *from* The Bystander, *1914.* (Below left) *A marked page from Shaw's personal rehearsal copy of* Pygmalion. (Below right) *The first Eliza: Lilli Marberg at the Hofburg Theatre, Vienna, 1913*

Patterson, for example, nor marry Florence Farr, nor bring himself to sexual intimacy with Stella Campbell. In one sense he understood women poorly since they were his own visionary creations, a fact that explains why, whether addressed to 'Alice, Alice, Alice' or 'Stella, Stella, Stella', his love letters in their religious imagery and ecstasy are all remarkably alike. 'If your part in my exaltation was an illusion,' he told Stella Campbell, 'then I am as lonely as God.' Hers and the parts of others *were* largely illusion; and although Shaw possessed 'a power of starving on imaginary feasts', the crash to reality was inevitable. The women themselves were left baffled, angry, or contemptuous.

If Shaw's puritanism caused many women pain and himself, after the brief rapture, only disillusion, it served his fictional women far better. Because Shaw could not easily bridge the chasm between intellect and body, he created protagonists out of the tissues of the former. Many writers created heroines out of the latter, dividing the human race into the tediously conventional camps of man – the mind and conscience, and woman – the body and temptation; and it was a division that Shaw could not always resist: Caesar-Cleopatra, Tanner-Ann, Higgins-Eliza, Marchbanks-Candida, Dudgeon-Judith, Magnus-Orinthia, A-Z. But Shaw was in nothing conventional. His weak sexual drive and androgynous nature led him to believe that the differences between the sexes were minimal: woman, he could say, is man in petticoats. And his most successful comic gambit proved to be the demonstration that men could be like women and women like men.

Thus in his first novel *Immaturity* Harriet Russell vigorously sculls the boat while her fiancé reclines upon pillows. Lydia Carew is a super-intellect who coolly looks over the pugilist Cashel Byron and decides to marry him for his body. Vivie Warren has a bone-crunching handshake and a taste for cigars. Ann Whitefield pursues the terrified Jack Tanner until she nails him. Lina Szczepanowska teaches Bentley Summerhays how to dare and Lavinia teaches the Captain how to die. Queen Elizabeth provides Shakespeare with his best lines. Lady Cicely's well-bred manners reduce brigands and sultans to helplessness. The Patient stuns the Burglar with a blow to the solar plexus and the Millionairess shoulder-throws her husband three times and flings him downstairs. The intellectuals who inherit the earth are the favourites not of Adam but of Eve. St Joan leads armies.

These wonderfully radical creations qualify Shaw as the most feminist of male writers. And in deciding that women were only males in petticoats, he had hit upon half a truth: that the division of the sexes is largely the artificial product of a society that finds it advantageous to render one half of the human race powerless. But women, under the very conditions Shaw attacked so vigorously, could not be like men. The typical heroines he deplored – Pamela, Little Nell, Esther Summerson, Amelia Osborne, Hetty Sorrel – are more real than Shaw supposed to the extent that women patterned themselves after an artificial ideal and believed in it. Conversely, the Shavian heroine is unreal in her incredible disregard for conventional feminine behaviour. Shaw's women are thus superb comic instruments for attacking convention, but are so despotic and self-sufficient that even today many of them are beyond imitation, although their very presence in dramatic literature is salutary.

But there was also for Shaw sex: the body which by his own admission he could not integrate with mind. And his distaste often proved hard on women, for his most powerful male characters either reject romantic passion altogether or put up a desperate struggle against it before capitulating; and in this duel it is woman who stands for temptation and man for conscience – a division widened by Shaw's belief that human nature had not essentially changed and his subsequent dealing in archetypes:

'He men and She women of his patent brand.' Shaw had once considered anti-romanticism diabolic; by the writing of *Man and Superman*, however, he fastened romance firmly on the Devil in hell: heaven is the place of pure intellectual contemplation. The Shavian hero has his eye on heaven: Dick Dudgeon who refuses to die for a woman; Caesar who hands Cleopatra over to Marc Antony with relief; Marchbanks who fastidiously rejects domestic bliss; Tanner who flees from Ann across Europe; Captain Shotover to whom dynamite and dreams are reality; Private Meek, envied by the wife-dominated Colonel Tallboys; A, the poet, who capitulates to Z, the materialist. The men who come off worst in a Shaw play are men deluded by romance or passion: Morell, Frank, Sergius, Octavius, Hector Malone, Mendoza, Randall the Rotter, Hector Hushabye.

This neurosis (whatever havoc it played in private) also proved progressive in Shaw's art. Because he disliked sex, he exposed it for what it was: a biological drive that seizes men and women by the scruffs of their necks and throws them into each other's arms. Sex was – sex. 'Woman, lovely woman' did not exist: woman was the female of the species as man was the male. This ruthless cutting away of romantic illusion exposed many lies: that marriage is essentially a matter of love; that chastity is a moral issue; that sexual attraction is founded on love; that sexual constancy is normal for women but abnormal for men; that lifelong intimacy is a rational state. And since women suffered more than men from these lies, Shaw's attack is indeed feminist.

Shaw's puritanism also glorified women in another sense. For Shaw life was duty. Unable to sanction physical pleasure for its own sake – as he could not sanction art for art's sake – he interpreted his own pursuit of it as obligation: sexual experience, he told Frank Harris in 1930, seemed to him a necessary completion of human growth. He altered the statement slightly in *Sixteen Self Sketches*, still stressing utility. 'Sexual experience seemed a natural appetite,' he wrote, 'and its satisfaction a completion of human experience for fully qualified authorship.' In his art he invested sex with a still higher purpose, thus bridging the chasm between body and mind he had not often bridged in life. The duty of the human race is the struggle towards the Superman; and women, because they bear the burden of this epic quest, are glorified by Shaw who willingly tosses any number of males into their open jaws as sacrifices to the great cause. And by making sexual attraction the Will of the Life Force, Shaw the puritan exonerates its helpless victims from the severest charge he could make: mere eroticism. As Z says simply to A in *Village Wooing*: 'Something above me and beyond me drove me on.'

But Shaw is really not happy with this state of affairs: he yearns to get above and beyond. At its most intense, sex could be for him a 'celestial flood of emotion and exaltation' – celestial because it provided 'a sample of what may one day be the normal state of being for mankind in intellectual ecstasy'. Sex therefore is a means to permanently overcoming the sensual, a state finally reached in *Back to Methuselah* with Shaw's vision of biology transcended: human beings hatched out of eggs in nurseries and human energy – both female and male – devoted to a permanent ecstasy of thought. At the end Shaw could not postpone sexlessness until the millennium: with his last breath he created a heroine in *Why She Would Not* who rejects even the imperative of the Life Force for chastity and a single life.

Shaw thus offers us the contradiction of the artist who dwelt on themes of sexual attraction, marriage, and procreation, yet longed for a sexless state; and of a man who sought and attracted women, yet evaded them. As he admitted, the steps to heaven were often taken on a woman's bosom. In his art, she rose with him; in life, however, he walked the high road 'as lonely as God'.

Benny Green

A FUNNY MAN

Among the vast accretions of tribal revelation compiled by Bernard Shaw throughout his life, there occurs one of the most revealing remarks he ever made. He was indulging at the time in that exercise so beloved of all writers, the marshalling in the salon of recollection of the immortal legions of the family, with particular reference to those aunts and uncles who, having been rendered giantesque through the telescopic sights of infancy, remain happily frozen in that flattering perspective for all time. It is our immediate relations who first impart to us the tremendous discovery that all men, so far from being created equal, are as unequal as quiddity of temperament and oddity of attitude can make them, and therefore provide us with a priceless portrait gallery of differentiated excess. In this regard Shaw was among the most fortunate of writers, being endowed with so outlandish a gallimaufrey of blood relations that had they never existed, then we feel it would have been necessary for Dickens to invent them. In recounting some of the spectacular indiscretions of his tribe, Shaw arrives at a maiden aunt

> whose conception of the family dignity was so prodigious, the family snobbery being unmitigated in her case by the family sense of humour that she would have refused an earl because he was not a duke, and so died a very ancient virgin.

As to the family dignity, we learn from the same context that the Shaws were so crazed by their own grandiloquent conception of themselves as to talk of the 'Shaws, as who should say the Valois, the Bourbons, the Hohenzollerns, the Hapsburgs or the Romanoffs'. But the family sense of humour, of which Shaw himself talks as if of the family crest or the family vault or the family nose, requires closer elucidation. Shaw made it clear on numerous occasions that in referring to this family sense of humour he is thinking exclusively of his paternal Shaws rather than his maternal Gurlys. 'My mother,' he insists, 'had no comedic impulses, and never uttered an epigram in her life: all my comedy is a Shavian inheritance', a claim he contradicts elsewhere by describing the aftermath of an incident involving the pretence by his father that he intended throwing his son into the canal: 'When we got home I said to my mother as an awful and hardly credible discovery, "Mamma, I think Papa is drunk". This was too much for her. She replied "When is he anything else?" '

Nor were the rest of the Gurlys quite devoid of a gift for the ridiculous. It was through an extraordinary virtuosity in familial mismanagement that Grandfather Gurly contrived to get himself arrested while en route to buy a pair of white gloves on the morning of his own wedding, a triumph much relished in later years by his son, Shaw's Uncle Walter, whose rabelasian excesses did something to extend Shaw's *GBS relaxes at the beach* juvenile knowledge of the world: 'To the half-dozen childish rhymes taught me by my mother, he added a stock of unprintable limericks that constituted almost an education in geography.'

Even so, Shaw was always quite clear in his own mind that it was in the Shaw family that the wellsprings of his own humour were located, a humour of a particular kind which he took some care to define in literary terms, saying that 'George Carr Shaw had a vein of humour which delighted in anti-climax and would have made him an appreciative listener for Charles Lamb'. What is more to the point, it made Shaw an appreciative listener for his own father, who appears to have delighted in giving copious demonstrations of his gift to his small son. When Shaw Senior's slapstick attempt to be a corn merchant collapsed in ruin irredeemable on the bankruptcy of one of his customers, 'he found the magnitude of the catastrophe so irresistibly amusing that he had to retreat hastily from the office to an empty corner of the warehouse and laugh until he was exhausted'.

Now a parent whose sense of the discrepancy between the world's view of things and his own is so acute as to reduce him to hysterical laughter even in the face of disaster, is perhaps not the man to instil conventional virtues into his children. In fact, George Carr Shaw was, according to his son – who was not merely being paradoxical when he said it – the most splendidly virtuous and dutiful of fathers, a status he achieved through the comically eccentric method of training, not by precept but by its reverse. George Carr Shaw strove to reveal to his child what nature of man he was, thereby hinting at the worldly advantages likely to accrue to anyone contriving to be the opposite, and thus demonstrating the truth in action of the ineffably Shavian theory that the man who is always wrong is just as infallible a guide to conduct as the one who is always right:

> He taught me to regard him as an unsuccessful man with many undesirable habits, as a warning and not as a model. In fact he did himself some unjustice lest I should grow up like him; and I now see that this anxiety on his part was admirable and lovable; and that he was just what he so carefully strove not to be; that is, a model father.

Clearly Shaw is resolved on loving his father no matter how damning the evidence against him, evoking overtones of an identical adamantine affection for a drunken sponger of a father displayed by Shaw's hero Charles Dickens. But there is a sense in which Shaw's deep love for his father was perfectly understandable. George Carr Shaw may have failed the family commercially; he may have been its Dublin ruin socially; he may have failed miserably to be grave at those junctures in his affairs when the world expected gravity. But had he not bequeathed to his son the most priceless item of cerebral equipment? Shaw later wrote: 'I have never aimed consciously at anti-climax: it occurs naturally in my work. But there is no doubt some connection between my father's chuckling and the enjoyment produced in the theatre by my comedic methods.'

Posterity's impression of this gift for Elian anti-climax of George Carr Shaw's might have remained too nebulous for the savouring had it not been for the significant persistence with which his son recorded instances of it in action. The two most notorious examples, because they embody heresies startling in the context of the complacent religious orthodoxies of mid-nineteenth-century Dublin, concern the postulations that a life saved is not necessarily a life gained, and that Christianity's holy writ is a tissue of moonshine:

> When I was a child, he gave me my first dip in the sea in Killiney Bay. He prefaced it by a very serious exhortation on the importance of learning to swim, culminating in these words: 'When I was a boy of only fourteen, my knowledge of swimming enabled me to

Killiney Bay

save your Uncle Robert's life.' Then, seeing that I was deeply impressed, he stooped, and added confidentially in my ear 'and, to tell you the truth, I never was so sorry for anything in my life afterwards'. He then plunged into the ocean, enjoyed a thoroughly refreshing swim, and chuckled all the way home.

As George Carr Shaw well knew, there was no point in so meticulously stage-managing this sort of charade unless it ridiculed the received truths of the outside world. 'His anti-climaxes,' Shaw wrote, 'depended for their effect on our sense of the sacredness he was reacting against':

> The more sacred an idea or a situation was by convention, the more irresistible was it to him as the jumping-off place for a plunge into laughter. Thus, when I scoffed at the Bible he would instantly and quite sincerely rebuke me, telling me, with what little sternness was in his nature, that I should not speak so; that no educated man would make such a display of ignorance; that the Bible was universally recognised as a literary and historical masterpiece; and as much more to the same effect as he could muster. But when he had reached the point of feeling really impressive, a convulsion of internal chuckling would wrinkle up his eyes; and (I knowing all the time quite well what was coming) would cap his eulogy by assuring me, with an air of perfect fairness, that even the worst enemy of religion could say no worse of the Bible than that it was the damndest parcel of lies ever written. He would then rub his eyes and chuckle for quite a long time. It became an unacknowledged game between us that I should provoke him to exhibitions of this kind.

All this constitutes very much more than the mere picturesque filial portraiture achieved by the inversion of Micawber's solemn invocations to young Copperfield as to the road to happiness. As Shaw said, 'I know how long such things stick', and might have added, 'a lifetime', for with the very last completed written work of his life, a preface to Stephen Winsten's *Salt and his Circle*, he is still savouring the ancient Shaw family joke of detested relations, reminding the reader of the scandal given by Cashel Byron's 'I hate my mother' which so shocked Mrs R. L. Stevenson that she shut the book with a bang and flung it away. All heroes in 1882 had to love their mothers and in due degree the rest of their relatives. I broke that convention because my father's relatives, though they quarrelled between themselves, combined against my mother, who one day, calling on one of my aunts, overheard her exclaiming to the servant who announced her 'Oh, that bitch!' After that we all boycotted one another; and I came to regard all paternal relatives as obnoxious persons, and to make a joke of it.

That passage, composed nearly ninety years after the dip in Killiney Bay, is an example of how Shaw contrived to resolve his father's intuitive skylarking into a rationale of family life; even more striking is the way in which George Carr Shaw's assault on the Holy Bible was appropriated by the son to become one of the main supports of the Shavian platform for Revolutionaries. And fifty years later was echoed in the text of *Misalliance*, the preface of which tells us more about Shaw's childhood than its author perhaps realized:

It is true that the Bible inculcates half a dozen religions: some of them barbarous; some cynical and pessimistic; some amoristic and romantic; some sceptical and challenging; some kindly, intuitional and simple; some sophistical and intellectual; none suited to the character and conditions of western civilisation unless it be the Christianity which was finally suppressed by the Crucifixion, and has never been put into practice by any State before or since. But the Bible contains the ancient literature of a very remarkable Oriental race; and the imposition of this literature, on whatever false pretences, on our children left them more literate than if they knew no literature at all, which was the practical alternative. And as our Authorized Version is a great work of art as well, to know it was better than knowing no art, which was also the practical alternative. It is at least not a school-book; and it is not a bad story book, horrible as some of the stories are. Therefore as between the Bible and the blank represented by secular education in its most matter-of-fact sense, the choice is with the Bible.

The ghostly laughter of George Carr Shaw drifts on the wind of every nuance of that passage, as it twists and turns through the labyrinth of Shavian paradox, exhorting the world to do the right thing for the wrong reasons. To quote the son once more, 'Parents know very well that the children are only themselves over again'. It is hardly surprising that when we come to examine the father, we find that he incorporated so many of the conventional antitheses of the failed pillar of the community who learns to live with his failure by dramatizing it as farce, the sad imbalance between the soul of a teetotaller and the inclinations of a tipsy buffoon, between the assumptions of commercial rectitude and the flounderings of the financial farceur, between the responsible husband and the pathetic domestic cipher baffled by his own ineffectuality. The victim of such contradictions usually reconciles them by recourse either to tears or to laughter. George Carr Shaw laughed, in which regard he was not altogether unlike John Dickens, who waited with such touching confidence for something to turn up; the difference between these two drunken fathers of two such remarkable sons is that a previous engagement with that deity in whose competence he had so little faith prevented George Carr Shaw from waiting quite long enough; he died in 1885, the very year that Shaw began at last to pay his way as a journalist in London. Shaw's awareness of the irony of the timing of these events emerges in a remark he once made which has been overshadowed by the celebrated masterpiece of anti-climactic facetiousness by which it is preceded. It is often forgotten that after Shaw's 'I did not throw myself into the struggle for life: I threw my mother into it', there comes 'I was not a staff to my father's old age: I hung on his coat tails. His reward was to live just long enough to read a review of one of my silly novels written in an obscure journal by a personal friend of myself.' At which, having sailed as close to the winds of filial contrition as his nature would allow, Shaw turns the comedian's guns on the arch-comedian with:

> I think, myself, that this was a handsome reward, far better worth having than a nice pension from a dutiful son struggling slavishly for his parent's bread in some sordid trade. Handsome or not, it was the only return he ever had.

The like-it-or-lump-it style of that announcement is no more than a wink from the son to the father who had instructed him from infancy in the art of cocking a snook at the self-importance of the adult world.

But George Carr Shaw's impotence in the face of the world's expectations dis-abused his son of something more than the conventional responses towards blood relatives; it taught him never to accept at face value those romantic impostures con-cerning life which are none the less impostures though their adherents may believe in them on pain of fire and sword, and whose negation is so aptly defined by George Carr Shaw's failure to realize any of them. By acting out the tragi-comedy of the gulf between posture and performance, Shaw's father provided him with the vital clue to the mystery of transmuting life into art:

> A boy who has seen 'the governor' with an imperfectly wrapped-up goose under one arm and a ham in the same condition in the other (both purchased under heaven knows what delusion of festivity), butting at the garden wall in the belief that he was pushing open the gate, and transforming his tall hat to a concertina in the process, and who, instead of being overwhelmed with shame and anxiety at the spectacle, has been so disabled by merriment (uproariously shared by the maternal uncle) that he has hardly been able to rush to the rescue of the hat and pilot its wearer to safety, is clearly not a boy who will make tragedies out of trifles instead of making trifles out of tragedies. If you cannot get rid of the family skeleton, you may as well make it dance.

Having realized soon enough that his own family was endowed with an unusual liberality of skeletons, Shaw set to work to make all of them dance simultaneously, to create a fandango of tribal eccentricity and ineptitude unmatched by any writer in English since Dickens. Thus posterity learns that his great-grandfather leads a double life as country gentleman and slum pawnbroker, that his grandfather is arrested on his own wedding day, that his mother loves him so little that she is never angry with him, that his Uncle Walter, so far from curbing the excesses of George Carr Shaw, actually encourages them, that he is so detached from his own sister Lucinda and she from him that neither is perturbed when she becomes the object of a seduction by his best friend, Pakenham Beatty, in the house of his mistress, Jenny Patterson. Most slapstick of all, there is evidently no single member of the Shaw family with enough literary acumen to take him seriously; when we read his advice to an aspiring novelist in 1882, 'If a rule can be said to exist for such a matter, it is that the author's friends flatter, and her family ridicules her work', we can only wonder at the dramas of rejection and derision which lay behind so rueful a fragment of worldly wisdom.

Whatever the sentiments of the precarious matriarchy at Victoria Grove, Fulham regarding Sonny's dogged attempts to be a writer, it seems that in later years the five novels of his nonage, the five 'brown paper parcels', came to stand as a symbol of the period in which he compiled them, a period when, although his parents had at last evolved an equitable method of conducting their marriage by allowing the Irish Channel to flow through the middle of it, the remnants of family cohesion still clung to the exiled Shaws, for whose son and heir the recollection of his aunts and uncles still belonged to a very recent past. For the rest of his life he was quick to throw in a family anecdote whenever the occasion seemed to demand it; that is, whenever recollection was revitalized by the exigencies of his work. And it was in 1930, writing a preface for the belated publication of his first novel, *Immaturity*, fifty-one years after its completion, that Shaw achieved his masterpiece of family portraiture.

Having observed that 'humour is one of the great purifiers of religion, even when it is itself anything but pure', he goes on to describe the affair of his father, the goose and the ham, and then arrives at the extraordinary spectacle of his Uncle William, 'a most amiable man, with great natural dignity'. The reader soon finds himself wondering where that dignity lay. We learn that Uncle William was a committed drunkard who suddenly reformed and devoted himself to an obsolescent Victorian musical blunderbuss called the ophicleide, defined in another context by Corno di Bassetto as 'a chromatic bullock'. Uncle William then renounced the ophicleide as adamantly as he had once renounced alcohol, exchanging one bullock for another by marrying a lady of such rampant sanctimonious piety that 'she declined, naturally, to have anything to do with us', and injected her unfortunate husband with an overdose of sacerdotal sedative whose effect was to induce in him a form of Fundamentalist lunacy which ingeniously incorporated his earlier taste for the jolly coarsenesses of life:

> I never saw her, and only saw my uncle furtively by the roadside after his marriage, when he would make hopeless attempts to save me, in the pious sense of the word, not perhaps without some secret Shavian enjoyment of the irreverent pleasantries with which I scattered my path to perdition. He was reputed to sit with a Bible on his knees, and an opera glass to his eyes, watching the ladies' bathing place in Dalkey; and my sister, who was a swimmer, confirmed this gossip as far as the opera glass was concerned.

Gradually Uncle William's enthusiasm for secular sport was stifled by his biblical frenzy:

> The fantastic imagery of the Bible so gained on my uncle that he took off his boots, explaining that he expected to be taken up to heaven at any moment like Elijah, and that he felt his boots would impede his celestial flight. He then went a step further, and hung his room with all the white fabrics he could lay hands on, alleging that he was the Holy Ghost.

His wife, like so many devout Christians of the period, believing in the Word rather more than in the Deed, at least where charity and compassion were concerned, had him committed to a local asylum, at which point what Shaw describes as the fantastic imagery of the Bible is quite eclipsed by his own, as the tragical comedy of Uncle William proceeds swiftly to its climax. Uncle William becomes obstinately mute. George Carr Shaw decides to use music to break the silence, only to discover that the ophicleide has disappeared, although how so formidable an item can be mislaid, even by a demented Shavian connection, is difficult to imagine. Shaw's father, evidently believing, like his son, that a little music is better than no music at all, takes a flute to the asylum instead. The rest of the sketch then soars to sublime heights of affectionate portraiture which eschews mere photographic likeness in its search for the poetic truth:

> My uncle, still obstinately mute, contemplated the flute for a while, and then played Home Sweet Home on it. My father had to be content with this small success, as nothing more could be got out of his brother. A day or two later my uncle, impatient for heaven, resolved to expedite his arrival there. Every possible weapon had been carefully removed from his reach; but his custodians reckoned without the Shavian originality. They had left him somehow within reach of a carpet bag. He put his head into it, and in a strenuous effort to decapitate or strangle himself by closing it on his neck, perished of heart failure. I should be glad to believe that, like Elijah, he got the heavenly reward he sought; for he was a fine upstanding man and a gentle creature, nobody's enemy but his own, as the saying goes.

The sketch is informed by the tenderest familial affection, and its comic insight so subtly applied that it is impossible to know at which point the facts retreat before literary artifice. However, Shaw will not have it that they retreat at all, asking 'what idle fancy of mine could have improved on the hard facts of the Life and Death of Uncle William?'. It is a rhetorical question which raises another: to what paroxysms of intellectual disarray was the English literate reading public reduced when this veteran son and nephew of a whole battalion of eccentric relations began addressing it on subjects it was accustomed to seeing treated with the same degree of solemnity that its bishops accorded to holy writ? Picture the English middle classes nurtured by the grave nonsense of musical quacks whose pseudo-technical rigmaroles filled column after column of weekly and daily criticism, suddenly exposed to the sniping of a bumptious young man who had decided that the time had come for the introduction into cultural circles of a touch of deflating levity. Predictably they assumed that the levity betokened ignorance, and were to grow weary over the next fifty years of having their noses put out of joint time and time again by Shaw's patient expositions for their benefit of the fact that the more facetious he appeared to be, the more he knew about the business at hand.

The refusal by the so-called educated public to believe he was educated, spurred him on to further flights of journalistic slapstick; in an essay published in 1893 he describes his meeting with a gentleman in Oxford Street who, 'after flattering me with great taste and modesty', asked him, 'Excuse me, Mr GBS, but *DO* you know anything about music?' Shaw goes on to explain how the reading public's belief that his musical criticisms are supposed to be an elaborate joke has finally dawned on him, and how, in an attempt to maintain the imposture and therefore his means of employment, he works at the task of feigning ignorance:

> When people hand me a sheet of instrumental music and ask my opinion of it, I carefully hold it upside down, and pretend to study it in that position with the eye of an expert. When they invite me to try their new grand piano, I attempt to open it at the wrong end; and when the young lady of the house informs me that she is practising the cello, I innocently ask her whether the mouthpiece did not cut her lips dreadfully at first.

As he sits there in the second-floor room in Fitzroy Square, surrounded by the debris of the vegetarian life, 'butter, sugar, apples, knives, forks, spoons, sometimes a neglected cup of cocoa or a half-finished plate of porridge', the wildest comic fancies bubble to the surface of his prose, irrepressible cerebral extravaganzas whose like the Victorians had never seen before, and whose barbs are intended for the most part for the kind of critical poseurs who 'can tell you how old Monteverdi was on his thirtieth birthday'. It seems almost as though he can hardly attend a musical performance of any kind without being visited by some fantastical flight of critical fancy. For instance he brings home the fundamental imbecility of the archetypal Italian opera libretto by asking himself how far he could survive in an exclusively Italian milieu:

> My command of operatic Italian is almost copious. I can make love in Italian. I could challenge a foe to a duel in Italian if I were not afraid of him; and if I swallowed some agonising mineral poison, I could describe my sensations very eloquently. And I could manage a prayer pretty well.

While squirming at the inanities of an opera called *Captain Therese*, he asks himself what needs to be excised from it in order to make it a coherent work of art, and comes to the conclusion that 'the first thing to do with it is to cut out the plot. The next step will be to cut out the music, even at the risk of leaving somewhat of a hiatus.' And then, pretending to a faint twinge of remorse, he adds, 'There is nothing

From an envelope which arrived safely at Shaw's London flat

else that I could wish to see excised, except perhaps all the incidents and most of the dialogue'. Most celebrated of all is his annihilation by ridicule of the school of analytical criticism in the person of one Heathcote Statham, whose work, *Form and Design in Music*, had happened to fall into Shaw's delighted hands in May 1893, and whose dreary scholarship is precisely what Shaw had in mind when he said later, 'I purposely vulgarised musical criticism, which was then refined and academic to the poit of being unreadable and often nonsensical.' The ceremony of genial critical homicide begins with a lengthy quote from the unfortunate Heathcote Statham on the theme of Mozart's G Minor Symphony:

> The principal subject, hitherto only heard in the treble, is transferred to the bass (Ex. 28), the violins playing a new counterpoint to it instead of the original mere accompaniment figure of the first part. Then the parts are reversed, the violins taking the subject and the basses the counterpoint figure, and so on till we come to a close on the Dominant of D Minor, a nearly related key (commencement of Ex. 29).

Pausing only to describe the use of the term 'the Dominant of D Minor' as Mesopotamian, Shaw then delivers the death-blow by the simple process of using his victim's methods to explain something couched in a language, that is, English, which requires no explanation. Adopting with glee the facetious posture of the suburban conjuror who announces that his next trick is impossible, he proceeds to analyse Hamlet's soliloquy on suicide (see page 66).

Understandably the genteel reading classes were bewildered by what was in effect a persistent barrage of erudite persiflage. One of Shaw's musical notices deploys the anti-climactic effects of his father far beyond the brink of absurdity with 'By the time I reached Paderewski's concert on Tuesday last week, his concerto was over, the audience in wild enthusiasm, and the pianoforte a wreck'; when perversely he decides to base his column on a recital at a High School for girls he remarks that 'when God Save the Queen was sung, the substitution of two quavers for the triple at the beginning of the last line so completely spoiled it that I instantly suspected the headmistress of being a Fenian'. And in reviewing a recital by Sherlock Holmes's favourite violinist, Sarasate, he says that the great musician 'left all criticism behind him. He also left Mr Cusins behind by half a bar or so all through the two concertos, the unpremeditated effects of syncopation resulting therefrom being more curious than delectable.' His readers laughed, sometimes uneasily, although the more perceptive of them might have noticed in the description of the accidental syncopation of Sarasate, evidence that only an experienced musician in full control of his journalistic powers could have conceived it. The truth was that after an unnaturally protracted period of neglect and apprenticeship, Shaw had at last got his foot in the door, having accumulated in the interim so vast a musical knowledge that the concert halls and recital rooms of late Victorian London must have seemed like so many toys spread out for his critical and journalistic delectation.

When the change of job came with his removal into theatre criticism the flow continued unabated. Hastening to give notice to anyone whom it concerned that he intended taking up where he had left off, he proceeded in only the third of his weekly theatre feuillitons to begin the long painstaking process of dismembering Henry Irving. After seeing the Great Thespian as King Arthur, he muses sweetly, 'I sometimes wonder where Mr Irving will go to when he dies – whether he will dare to claim, as a master artist, to walk where he may any day meet Shakespear whom he has mutilated, Goethe whom he has travestied, and the nameless creator of the hero-king out of whose mouth he has uttered jobbing verses.' A Sardou production is 'surpassingly dreary, although it is happily relieved four times by very long waits between the acts'. In reviewing a play about the Dreyfus Affair he observes that 'our plan is to govern by humbug, and to let everybody into the secret. The French govern by melodrama, and give everybody a part in the piece. The superiority of our system lies in the fact that nobody dislikes his share in it.' One night, at the Princess Theatre for a performance of Boucicault's *The Colleen Bawn* he reports:

> I regret to say that the patrons of the gallery at the Princess, being admitted at half the usual west end price, devote the saving to the purchase of sausages to throw at the critics. I appeal to the gentleman or lady who successfully aimed one at me to throw a cabbage next time, as I am a vegetarian, and sausages are wasted on me.

In describing the musical accompaniment to an Irving adaptation of *Cymbeline* he is amused by the juxtaposition in the printed programme of the list of musical items and the letters, printed in the margin in red capitals, 'LOST PROPERTY':

> Perhaps I can be of some use in restoring at least some of the articles to their rightful owner. The prelude to the fourth act belongs to Beethoven – first movement of the Seventh Symphony. The theme played by the 'ingenious instrument' in the cave is Handel's, and is familiar to lovers to Judas Maccabeus. . . .

A photograph of Sir Henry Irving signed by himself

In the sense that it must have mortified its victims, delighted their enemies, and bemused the general reader, this famous review of *Cymbeline*, published in the *Saturday Review* for 26 September 1896, is the archetypal fireworks display of Shavian erudition larded with slapstick. Even Sir Henry must have perceived from its contents that there was some truth in Shaw's modest claim that 'when I was twenty I knew everybody in Shakespear, from Hamlet to Abhorson, much more intimately than I knew my living contemporaries, and to this day, if the name of Pistol or Polonius catches my eye in a newspaper, I turn to the passage with more curiosity than if the name were that of – but perhaps I had better not mention any one in particular.' Whatever his limitations, Shaw was clearly not unversed in the great literature of the theatre. How serious, then, the reader found himself wondering, was this well-read buffoon when he suggested, as he did in the *Cymbeline* review, that Shakespeare was guilty of reducing 'the subtlest problems of life to commonplaces against which a Polytechnic debating club would revolt'? How much truth was there in his insistence that Irving 'does not merely cut plays; he disembowells them'? A cheap joke, perhaps? And yet the joker had taken care to give chapter and verse with regard to Irving's mutilation of *Cymbeline*.

Five months later Shaw returns to the Irving campaign with comically feigned reluctance:

> My regard for Sir Henry Irving cannot blind me to the fact that it would have been better for us twenty-five years ago to have tied him up in a sack with every existing copy of the works of Shakespear, and dropped him into the crater of the nearest volcano.

There was a simple enough explanation for all this insult and invective. Having been instructed by his father that an excess of vituperation is a priceless comic effect, and having perceived even as a child that by the sheer law of creative averages most works of art, whether literary, musical or painted, are merely either commercial speculations or milestones on the by-road of some insignificant life, he came late into art journalism to discover that the entire cultural domain of England lay under a permanent and very nearly impenetrable fog of ignorance and pretension, or to put it another way, weather conditions were perfectly normal. And having confirmed his exultant suspicion that he had forgotten more about Shakespeare and Beethoven than the experts had ever known, he went about his weekly duties with the genial heartlessness of a man so long inured to his own failure as to give even less for his own prospects than for the reputations of his victims. There is a curious moment in May 1896 which expresses to perfection his intellectual detachment from the world he was already beginning to dominate. Most uncharacteristically he attends a supper party organized for the recondite purpose of congratulating Sir Charles Wyndham for having succeeded in remaining Sir Charles Wyndham for so long:

> It was an amazing spectacle. There we were in our thousands – players and authors and critics – geniuses and beauties – lost sheep strayed from the Philistine fold of respectability – the disgraces of our own families – the delight of everybody else's families – the mighty *cabotinage* of London in all its fascination, and all its unlimited capacity for flattery, champagne and asparagus. Nine out of every ten guests were players by profession; and fully one out of every two hundred and fifty could really act – first among these, beyond all challenge, Wyndham himself, whose health was proposed by that tragic comedian the Lord Chief Justice. . . .

Shaw's view of his fellow-Bohemians as outcasts from the Eden of respectability was none the less sincere for being expressed humorously; it was unique in that the world of the theatre was, as usual, so enclosed and narcissistic a society as never to perceive the quaintness of its own absurdity. Shaw the foreigner, the economist, the revolutionary theorist, the vegetarian, the personification of abstinence in the midst of self-indulgence, was enabled by his detachment not only to see this community plain, but to relate it to that outside world of death and taxes with which it was never associated either by critics or players or speculators. The air of faint raillery in the Wyndham notice, culminating unexpectedly in the contemptuous metamorphosis of a pillar of juridical society into a bladder of lard, was precisely the sort of thing to have reduced George Carr Shaw to convulsions of irreverent joy; more to the point, it was Shaw's chosen weapon in his assault on a fundamentally frivolous community with a view to persuading it to be a little more serious. That slapstick should be recruited in the cause of seriousness was a little too much for a professional coterie devoted to the charade of pretending to drown in Sir Arthur Pinero's teacups. The device of anti-climax was perfectly suited to the job at hand, and remained so when the *brio* of the weekly journalism gradually moved over from the critic's stall to the far side of the footlights. George Carr Shaw would have been pleased to note the extent to which John Tanner was addicted to the anti-climactic form:

> The essential function of marriage is the continuance of the race, as stated in the Book of Common Prayer.
>
> The accidental function of marriage is the gratification of the amoristic sentiment of mankind.
>
> The artificial sterilization of marriage makes it possible for marriage to fulfil its accidental function while neglecting its essential one.
>
> The reasonable man adapts himself to the world: the unreasonable man persists in trying to adapt the world to himself. Therefore all progress depends on the unreasonable man.

The challenge presented by this style of paradoxing is to know where tomfoolery ends and serious invocation begins, or indeed if there is any obligation to separate them at all. Every joke, Shaw once said, is in earnest in the womb of time.

The method was straightforward enough; to take on apparent trust the lunacy of a dialectical rival, and by proceeding on that rival's assumptions, reduce him to the status of a solemn booby; and if, in the process, the letter of truth was bent a little, nobody was likely to complain, except possibly the victim. In 1888, a young, impoverished writer, Shaw regards the case of the impresario Sir Augustus Harris, a man whose manners were so regrettable that he committed the ultimate solecism of obliging others to appear in clothes as idiotic as his own.

> I complain of Mr Augustus Harris taking upon himself to dictate to me what sort of coat I shall wear in a public theatre, merely because he happens to be the manager of that theatre. Next season, I shall purchase a stall for the most important evening I can select. I shall dress in white flannels. I shall then hire for the evening the most repulsive waiter I can find in the lowest oyster shop in London. I shall rub him with bacon crackling, smooth his hair with fried sausages, shower stale gravy on him, season him with Worcester sauce, and give him just enough drink to make him self-assertive without making him actually drunk. With him I shall present myself at the stalls; explain that he is my brother; and that we have arranged that I am to see the opera unless evening dress is indispensable, in which case my brother, being in evening dress, must take my place.

Most remarkable of all, and significant for the light it sheds on the Shavian stratagem of improvising on a factual base, is the performance in *The Star* for 21 February 1890. Shaw has witnessed an exhibition by a dancer called Vincenti, and is so taken with the latter's mastery of the art of the pirouette that on his return home to Fitzroy Square in the small hours, he is tempted by the 'magnificent hippodrome of the Square' to emulate the artist. At first he falls repeatedly, and is eventually picked up by a policeman, who asks Shaw what he thinks he is up to. Shaw tells him, at which the policeman says, 'Would you mind holding my helmet while I have a try?', at which point the reader suspends the suspension of his disbelief and settles down to an extravaganza. Eventually an inspector arrives, asking the policeman 'whether that was his notion of fixed point duty'. Soon the inspector is joining in. The episode then spins to a furious climax:

> We were subsequently joined by an early postman and a milkman, who unfortunately broke his leg and had to be carried to hospital by the other three. By that time I was quite exhausted and could barely crawl into bed. It was perhaps a foolish scene; but nobody who has witnessed Vincenti's performance will feel surprised at it.

Hesketh Pearson.
7/11/42.

Also his humble collaborator
G. Bernard Shaw
21ˢᵗ August 1945.

Hesketh Pearson's and Shaw's signatures on the flyleaf of Pearson's biography of Shaw

When his biographer Hesketh Pearson taxed Shaw on this 'tissue of lies', he replied by saying that 'a literal account is neither true nor false; it tells just nothing. You may read the Annual Register from end to end and be no wiser. But read *Pilgrim's Progress* and *Gulliver's Travels* and you will know as much human history as you need, if not more.' Or, as he once confessed, 'I am the victim of an unsleeping and incorrigible sense of humour.' And again, in a letter to Florence Farr, 'It is by jingling the bells of a jester's cap that I, like Heine, have made people listen to me. All genuinely intellectual work is humorous.' As to the source of that humour, it is revealing that the most ambitious of all his plays, *Back to Methuselah*, that long metabiological trek through the jungles of speculative science, begins with a childhood anecdote. The voyage 'as far as thought can reach' has not arrived at the end of the street before 'the richest and consequently most dogmatic of my uncles came into a restaurant where I was dining, and found himself, much against his will, in conversation with the most questionable of his nephews.' A violent argument follows as to the nature of Darwinism. 'He died impenitent,' Shaw says of his uncle, 'and did not mention me in his will.' By embracing such family skeletons and making them dance, Shaw was able for the rest of his life to domesticate, to personalize, and therefore to render infinitely comic, the most abstruse flights of philosophic fancy, the most dogmatic assertions of unpalatable truths, the most hair-raising instructions as to how humanity should proceed. 'If you don't listen,' Shaw seems to be saying, 'well then, you will end up like my family.' One imagines there are worse fates.

Barbara Smoker

MAN OF LETTERS

The usual literary sense of my title is covered by other contributors. Here it is used literally – in the alphabetic sense.

Always convinced, from boyhood, that he would be a great man, Shaw left Dublin for London with a determination and faith in himself that never deserted him. Where his talents lay, however, he had no idea. His 'gift of the gab', his knack of absurd anti-climax, his comic exaggeration to make a serious point: these were just part of his essential Irishness (even if his forbears did hail from Yorkshire), and came so naturally to him that he was always looking for some other way of proving himself.

One of his closest friends during his first few years in London was James Lecky who, besides sharing his Irishness, shared his enthusiasm for music. But Lecky had other enthusiasms too – notably linguistics, phonetics, and phonetic shorthand. And these he passed on to Shaw.

It was Lecky who introduced him to the irascible Oxford lecturer in phonetics, Henry Sweet, who 'claimed that he could distinguish 11,000 sounds in spoken English'.[1] (No prizes for recognizing Sweet as the primary model for Professor Henry Higgins, anti-hero of *Pygmalion*.)

It was also Lecky who, in 1879, took Shaw along to the Zetetical Society, a debating club founded for 'the unrestricted discussion of Social, Political, and Philosophical subjects' where Shaw (apart from meeting the young Sidney Webb, hearing about Marxism, and being converted to vegetarianism) began to train himself in the arts of debate and platform oratory. He soon discovered that his natural trick of expressing serious ideas in a comic way was surprisingly effective with an audience, and a much rarer gift than he had supposed. Thenceforth, verbal communication was the tool with which he would carve his niche of fame – at first, mainly through public speaking; but then, for the sake of permanence, through the written word.

Serving his professional 'apprenticeship' in the British Museum Reading Room, the embryonic GBS would spend part of each day studying, part writing. From 1879 to 1882, his writing chiefly comprised his first four novels, written at a steady rate of five neatly handwritten pages of a notebook each day: a self-imposed stint which he kept up doggedly, 'rain or shine, dull or inspired', often finishing with relief in the middle of a sentence at the bottom of the fifth page. And 1500 words of creative writing remained his daily target for the next seventy years.

By the beginning of 1882, while continuing to use longhand for work intended for publication, GBS was using Pitman's shorthand for his personal notes, doggerel verses, the drafts of important letters, and so on.

GBS with notepad and pen, 1914

In 1944, Shaw declared: 'I learnt Pitman's phonetic alphabet in my teens easily in six weeks or thereabouts. Any author can. But I was put off it by the absurd notion that I could not be fully qualified as a shorthand writer until I could report human utterance verbatim, which means writing 150 words a minute. Now this cannot be done by an alphabet. . . . To do this the alphabet must be contracted and contorted. . . .'[2]

If he really did begin to learn Pitman's in his teens (that is, before he left Dublin), he probably embarked on it as a marketable office skill, without persevering long enough for it to be of any practical use, and took it up again only after meeting Lecky. This would explain why he never used shorthand before the age of twenty-five. His having a prior knowledge of Pitman's would also explain his choice of this system in spite of Lecky's persuading him that it was 'drawing, not writing', and 'probably the worst system of shorthand ever invented', and that Sweet's 'Current' shorthand was far superior.

In 1902 GBS tried to change over to Sweet's system, but he soon went back to Pitman's. The reason, he always said, was that Pitman's being 'the best pushed on its business side', his secretaries were inevitably Pitman-trained. But in fact he had no secretary in 1902 except his wife, and she never learnt shorthand at all. The true reason was probably that, though he theoretically preferred Current shorthand, he never managed to acquire the fluency in it that he had acquired by now in Pitman's. Forty-six is late to begin a new notation.

Besides, though Current shorthand is supposed to be easier to write than a geometric system, while the latter is supposed to be easier to read, Shaw seems to have held the opposite view. Pitman's, he said, he could write 'at the rate of 20 words per minute and could not read afterwards on any terms'. And in a statement he wrote for a Pitman advertising leaflet, he said: 'Much of my writing is done in trains, where . . . I cannot write longhand, nor any cursive shorthand, legibly, though I can make any geometrical shorthand, like Pitman's, sufficiently plain to ensure a correct transcript from the typist.' (The leaflet contained a facsimile shorthand note, written by Shaw specially for it, and reproduced here.)

Facsimile Note in Pitman's Shorthand by GEORGE BERNARD SHAW, the famous Playwright, Essayist and Novelist

BERNARD SHAW preferred Pitman's Shorthand, although he was acquainted with other systems. Read carefully the excellent reasons given overleaf

Facsimile shorthand note written by Shaw for a Pitman advertising leaflet. It reads:

This is the way I write. I could of course substitute 'This-is-the-way-I-write' with an apparent gain in brevity; but as a matter of fact it takes longer to contract. Writing shorthand with the maximum of contraction is like coding telegrams: unless one is in constant practice it takes longer to devise the contractions than to write in full; and I now never think of contracting except by ordinary logograms.

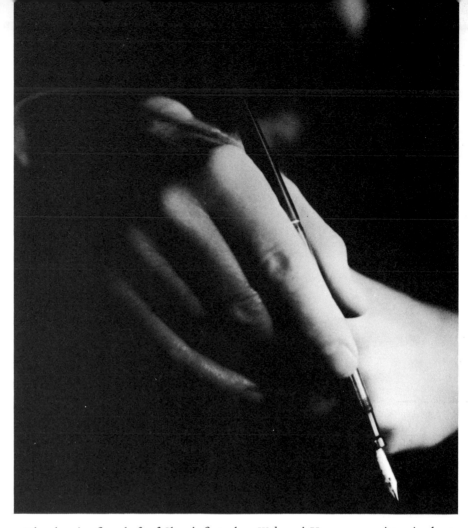

The hands of GBS

The abortive first draft of Shaw's first play, *Widowers' Houses*, was written in short-hand. (This draft, now owned by the University of Texas, I have myself transcribed; and the inscribed date of Shaw's last day's work on it, at the beginning of Act III, was 14 October 1884 – not 1885, as given on the 1892 manuscript and in every Shaw biography.) It was not until 1908 that GBS first had the shorthand draft of a play (*Getting Married*) transcribed by someone else. That was his half-cousin, Georgina Gillmore, who had become his secretary the previous year. She was succeeded in 1912 by Ann M. Elder who, on her marriage in 1920, was in turn succeeded by Blanche Patch – and they all transcribed his shorthand drafts.

Short letters he would sometimes dictate, or type himself. Creative writing, how-ever, he would never dictate, for dictating would have come between him and his inspiration. In describing his inspirational experience, he said it felt as though he were an amanuensis, not the originator of the phrases he wrote. It therefore seemed most natural for him to use the notation of the amanuensis – phonetic shorthand.

Whereas Shaw's longhand drafts are often very heavily corrected, his shorthand drafts are scarcely corrected at all, and comparison of them with the published works reveals remarkably little variation.

Being phonetic, shorthand could follow the sound of his inner voice and the voices of his characters in his mind's ear, with no capricious spelling to distract him. And it could keep pace with his inspiration: while his average speed of writing in shorthand was well within his longhand capability (sometimes he estimated it at a mere twelve words a minute, sometimes twenty – and it is possible to scribble longhand at thirty), he could step up the speed for brief bursts as his thoughts quickened. Besides, the sheer physical labour of his writing in shorthand was less than half that of either longhand or typing; so he was able to keep it up for hours at a time, even in extreme old age.

Shakespeare and Dickens, opined GBS, might 'in their short lives . . . have written two or three more plays and novels than they had time to get through',[3] had the players and printers been literate in a phonetic notation.

Though easier to write than longhand, shorthand (whatever the system) is more difficult to read back – at least for those who, having learnt the ABC in early childhood, are adults before they learn shorthand. In her book *Thirty Years with GBS*, Blanche Patch comments:

> When one thinks of it, it is something of a feat to write a play like *Saint Joan* straight off in shorthand, even although this was the play Shaw said he found easiest to get down on paper. True, his thoughts flowed easily; yet, when all is said, it must be uncommonly difficult to write dialogue in shorthand which cannot be visualised as you go along.

GBS with his secretary, Blanche Patch

A few years after Shaw's death, Miss Patch helped me fill some gaps in my transcriptions of Shaw's drafts of letters for the first volume of the *Collected Letters* compiled by Dan H. Laurence, and I was both amused and amazed at her casual attitude in contrast to Professor Laurence's scholarly regard for accuracy. Why not just put such-and-such, she suggested: 'I know that's not what it says, but it would make sense.'

During Shaw's lifetime this would not usually have mattered, as GBS generally checked the typescript and corrected any mistranscriptions. Occasionally, however, they found their way into print and were never put right. For instance, in Shaw's article 'The Author as Manual Laborer', I noted the nonsensical 'a dozen or so of vowel syllables are quite sufficient to make English writing as intelligible as English speech'. What GBS intended here was obviously 'vowel symbols' and, since the only difference in Pitman's shorthand between *symbols* and *syllables* is the difference between a horizontal curve and a diagonal curve, there can be no doubt how the error came about.

When writing an unusual word for which he had no habitual outline, Shaw would generally write it in longhand. 'In thirty years,' writes Blanche Patch, 'I can recall only one spelling error: for a time he omitted the third *i* of "*millionairess*", but he had reformed before the curtain went up.'[4] However, Shaw was guilty of many more misspellings than that. There is one in the handwritten postcard reproduced on page 220; and Dan Laurence, in his Introduction to the second volume of the *Collected Letters*, notes that 'his correspondence is strewn with such exotic formations as "quarrell", "parralel", "suddeness", "noticable", "withold", and "wheras".' But GBS disdained, as both time-wasting and humiliating, the consultation of a dictionary to ascertain merely the approved spelling of a familiar word in one's own mother tongue. The fault was in the spelling, not the speller; and 'correct' spelling, like 'correct' grammar, was for pedants to bother about. ('If the grammarian cannot square his pedantries with my English, why, so much the worse for his pedantries.'[5])

Nevertheless, GBS was as insistent as any pedant on the use of his own preferred spellings and his own rules of punctuation in the printing of his books. Being his own publisher (he used publishing firms only as distribution agents, never selling his copyrights or delegating decisions as to format, type-face, and so on), he was able to make his own printing rules. He indicated emphasis by having the letters spaced out, instead of by the use of italics or underlining; and he omitted (for aesthetic, as well as economical reasons) the apostrophes from common abbreviations, e.g. *shant*, *wont*, except where ambiguity might arise (e.g. *he'll*).

Without going so far as to adopt a phonetic system, he adopted the economical American usage in such words as *labor* and *program*, plus a few simplifications of his own, such as *Shakespear*, and (in his last years) *alfabet* and (inconsistently) *fotograph*. Less acceptable, perhaps, to modern eyes, is his insistence on *shew* – but in his youth this had been a common alternative to *show*, and the more modern spelling did not strike him as an improvement, since it suggested rhyming with *now*.

In common with John Milton, Benjamin Franklin, Mark Twain, Andrew Carnegie, and many other eminent men, GBS interested himself in several systems of simplified spelling, but he finally came down in favour of reforming the alphabet itself rather than tinkering with the spelling within the inadequate 'Phoenician' alphabet, as he called it. Tampering with the traditional spelling – 'Johnsonese' – would be up against the emotional hostility with which we all defend our habitual mental processes. ('No Englishman will ever have himself set down as illiterate, ignorant, ridiculous, and even occasionally indecent, by beginning his epistles with "Deer Sur"....'[6]) An entirely new alphabet, on the other hand, could be used 'side by side with the present lettering until the better ousts the worse'.[7]

As Shaw's epithet 'Phoenician' indicates, our alphabet is basically the one developed by the Phoenicians some 3500 years ago – and even they did not design the letters from scratch, but took them from traditional pictographs, which had in turn evolved from prehistoric cave drawings! So it is hardly surprising that they fall short of modern needs and are inadequate for some modern languages.

It is absurd that any letter should require four or five strokes of the pen (like *m*) or a dot to be added afterwards (like *i*); it is absurd that similar shapes (such as *u* and *n*, E and F) should represent such dissimilar sounds, whereas similar sounds (e.g. *k* and hard *g*) are represented by such dissimilar shapes; it is absurd to use two series of letters – capital and small – to represent the same series of sounds.

However, the main defect of our alphabet is its insufficiency. Most European languages have about thirty phonemes (meaningful speech-sounds) to be spelt with twenty-one to twenty-seven letters; English (a hybrid language) has about forty phonemes (the exact number varies, according to choice of phonetician and degree of precision, from thirty-seven to forty-eight), and struggles along with twenty-six letters – of which, moreover, C and Q are a dead loss and X is something of a luxury. Some of the letters therefore have to do double duty for two or more different phonemes, and we also fall back on digraphs (pairs of letters for single sounds) such as *aw*, *sh*, *ng*. This, plus the use of silent letters for historical reasons, means that we are constantly using two or more letters where one should do. GBS hated such inefficiency: 'As to spelling the very frequent word *though* with six letters instead of two, it is impossible to discuss it, as it is outside the range of common sanity.'[8]

Not only does the pronunciation of an English word fail to indicate how it is spelt (a defect shared with French), but the spelling is not even a sure guide to its pronunciation. This puts a brake on the adoption of English as a universal second language for international communication, as well as on the literacy of many English-speaking people. It also leads to rapid distortion of the spoken language through 'eye-pronunciation' – and Shaw was a pedant indeed in the matter of English pronunciation. 'Absurd pseudo-etymological spellings are taken to be phonetic, very soon in the case of words that are seldom heard, more slowly when constant usage keeps tradition alive, but none the less surely.'[9]

Alphabet reform schemes are of two kinds: augmented roman alphabets, where a few extra letters are added to the ABC; and entirely new alphabets, where the opportunity can be taken to introduce more economical and more phonetically logical letter-shapes.

So conscious was GBS of the amount of 'manual labor' he had been spared by using shorthand, instead of 'Johnsonese' spelling with the 'Phoenician' letters, for his half-million words a year during seventy years, that it became his 'particular fad', as he put it, to be instrumental in 'the establishment of a fit British alphabet'.[10] In each of his six wills from 1913 onwards he left money for this purpose, though in the earlier years it was subsidiary to his concern for elocution, and only gradually became a primary purpose with the emphasis on economy.

Among the items salvaged from Shaw's wastepaper basket that found their way onto the American market after his death was a sheet of his shorthand, which I transcribed for a California dealer who bought it 'blind' at auction in 1970. It turned out to be draft notes for his last will, of which the following paragraph was completely omitted from the final document drawn up by solicitors a few months later:

Having regard to the fact that all considerable printers include in their plant Greek, Russian and algebraic founts of type from which the extension of Doctor J's alphabet to 40 letters could be supplied, my Trustee shall nevertheless be empowered but not obliged to employ an artist calligrapher professional or amateur to design an alphabet which may or may not include Dr Johnson's alphabet capable of fulfilling the phonetic function of the PBA (Proposed British Alphabet).

Neither this draft nor his final will stipulates that his PBA must be an entirely new alphabet, but his preference for this is clearly indicated elsewhere:

The new alphabet must be so different from the old that no one could possibly mistake the new spelling for the old. . . . The first step is to settle the alphabet on purely utilitarian lines and then let the artists make it as handsome as they can. For instance, a straight line, written with a single stroke of the pen, can represent four different consonants by varying its length and position.[11]

As he grew older and his correspondence became vast, Shaw coped with it by using part-printed postcards

Several possible alphabets were submitted to Shaw, one of them being *Sprechspur* (Speech-tracing), invented for German in 1927 by Felix von Kunowski, and expanded for English. It was sent to GBS in 1950 by Mr Russell Scott (nephew of the famous editor, C. P. Scott), but, at ninety-four, Shaw was too tired to examine the system minutely or to consider changing his will yet again. He dismissed Speech-tracing as just another shorthand. Scott insisted it was not; and Shaw's postcard in reply (which the recipient gave me before he died) is reproduced here.

Mr. Bernard Shaw, though he is always glad to receive interesting letters or books, seldom has time to acknowledge them; for his correspondence has increased to such an extent that he must either give up writing private letters or give up writing anything else. Under the circumstances he hopes that writers of unanswered letters and unthanked friendly donors of books and other presents will forgive him.

Never waste your time writing to very old men. I am 94, finished. I can do no more. You must carry on from where I left off. No use bothering me about it. I have said my say about Kunowski and have not changed my mind. Thank you all the same for your letter. G. B. S.

Ayot Saint Lawrence, Welwyn, Herts. 26/8/1950

The main reason, however, for Shaw's declining to select an alphabet himself to name in his will (though he knew this would give his trusts a better chance of being upheld in an English court of law) was that he thought the 'PBA' would stand a better chance of public acceptance if selected and launched by an official institution, to give it an aura of authority.

The body he first chose for this purpose, in 1943, was the Orthological Institute, set up by C. K. Ogden to promote his invention, Basic English. 'Basic', Shaw wrote to Ogden, 'can hardly become a universal spoken language without a phonetic script: its pronunciation would soon be all over the shop in a dozen dialects.' A few months later, however, he had changed his mind: 'The two reforms had better be kept separate.'[12] Though a rational decision, it was to prove fatal to both brain-children. Shaw's money would have enabled the Orthological Institute to stay in business, while the Institute would have enabled Shaw's 'PBA' to inherit money under English law.

Instead, in 1944, prior to making his penultimate will, Shaw wrote a long letter (the text of which is appended to 'The Author as Manual Laborer') to a large number of public bodies – government departments, trusts, educational establishments, voluntary societies, etc. – offering to leave them his money for a new alphabet. None of them accepted, so he had to fall back on the creation of a private trust, knowing that it could be invalidated in law unless held to be legally 'charitable'. There was some consolation in the thought that a court case held after his death to settle the charity question would provide valuable publicity for the cause of alphabet reform, well worth the few thousand pounds of lawyers' fees it would cost, though he hoped the alphabet trusts would be upheld. In the event, however, the decision of Mr Justice Harman in the Chancery Court in February 1957 was that Shaw's alphabet bequest was not charitable in law, and must therefore be declared invalid.

Although reluctant to choose a particular alphabet, or even to choose between an augmented 'Phoenician' alphabet and an entirely new one, GBS did attempt the phonetic analysis on which the alphabet should be based. In a handwritten postcard (see below), he has set out the minimum number of letters as a sum, totalling forty-two. The recipient of this postcard presumably pointed out to him that he had forgotten to subtract the redundant letter *q* and that the medial consonants of *million* are really *l-y*, for these are excluded from the final version of his printed postcard on the subject – one of the famous printed cards with which he contrived to cope with his huge daily correspondence. But it does not seem to have been pointed out to him (or else he refused to accept it) that *ch* and *j* are likewise superfluous, since they are the double sounds *t-sh* and *d-zh* respectively. In his last will (dated 12 June 1950), GBS stipulated that the minimum number of letters should be forty, of which sixteen should be vowels, but he did not specify them.

It may seem insular to advocate a new alphabet for Britain alone, but Shaw had good reason for this. Not only because it is the world's most widespread language, but also because of its large number of phonemes, since it is easier to adapt an alphabet from one language to another by eliminating letters rather than by designing extra

Shaw outlines his plan, later amended

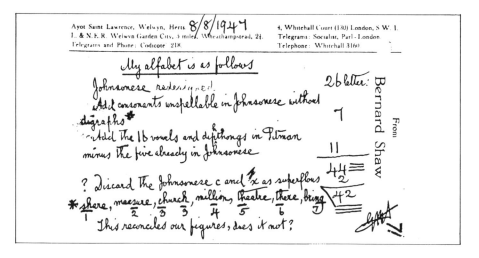

characters to fit in; so English is the most suitable language on which to base a new world alphabet. But the phonemic structure of English varies from one English-speaking region to another, so one particular pronunciation has to be chosen in the first instance: hence 'British'. And on this point Shaw's will is even more specific: 'the pronunciation to resemble that recorded of His Majesty our late King George V and sometimes described as Northern English.' (Whether George V's pronunciation was in any sense 'Northern' is doubtful, but what Shaw presumably had in mind was open vowels.)

An appeal against Harman's judgment produced an out-of-court settlement of £8300, granted by the three institutional beneficiaries for the implementation of Shaw's alphabet instructions: (a) for a suitable alphabet to be chosen; (b) for a bi-alphabetic edition of his play *Androcles and the Lion* to be published; and (c) for a statistical enquiry to be carried out into the potential saving of time, labour, and money, were the alphabet universally adopted for the English language.

Accordingly, the Public Trustee, as Shaw's executor, announced a prize of £500 in open competition for a suitable alphabet. Of 467 entries, four shared the prize, and an improved version of one of them was finally adopted as 'the Shaw Alphabet' and used for a Penguin Books edition (1962) of *Androcles and the Lion* 'with the original Dr Johnson's lettering opposite the transliteration page by page' (as directed in Shaw's will). A somewhat half-hearted statistical enquiry ensued, but when its findings eventually came out they hardly caused a ripple of public interest. This was not surprising in view of the miserly sum of money available for propaganda – the total grant of £8300 being only about one-thousandth part of the royalties accruing to the Shaw estate during the twenty-one-year period he had set aside for the alphabet trusts.

In any case, statistical arguments, however conclusive, would never break through the wall of prejudice with which we all defend the vested interest of our literacy. Instead of appealing to the rationality of adults, GBS would perhaps have been better advised to concentrate on the infant school, where the alphabet of the future could serve first as a stepping-stone to the ABC. Only when everyone living had grown up with both notations would the new one gradually supersede the old – relegating it at last to the level of an academic subject, unwanted except for research into musty books and documents.

Had GBS forgotten the Fabian principle?

From the bi-alphabetical edition of Androcles and the Lion

ANDROCLES AND THE LION

FERROVIUS. I only meant that they have no souls.

ANDROCLES [*anxiously protesting*] Oh, believe me, they have. Just the same as you and me. I really dont think I could consent to go to heaven if I thought there were to be no animals there. Think of what they suffer here.

FERROVIUS. Thats true. Yes: that is just. They will have their share in heaven.

SPINTHO [*who has picked himself up and is sneaking past Ferrovius on his left, sneers derisively*]!!

FERROVIUS [*turning on him fiercely*] Whats that you say?

SPINTHO [*cowering*] Nothing.

FERROVIUS [*clenching his fist*] Do animals go to heaven or not?

Colin Wilson

A PERSONAL VIEW

In November 1919, the composer Busoni described a meeting with Shaw in a letter. 'Yesterday afternoon GBS came to tea. He talks too much and cannot cloak his vanity.' And when Busoni remarked that he would like to write music for the hell scene in *Man and Superman*, Shaw told him it wouldn't bring in any profit. 'That is not what attracts me,' said Busoni. 'Oh, but you *must* reckon with that,' said Shaw. 'Everybody has to reckon with it. Of course, I am now a famous artist' (he added half jokingly), 'and I can allow myself to ride hobby horses.' To a man who had been a world-famous pianist for more than three decades this was a singularly tactless remark.

It helps to explain why Shaw aroused such curious hostility during his lifetime – a hostility that is still remarkably widespread, considering that he has been dead for more than a quarter of a century. Edmund Wilson, a thoroughly sympathetic critic, remarked: '. . . egoism like Shaw's was a disability like any disability – which you had to carry with you all your life. When he was young, it had been amusing, he had carried it off with panache; but it had become disagreeable with his later years, and one saw then that it was compulsive, incurable.'

The interesting consequence was that most of Shaw's contemporaries regarded him as an irritating egoist who also happened to possess talent – rather, I think, as most people still feel about Salvador Dali and Cassius Clay. In the first decade of his fame – from 1905 to 1915 – the British were impressed; after that, there was a widespread feeling that he was rather a 'cad', a self-advertiser, and they did their best to show their disapproval by ignoring him. Impossible, of course, but they tried.

The attitude still persists among those who actually recall Shaw as a contemporary. In 1956, the centenary of Shaw's birth, I wrote a memorial article for the *Sunday Times* in which I expressed my feeling that Shaw was a major writer who had been strangely underrated by his contemporaries. When the pieces appeared, I found that *The Times* had also commissioned an article from A. J. P. Taylor, in which Shaw was dismissed as an outmoded exhibitionist whose works would soon be forgotten. The difference in attitude can be explained by noting that A. J. P. Taylor is some quarter of a century my senior, and was old enough to remember Shaw at the height of his fame; whereas I was born in 1931, and knew next to nothing of the Shaw personality when I went to see the film of *Caesar and Cleopatra* in 1946. I came to know Shaw purely through his work.

It was not until some time after the publication of my first book, *The Outsider*, in 1956 that I fully understood the nature of the trap Shaw had fallen into. Because the book became a freak 'bestseller', because I found myself bracketed with the 'Angry Young Men 'of the period, I found myself carried to 'fame' on a wave of publicity –

GBS: Gerald Karsh

only to discover that this kind of fame is one of the subtlest forms of obscurity. Everybody knew who I was, and nobody knew what I stood for. The public image meant that nobody was interested in what I had to say, for everybody was convinced that they already knew. I could talk until I was blue in the face about my attempt to revise the pessimistic existentialism of Heidegger, Camus and Sartre; as far as most people were concerned, I was an autodidact who was angry about something or other.

It took me only a few months to realize that the sensible thing was to get out of London and avoid publicity; even so, it took well over a decade to live down the Angry Young Man image. Shaw never had the opportunity to live down his own miscalculation about publicity. The first night of *John Bull's Other Island* in 1904 made him a celebrity at the age of forty-eight – exactly twice the age at which I published *The Outsider*. He had been waiting far too long. He fell upon fame like a starving man on food; he repeated in the limelight all the tricks he had developed as a defence against neglect. Oblivious of the rising tide of irritation – or incapable of grasping its implications – he continued doing this until 1914, when his attitude to the war caused the British public to express its contempt so violently that even Shaw was taken aback. By that time it was too late to back-pedal – although *Heartbreak House* seems to me an attempt to acquire a new personality. From then on, every literate contemporary thought he knew all about Shaw without the necessity of finding out what he really stood for. Like 'Professor' Joad of the Brains Trust – a devout Shavian – he had become a self-caricature. The only way to discover the essential Shaw was to read his works without knowing anything about him; and Shaw's innate exhibitionism meant that few people were in this position.

In this respect, I was incredibly lucky; I still regard my own discovery of Shaw as the most important single event of my early teens. My background was working class; my parents probably knew nothing of Shaw except that he had a beard. I had heard of Shaw – everybody had – but had no idea whether he was a writer, a politician or an inventor. My training was scientific rather than literary; from the age of ten I wanted to become an atomic physicist; all my adolescent hero worship was directed at Einstein. This preoccupation with atoms and stars turned me into a pessimist. The more I thought about the nature of life, the more I became possessed of the conviction that our human values are trivial and parochial, mere expressions of biological needs. The scientist seemed the highest type of man; yet even his 'love of truth' struck me as an illusion; human beings have no more need for absolute truth than a baby has for a table of logarithms. At fifteen I had passed beyond pessimism into a kind of nihilism; I felt that no one had ever fathomed the appalling truth of Koheleth's 'All is vanity'.

The worst thing about it was the feeling of total aloneness, of alienation from the rest of the human race. It lasted until the evening in 1946 when I came home from the cinema, switched on the BBC's new Third Programme, and heard the opening words of Act 3 of *Man and Superman*, spoken by a narrator: '*Evening in the Sierra Nevada. Rolling slopes of brown with olive trees . . .*' At first I was amused and excited – it was more witty and intelligent than anything I had ever heard on the radio. And then as Don Juan began to speak about the purpose of human existence, I experienced a sensation like cold water being poured down my back. 'Life was driving at brains – at its darling object: an organ by which it can attain not only self-consciousness but self-understanding.' It was as if a bubble had burst; that deep underlying sense of detachment and futility disappeared; someone else was talking about the problem that I thought incommunicable. When I went to bed, after midnight, I felt exhausted and slightly stunned; yet underneath the confusion, there was a deep certainty that my life had changed.

Shaw's sartorial tastes could be as surprising as they were various

Later that week, when the play was repeated, I listened to it from beginning to end
– all five hours of it. Then I borrowed the book from the library and read it over and
over again until I knew whole passages by heart. It confirmed that my original insight
had not been a misunderstanding. Shaw was saying that to regard most human existence as futile is not necessarily a disadvantage – only the first step in becoming a
philosopher. 'No: I sing, not arms and the hero, but the philosophic man: he who
seeks in contemplation to discover the inner will of the world, in invention to discover
the means of fulfilling that will, and in action to do that will by the so-discovered
means.' In which case, it seemed clear that my business in life was not to become a
scientist, but one of Shaw's 'artist-philosophers'. Accordingly, I pushed aside my
textbooks of physics and chemistry, and began writing plays instead. The result was
that I failed to pass the examination that might have opened the way to a career in
science, and so became an educational 'drop out' at the age of seventeen.

The next two years were the worst of my life – I still wince when I look back on
them. I worked at jobs I hated, and felt myself to be trapped on a treadmill. I experienced intense depressions, and once came close to suicide. I read a great deal of poetry,
listened to a great deal of music, and envied writers like Henry James who had been
rich enough to spend their lives as detached observers. I brooded on the fate of poets
who had been destroyed by this 'real world' that I detested so much: Keats, Schiller,
Beddoes, Poe, James Thomson, and was inclined to accept the notion that I would
end the same way. And again, it was Shaw who kept me basically sane and optimistic.
This was because it seemed obvious that his starting point had been the same as mine
– as a world-rejecting romantic. His comments on Shelley, on Poe, on Wagner, reveal
that Shaw understood the romantic mentality because he shared it. In *Candida*, it is
the Shelleyan poet, not the crusading social reformer, who comes off best. In the
preface to *Misalliance*, Shaw distinguishes between two types of imagination: the
romantic imagination, that would like to escape into a realm of fairy tales ('from a
world more full of weeping than you can understand'), and the realistic imagination
that can grasp things as they are 'without actually sensing them' – the imagination
that can change the world. And since Shaw had managed the transition from one to
the other, it no longer seemed impossible that I might succeed in doing the same. . . .
This was the basic theme of *The Outsider* (a term I also borrowed from Shaw): that the
'alienated man' has to rouse himself out of his self-pity and set about transforming
the society he finds so uncongenial. (Later still, Shaw's concept of the realistic imagination was developed into my notion of 'Faculty X' – the mystic's ability to grasp
the *reality* of other times and places.)

The odd thing is that although I had read every Shaw play by the time I was seventeen
and most of the novels and prefaces, I never became a 'complete Shavian'. I felt that
after *Man and Superman*, Shaw had made no real effort to analyse the central problem
of *what human beings are supposed to do with their lives*. Don Juan could speak about the
need to 'help life in its struggle upward', about 'Life's incessant aspiration to higher
organisation, wider, deeper intenser self-consciousness and clearer self-understanding'
but how does the individual actually go about it? Shaw's political solutions always
aroused my deepest scepticism. Shaw once remarked that Jesus's miracles were
irrelevant because it would be absurd to say: 'You should love your enemies; and to
convince you of this, I will now proceed to cure this gentleman of a cataract.' It
seemed to me equally irrelevant when Shaw said: 'Life aims at deeper self awareness,
therefore we must abolish capitalism.' Then, as now, Shaw's socialist dogmas struck
me as largely fallacious. Similarly, the intellectual content of most of the major plays

*Shaw was honoured by issues of
a commemorative stamp in
Russia and Rumania on 26
July, the centenary of his birth*

seemed to me oddly disappointing. I wanted him to talk about ultimate problems of philosophy, and he insisted on talking about politics and education and marriage and the iniquities of the medical profession (another matter on which I felt he was mildly cranky). The result was that in my first book on Shaw (*The Quintessence of Shavianism*, written at sixteen) I remained more than a little critical, and ended by implying that I would one day do better.

But then, the moment I actually opened a volume of Shaw, this hypercritical attitude vanished; I found it impossible not to keep on reading with a kind of excited approval, like a spectator at a boxing match who has to shout his enthusiasm. Johnson once told Boswell that when he first read Law's *Serious Call* he expected to find it rather beneath him, 'but Law proved to be quite an overmatch for me'. When it actually came down to it, Shaw always proved an overmatch for me. Within a few lines, I was chuckling, then shouting with laughter – not so much because I found it funny as because it was so exhilarating. It made no difference whether I opened the *Collected Plays* at *Widowers' Houses* or *Farfetched Fables*; the effect was always the same: a sense of revitalization, of excitement, like setting out on a holiday.

Oddly enough, it never struck me to try and analyse the source of this effect until I was asked to write the present essay. And then I found it fairly easy to track down. It is the fact that, embedded in its very syntax, Shaw's prose has an irresistibly *optimistic* forward movement.

> Then there was my Uncle William, a most amiable man, with great natural dignity. In early manhood he was not only an inveterate smoker, but so insistent a toper that a man who made a bet that he would produce Barney Shaw sober, and knocked him up at six in the morning with that object, lost his bet. But this might have happened to any common drunkard. What gave the peculiar Shaw finish and humour to the case was that my uncle suddenly and instantly gave up smoking and drinking at one blow, and devoted himself to the accomplishment of playing the ophicleide. . . .

As I now read these words, I find myself beginning to smile halfway through the first sentence: 'a most amiable man, with great natural dignity' – for I know this is going to be the prelude to some anticlimactic absurdity. And then there is an element in the prose which in a comedian like Groucho Marx would be called perfect timing. If Shaw had written: 'my uncle suddenly gave up smoking and drinking, and devoted himself . . .' etc., it would not be funny; to say: 'suddenly and instantly gave up smoking and drinking at one blow' produces a kind of shock effect, like a clown walking into a custard pie.

All Shaw's prose produces an effect of determined clarity, and it is this clarity that causes our ears to prick up: he is obviously saying something important or he wouldn't be making such an effort. And the air of optimism is a consequence of the directness. Inability to express ourselves makes us feel depressed and defeated – a gloomy conviction that the world is too complicated for our limited powers of assimilation. Kafka's effects of nightmare are produced by piling up dreamlike ambiguities and complications until the mind is hypnotized into a sense of helplessness. Shaw's clarity produces exactly the opposite effect, for it is obviously inspired by a conviction that any problem will yield to a combination of reason, courage and determination. 'The brain will not fail when the will is in earnest.' No matter what Shaw happens to be saying – whether he is talking about human evolution or municipal trading – it is this underlying tone of sanity and optimism that produces the exhilarating effect.

All this helps to explain why the inevitable period of devaluation and neglect that followed Shaw's death was shorter than usual, and why his plays are now more popular than ever. It is a case of rediscovery in the most precisely literal sense. When *Man and Superman* and *John Bull's Other Island* burst on London in 1904, his contemporaries were dazzled; it was like a firework display. But even in those early years, there must have been admirers who were worried that a man of Shaw's genius could present a piece as feeble and silly as *How He Lied to Her Husband* on the same bill as *The Man of Destiny*. During the next ten years or so, Shaw repeated the offence with pieces like the atrocious *Shewing Up of Blanco Posnet, Overruled, Press Cuttings, The Fascinating Foundling* (he even enjoyed giving them defiant sub-titles like 'A Piece of Utter Nonsense' and 'A Disgrace to the Author'). And plays like *Getting Married, Misalliance, Fanny's First Play* revealed the odd streak of complacency that Busoni noted later. By 1920, as far as the public was concerned, the Shaw genius had been completely over-shadowed by the Shaw silliness and egoism – that is, by the posturings of the puppet called GBS. Before Shaw could be truly appreciated again, he had to shut up for a long time – in short, to die. When that happened, it was only a matter of time before the genius of his plays could once again compel the respect and enthusiasm of audiences. And this had happened by 1961.

And what about Shaw as a thinker? Shaw liked to regard himself as an artist-philosopher. Most of us will concede that he was an artist, but we have our doubts about the philosopher. Again that could be due to our lack of perspective. We think of a list of typical philosophers – Plato, Spinoza, Locke, Hegel, Whitehead – ask if Shaw belongs on it, and decide he doesn't fit. But philosophers cannot be judged simply as abstract thinkers; what is equally important is their place in the history of ideas. And here Shaw undoubtedly qualifies. He was born in the middle of the Romantic era, the century of pessimism. The materialist philosophers announced that man is a machine and that free will is a delusion; the idealists said that mind undoubtedly exists but that matter may be a delusion. And all the romantic poets from Shelley to Yeats agreed that life is a dim vast vale of tears and that the human condition is tragic. When Shaw came on the literary scene, in the early 1880s, the romantics had decided that mankind can be split into two groups: the stupid go-getters and the sensitive world-rejectors. You were either a shallow-minded optimist or an intelligent pessimist. (Thomas Mann made this antimony the basis of all his work.)

Shaw's revolt was instinctive. If he was a romantic, it was not of the self-pitying variety that regards the universe as cruel and meaningless because it refuses to treat them as exceptions. And it was Shaw's intuitive intelligence that made him aware that no healthy civilization can embrace a philosophy of pessimism. In *Man and Superman* he points out that man is the only animal who can be nerved to bravery by putting an *idea* into his head: that is to say, that man's inner strength depends on his beliefs; in *Back to Methuselah* he shows the other side of the coin when Pygmalion's two human creations lie down and die when they feel discouraged. It follows that a civilization that believes that Darwin and Freud are right about human nature is going to deflate like a tyre with a slow puncture. Shaw was not capable of analysing the history of philosophy since Descartes, the history of science since Newton, the history of religion since Luther, the history of romanticism since Rousseau and writing his own *Decline of the West*, yet he recognized that all have converged into the conviction that made Sartre write: 'Man is a useless passion.' He knew only one thing: *that somehow, sooner or later, the trend will have to be reversed.* His own age was not ready for that insight, and a younger generation of writers – Proust, Eliot, Joyce *et al* – continued the tradition of romantic pessimism as if Shaw had never existed. Most of

GBS at the gates of Shaw's Corner, 1948

them took the opportunity to denounce Shaw for failing to recognize the seriousness of the situation. Yet as this century of confusion and anxiety enters its last decades, it becomes clear that Shaw's instinct was correct. Somehow, whether we like it or not, we have to start believing in the future, and in man's power to transform it. At the end of *Too True to be Good*, the rascally clergyman declares: 'We have outgrown our religion, outgrown our political system, outgrown our own strength of mind and character. . . . But what next? Is NO enough? For a boy, yes: for a man, never. Are we any the less obsessed with a belief when we are denying it than when we are affirming it? No, I must have affirmations to preach. . . .'

The affirmations are still in the painful process of being born. When it finally happens, we shall recognize that Shaw did more than any other man to bring them into being.

Contributors

JOHN O'DONOVAN was born in Dublin (1921), started his career by combining clerking and auxiliary firemanship in a Belfast hospital during the war, thereafter changing the combination to journalism and dramatic authorship in Dublin. Author of *Shaw and the Charlatan Genius* and *The Shaws of Synge Street:* a play produced at the Abbey Theatre in 1962. Half a dozen of John O'Donovan's stage plays have been produced at the Abbey Theatre, and a couple of dozen other plays and documentaries have been done on radio and television. He is Chairman (1977–78) of the Society of Irish Playwrights.

TERENCE DE VERE WHITE was Literary Editor of the *Irish Times* until he retired in 1977. He is the author of biographies, travel books, novels and short stories. His most recent books are a *Life* of Tom Moore and a novel *My Name is Norval*. Vice-Chairman of the National Gallery of Ireland, he is their representative on the Shaw Estate's Committee of Management.

STANLEY WEINTRAUB is Research Professor and Director of the Institute for the Arts and Humanistic Studies at The Pennsylvania State University. He has edited *The Shaw Review* since 1956, and *Shaw: An Autobiography* (1969, 1970), *The Nondramatic Literary Criticism of Bernard Shaw* (1972), *Saint Joan: Fifty Years After* (1973) and *The Portable Bernard Shaw* (1977); and he is the author of the biographies *Private Shaw and Public Shaw* (1963) and *Bernard Shaw 1914–1918: Journey to Heartbreak* (1971). Among his non-Shavian biographies are *Reggie* (1965), *Beardsley* (1967, rev. ed. 1976), *Whistler* (1974) and *Four Rossettis: A Victorian Biography* (1978).

CHARLES OSBORNE is Literature Director of the Arts Council of Great Britain, and the author of several books on musical and literary subjects, among them *Kafka* (1967), *The Complete Operas of Verdi* (1969), *Wagner and his World* (1977) and *The Complete Operas of Mozart* (1978). *Swansong*, a volume of his poems illustrated by Sidney Nolan, was published in 1968. Born in Brisbane in 1927, he completed his musical studies in Australia and then worked as an actor for several years. His interest in Shaw dates from his appearance as Marchbanks in an Australian production of *Candida* in 1947. Since 1953 he has worked in London, as a free-lance literary journalist and broadcaster on musical subjects, and later as Assistant Editor of *The London Magazine*. He joined the Arts Council in 1966. He is currently writing a life of W. H. Auden.

JOHN STEWART COLLIS published his first book in 1925 – it was on Bernard Shaw. He went on to write biographies of Havelock Ellis, Strindberg, Tolstoy, the Carlyles, and Christopher Columbus. He is perhaps best known for his series of books on natural phenomena (one of which won the Heinemann Foundation Award in 1947). His friendship with Shaw is recorded in his autobiography, *Bound Upon a Course* (1970).

BRIGID BROPHY is a middle-aged Londoner who shares Shaw's vegetarianism, anti-vivisectionism and Irish descent. She writes non-fiction books and novels (most recent: *Palace Without Chairs*; most Shavian: *The Adventures of God in his Search for the Black Girl*) and has twice contributed programme notes to the Shaw Festival in Ontario. She is an active trade unionist in the Writers' Guild of Great Britain. She is married to Michael Levey, writer and director of the National Gallery, London, and they have a grown-up daughter.

ROBERT SKIDELSKY is the author of *Politicians and the Slump* (1967), *English Progressive Schools* (1969) and *Oswald Mosley* (1975). He is Professor of International Studies at Warwick University and at present working on a biography of John Maynard Keynes.

HILARY SPURLING was theatre critic of the *Spectator* from 1964 to 1970, and has since published *Ivy When Young, The Early Life of I. Compton-Burnett 1884–1919* (Gollancz, 1974) and a *Handbook to Anthony Powell's 'Music of Time'* (Heinemann, 1977). She is married to the playwright John Spurling and has three children.

IRVING WARDLE was born in Bolton, Lancashire in 1929 and was educated there and at Wadham College, Oxford and the Royal College of Music. He was assistant theatre critic of the *Observer* 1960–63 and has been theatre critic for *The Times* since 1963. He is the author of a play, *The Houseboy*, and a biography, *The Theatres of George Devine* (Cape, 1978).

MICHAEL HOLROYD has written one novel, a collection of essays entitled *Unreceived Opinions*, and lives of Hugh Kingsmill, Lytton Strachey and Augustus John. He is at present working on the authorized biography of Bernard Shaw.

MARGOT PETERS is a Professor of Victorian Literature and Linguistics at the University of Wisconsin. She is the author of *Shaw and the Actresses* (1979), the prize-winning *Unquiet Soul: A Biography of Charlotte Brontë* (1975), and *Charlotte Brontë: Style in the Novel* (1973), as well as of numerous articles on the Brontës, stylistics, detective fiction and women's studies.

BENNY GREEN is a musician and writer whose journalistic posts have included jazz critic of the *Observer* and currently television reviewer for *Punch*, book critic for the *Spectator* and weekly columnist for the *Daily Mirror*. His several published works include *Shaw's Champions: a Study of GBS's Lifelong Infatuation with Prizefighting*. He has also written libretto and lyrics of a musical version of Shaw's life which was produced at the Nottingham Playhouse in 1968.

BARBARA SMOKER is a journalist, political campaigner, competition enthusiast, crossword compiler, shorthand expert; the author of *Humanism* (Ward Lock Educational, 1973 and 1976) and of *Good God!: a string of verses to tie up the deity* (B. & T., 1977); publisher of Heretic Cards; and, since 1971, President of the National Secular Society – an office for which GBS said he was once nominated. She became a keen Shavian in her twenties (Shaw's nineties) and, from the mid-1950s to the late 1960s, was Hon. Sec. of the Phonetic Alphabet Association, and successively Editor of *The Shavian* and Hon. Sec. of the Shaw Society.

COLIN WILSON, son of a boot and shoe worker, was born in Leicester in 1931. He became interested in writing (plays) while he held a variety of jobs including working as a navvy. Married with one son, he wrote his first novel *Ritual in the Dark* in 1954 and began *The Outsider* in 1956. He has lived in Cornwall since then with his second wife and three children and has now written some forty-five books, including *Bernard Shaw, A Reassessment*.

Notes on the Text

THE FIRST TWENTY YEARS

1. *Shaw and the Charlatan Genius* (Dolmen Press/OUP), 1965
2. Lee was successively George John Lee, George Vandeleur Lee and finally just Vandeleur Lee. He never used the George John Vandeleur Lee version adopted by Shaw
3. Note in Stewart's copy of *Annals of the Theatre Royal*, now in Dublin's City Library

IN THE PICTURE GALLERIES

1. *Collected Letters*, ed. Dan H. Laurence (London, 1965), I, 145–7 (Shaw to Archer, 12 December 1885 and 14 December 1885)
2. Bernard Shaw, 'Acting, by One Who Does Not Believe in It', a paper read to the Church and Stage Guild, London, 5 February 1889, in *Platform and Pulpit*, ed. Dan Laurence (New York and London, 1961), p. 19
3. 'Art Corner', *Our Corner*, May 1886, p. 310. (Where not otherwise noted, further quotations from Shaw's art criticism are from his 'In the Picture-Galleries' columns in *The World*
4. Barnard, known to his contemporaries as 'the Charles Dickens among black-and-white artists', did many of the illustrations in the (London) Household Edition of Dickens, including *A Tale of Two Cities*. He also published three sets of six-lithograph depictions of Dickensian characters as 'Character Sketches from Dickens', each afterwards issued as a 20 × 14½ inch, one-guinea photogravure. The first set (1879) included a Sydney Carton

5. Shaw to William Archer, 23 April 1894; in *Collected Letters: I*
6. Shaw to Ellen Terry, 6 April 1896; Shaw to Janet Achurch, 20 March 1895; in *Collected Letters: I*
7. Shaw to Siegfried Trebitsch, 16 August 1903, in *Collected Letters: II: 345*
8. Martin Meisel, 'Cleopatra and "The Flight into Egypt"', *Shaw Review* (1964), pp. 62–3
9. George W. Whiting, 'The Cleopatra Rug Scene: Another Source', *Shaw Review* (1960), pp. 15–17
10. 'Mr. Shaw's Roderick Hudson', *The Saturday Review*, 24 November 1906
11. Preface to *Saint Joan*
12. Shaw to Mrs Campbell, 8 September 1931; *Bernard Shaw and Mrs Patrick Campbell: Their Correspondence*, ed. Alan Dent (New York, 1952)
13. Preface to *Saint Joan*
14. *Daily Chronicle*, 5 March 1917
15. Shaw may also have known William Hilton's *The Citizens of Calais delivering their Keys to King Edward III* (1910), an early nineteenth-century favourite
16. F. R. Rattray, *Bernard Shaw: A Chronicle* (London, 1951), p. 283
17. 'Rodin', *The Nation*, 9 November 1912, reprinted in *Pen Portraits and Reviews* (London, 1931), pp. 226–31
18. *Table Talk of George Bernard Shaw*, ed. Archibald Henderson (London, 1925), pp. 90–1
19. Quoted from Epstein in Richard Buckle, *Jacob Epstein, Sculptor* (London, 1963), p. 210
20. Shaw, preface to the catalogue of the exhibition of Sigismond de Strobl's sculptures, London 1935
21. Letter to Epstein, quoted in Buckle, p. 211
22. Shaw to Curtis Freshel, tls,

27 November 1936, Southern Historical Collection at the University of North Carolina Library, Chapel Hill, N.C.
23. Michael Holroyd, *Augustus John* (New York and London, 1975), p. 436
24. Harold Nicolson, diary entry for 11 December 1950 in *Harold Nicolson: Diaries and Letters. The Later Years*, ed. Nigel Nicolson (New York and London, 1968)

THE FABIAN ETHIC

I have kept references to a minimum. Most of the Shaw quotations are from the *Collected Letters*, I and II, edited by Dan H. Laurence. The Webb quotations are from Beatrice Webb's *My Apprenticeship* and *Our Partnership* (the latter edited by Barbara Drake and Margaret Cole); and from *The Letters of Sidney and Beatrice Webb* in three volumes, edited by Norman MacKenzie.

1. Sheila Rowbotham and Jeffrey Weeks, *Socialism and the New Life: The Personal and Sexual Politics of Edward Carpenter and Havelock Ellis*, p. 15
2. These quotations are from Edward Carpenter's *England's Ideal* (1887)
3. Norman MacKenzie (ed), *The Letters of Sidney and Beatrice Webb*, i, p. 2

THE CRITIC'S CRITIC

(OTN I, II & III: *Our Theatres in the Nineties*, vols. I, II & III)
1. OTN I, 65
2. OTN II, 161
3. OTN II, 159
4. OTN I, 98
5. OTN II, 62
6. OTN I, 94
7. OTN I, 263
8. OTN II, 74

9. OTN I, 271
10. OTN I, 281
11. OTN I, 17
12. Michael Orme, *J. T. Grein by His Wife* (John Murray, 1936), p. 87
13. Mrs Clement Scott, *Old Days in Bohemian London* (Hutchinson, 1919), p. 129
14. Clement Scott, *The Drama of Yesterday and Today* (Macmillan, 1899), vol. II, 396
15. *Ibid.*, 390
16. *Bohemian London*, p. 184
17. William Archer, *The Theatrical World of 1893* (London, 1894)
18. OTN I, 45
19. Max Beerbohm, *Around Theatres* (2nd ed.), (Hart-Davis, 1953), p. 235
20. *The Theatrical World of 1896* (London, 1897)
21. OTN III, 157
22. *Bohemian London*, p. 268
23. *The Drama of Yesterday and Today*, vol. II, 398
24. *The Drama of Yesterday and Today*, vol. I, x–xi
25. OTN III, 1–2
26. OTN III, 268
27. OTN III, 298
28. OTN II, 195
29. OTN III, 207
30. *Ellen Terry and Bernard Shaw. A Correspondence* (Reinhardt & Evans, London, 1949), p. xxiv
31. Martin Meisel, *Shaw and the Nineteenth Century Theatre* (Oxford University Press, 1963), p. 29
32. Preface to *Three Plays for Puritans* (London, 1900)
33. Preface to *Widowers' Houses*, Independent Theatre Edition, 1893
34. *Ellen Terry and Bernard Shaw*, p. 18
35. Preface to *Three Plays for Puritans*
36. *Ibid.*
37. OTN I, 60
38. *Ellen Terry and Bernard Shaw*, p. 22
39. OTN I, 60
40. OTN I, 266

'AS LONELY AS GOD'

1. Eric Bentley interprets these contradictions as the Both/And principle in *Bernard Shaw: A Reconsideration* (New York: New Directions, 1947 and New York: Norton, 1976). I would also like to express my debt to Barbara Bellow Watson's *A Shavian Guide to the Intelligent Woman* (New York: Norton, 1972); Daniel Dervin's *Bernard Shaw: A Psychological Study* (Lewisburg: Bucknell University Press, 1975); C. G. L. DuCann's *The Loves of Bernard Shaw* (New York: Funk and Wagnalls, 1963); and G. K. Chesterton's *George Bernard Shaw* (New York: Hill and Wang, 1956)

2. Elinor Huddart to Shaw: 17 April 1882. Holograph: British Library. Letters from Elinor Huddart, a novelist who wrote under various pseudonyms and Shaw's first important female correspondent, survive from 21 July 1878 to 8 July 1894

3. Quoted in *Bernard Shaw: Collected Letters*, ed. Dan H. Laurence (London: Max Reinhardt, 1965): pp. 62–3

4. *Sixteen Self Sketches*: III: 29

5. 11 September 1883. *Collected Letters*: I: 65–7

6. 9 September 1883. *Collected Letters*: I: 62–4

7. 11 September 1883. Quoted in *Collected Letters*: I: 65

8. Preface to *Immaturity* (London: Constable, 1930): p. xix. *Immaturity* written between 5 March and 5 November 1879

9. *An Unsocial Socialist* (London: Constable, 1930); Chapter 5. Written 1883

10. *An Unsocial Socialist*: p. 257

11. *Collected Letters*: II: p. 73

12. Jane (Jenny) Patterson. Born 1844? – died 14 September 1924. Shaw's letters to her do not survive; there are 373 letters from her to Shaw, 1886–88, in the British Library

13. 12 May 1886. Holograph. British Library

14. Jenny Patterson to Shaw. Christmas Day, 2 a.m. 1887

15. Shaw to Stephen Winsten, quoted in C. G. L. DuCann, *The Loves of Bernard Shaw* (New York: Funk and Wagnalls, 1963): p. 57

16. See Josephine Johnson's biography *Florence Farr: Bernard Shaw's 'New Woman'* (Totowa, N.J.: Rowman and Littlefield, 1975)

17. Letters of 1 May 1891 and 7 October 1891. *Collected Letters*: I: 295–7, 313

18. 28 January 1892. *Collected Letters*: I: 331–2

19. 27 April 1893. *Collected Letters*: I: 391–2

20. 28 January 1892. *Collected Letters*: I: 331–3

21. 17 June 1889. *Collected Letters*: I: 215–16

22. 9 December 1897. *Collected Letters*: I: 827–8

23. 23 March 1895. *Collected Letters*: I: 503–7

24. *Collected Letters*: I: 624–7

25. *Collected Letters*: I: 590–2

26. 14 April 1896. *Collected Letters*: I: 624–7

27. Letters of 25 September 1896, 5 November 1896, 12 October 1896 in *Ellen Terry and Bernard Shaw: A Correspondence*, ed. by Christopher St John (New York: G. P. Putnam's, 1932): pp. 61–3, 87–9, 72–4

28. 8 August 1899. *A Correspondence*: pp. 247–9

29. Charlotte Shaw to T. E. Lawrence. 17 May 1927. Holograph: Humanities Research Center, University of Texas, Austin

30. 16 June 1884. Holograph letter. British Library

31. Preface to *Three Plays for Puritans* in *Collected Plays*: II: 18

32. *Bernard Shaw and Mrs. Patrick Campbell: Their Correspondence*, ed. Alan Dent (London: Victor Gollancz, 1952): p. 20

33. 10 December 1912. *Their Correspondence*: pp. 65–9

34. 6 August 1913. *Their Correspondence*: pp. 136–7

35. 11 August 1913. George Cornwallis West was not yet divorced from his wife, formerly Jennie Jerome Churchill. A few hours after the decree became final Stella Campbell and Cornwallis West were married 6 August 1914

36. Diary: British Library. Travel records: Humanities Research Center, University of Texas, Austin

37. *Shaw and Molly Tompkins in Their Own Words*, ed. Peter Tompkins (New York: Clarkson N. Potter, 1961): p. 170. See also *To A Young Actress: The Letters of Bernard Shaw to Molly Tompkins*, ed. Peter Tompkins (New York: Clarkson N. Potter, 1960)

38. 'Woman—Man in Petticoats' in *Platform and Pulpit*, ed. Dan H. Laurence (London: Rupert Hart-Davis, 1962): pp. 172–8

39. November 1945: Holograph: British Library

MAN OF LETTERS

1. An 'open letter' issued by Shaw as a brochure *Colossal Labor Saving*, May 1947: reprinted in *George Bernard Shaw on Language*, ed. Abraham Tauber (Peter Owen, 1965)

2. Shaw's article 'The Author as Manual Laborer', published in *The Author* (organ of the Society of Authors), Summer 1944; reprinted in *The Shavian*, September 1958, and subsequently in Tauber: *Shaw on Language* and in Allan Chappelow's *Shaw – 'the Chucker-Out'* (Allen & Unwin, 1969)

3. Shaw's preface to the Guild Books edition (1941) of *The Miraculous Birth of Language* by Richard A. Wilson

4. *Thirty Years with G.B.S.* by Blanche Patch (Victor Gollancz, 1951)

5. Letter from GBS to W. E. Henley, 1 July 1890; published in *Bernard Shaw: Collected Letters, 1874–1897*

6. Letter from GBS to *The Times*, published 27 December 1945; reprinted in Tauber: *Shaw on Language*

7. Preface *The Miraculous Birth of Language*

8. 'The Author as Manual Laborer'

9. Preface *The Miraculous Birth of Language*

10. 'The Author as Manual Laborer'

11. Preface *The Miraculous Birth of Language*

12. 'The Author as Manual Laborer'

Notes on the Illustrations

Despite diligent enquiries it has not been possible to trace the photographers of some of the illustrations in this book. Our apologies are due to those copyright holders who can substantiate their claims. In application to the Publishers they will receive the usual fee for reproduction.

The following abbreviations are used:
BL: The Trustees of the British Library. NPG: National Portrait Gallery. NT: National Trust. RADA: Royal Academy of Dramatic Art. RM & JM TC: Raymond Mander and Joe Mitchenson Theatre Collection. RTHPL: Radio Times Hulton Picture Library. SMNT: The Trustees of the Shakespeare Memorial Theatre. V & A: The Trustees of the Victoria & Albert Museum. V & A TC: Victoria & Albert Museum Theatre Collection.

Index